T0329024

*'A delightful and insightful read for
faerie enthusiasts everywhere.
Jacky and Alicen have created what I believe
will be a bestseller for faerie fans across the world.'*

Karen Kay, Editor, *Faeries and Enchantment Magazine*

A
Fairy
Treasury

A
Fairy
Treasury

The Ultimate Guide
to the Enchanted
Fairy Realm

JACKY NEWCOMB &
ALICEN GEDDES

HAY HOUSE

Carlsbad, California • New York City
London • Sydney • New Delhi

Published in the United Kingdom by:
The Sixth Floor, Watson House, 54 Baker Street, London W1U 7BU
Tel: +44 (0)20 3927 7290; Fax: +44 (0)20 3927 7291; www.hayhouse.co.uk

Published in the United States of America by:
Hay House Inc., PO Box 5100, Carlsbad, CA 92018-5100
Tel: (1) 760 431 7695 or (800) 654 5126
Fax: (1) 760 431 6948 or (800) 650 5115; www.hayhouse.com

Published in Australia by:
Hay House Australia Ltd, 18/36 Ralph St, Alexandria NSW 2015
Tel: (61) 2 9669 4299; Fax: (61) 2 9669 4144; www.hayhouse.com.au

Published in India by:
Hay House Publishers India, Muskaan Complex, Plot No.3, B-2,
Vasant Kunj, New Delhi 110 070
Tel: (91) 11 4176 1620; Fax: (91) 11 4176 1630; www.hayhouse.co.in

Text © Jacky Newcomb and Alicen Geddes, 2007, 2018

The moral rights of the authors have been asserted.

The information given in this book should not be treated as a substitute for professional medical advice; always consult a medical practitioner. Any use of information in this book is at the reader's discretion and risk. Neither the authors nor the publisher can be held responsible for any loss, claim or damage arising out of the use, or misuse, of the suggestions made, the failure to take medical advice or for any material on third-party websites.

A catalogue record for this book is available from the British Library.

Previously published in 2007 as *A Faerie Treasury* (ISBN: 9781401915537).

ISBN: 978-1-4019-6841-0

Dedication

Alicen:
I dedicate this book to
someone who knows all about the faeries,
HRH The Faerie Queene Rose Petal (Aimee Butler)
and 'The Fairy Box' children's charity.

Jacky:
I dedicate this book to the kindest woman
who ever walked this earth,
my lovely Mum,
and to dearest Dad …
who is clearly the biggest fan
a girl could ever wish to have!

Faerie Blessings

~~~

From Alicen:

There are so many people to thank for making this book possible as it would not have happened without them …

Lots of love and appreciation to Jacky Newcomb for being my very supportive co-author and friend.

Thank you to Llewellyn for suggesting the book in the first place and shoving me in the right direction!

Special mentions to Be and Drew and family at I Do Believe for all their magic, which they are always sending in my direction. Love and faerie wishes to Aimee and the Butler family who have given me so much inspiration while writing this book.

All good wishes and thanks to Michelle Pilley and everyone at the Hay House UK office for their continuing support of my faerie work.

To all those of the faerie community worldwide and the loyal readers of *Faeriecraft* who have been so encouraging to me while writing this book. A big thank-you also to all those faerie-blessed people who have sent in their fey experiences to contribute to the book.

Thanks to all my friends, family and neighbours who put up with me being a recluse while writing this book – now I can come out of the woodwork!

Merlyn and Epona and their team at The Children of Artemis, thanks for your help over the many years you have continued to believe in me.

Blessed Be to Queen Mab and the faeries for inspiration, love and guidance.

From Jacky:

To Alicen Geddes, without whom there would be no *Fairy Treasury*. I have learned so much more about the faerie realm – you are a wonderful co-author.

Llewellyn for bringing Alicen and me together in the first place. To Juliana and Holly – for believing in faeries too.

To my husband John, who cooks my tea and brings me regular refreshments whilst I work ... and most of all to my children who listen to my moans and groans and usually end up cooking for themselves ...

Thank you to everyone at Hay House for taking a chance on *A Fairy Treasury* ... and now the real work begins.

... But most of all I want to thank all the people who have shared their amazing stories of faerie intervention in their own lives. Belief in the magic of the unseen worlds is hard for many – but your stories bring the faerie realms alive to those who have yet to experience them.

From both of us ...

A big thank-you to Neil Geddes-Ward for researching and compiling the Faerie Resources Directory at the back of this book.

We believe in faeries!

Contents

The Birth of A Fairy Treasury

Alicen and Jacky have never met – at least not on the earth plane. I know that sounds strange, but in this day of emails and the Internet, it really is possible to write a book with someone over long distances …

Jacky first heard of the work of Alicen and her ex-husband Neil, the pagan and visionary artist, when Neil and Alicen came to her local town of Burton upon Trent (where Jacky lived at that time). Neil was giving a talk about his artwork and the faerie realms. Jacky was very attracted to a greetings card in a local shop and it contained artwork which Neil had painted … a woman holding an owl. The owner of the shop had been the one to then tell her about their visit. Sadly, Jacky missed the talk but felt that there was a connection and that their paths would cross again. She was right …

Years later, Jacky was writing an article for a magazine about faeries and came across Alicen's name during an Internet search. Alicen was good enough to give Jacky an interview over the telephone, and she was featured in the article … their spiritual paths had crossed again … but they still hadn't met!

In the meantime, Jacky had begun writing about angels and was searching for stories for a book one day when she once again came across Neil and Alicen's website. Neil had a wonderful afterlife communication story which Jacky was thrilled to include in one of her books … their spiritual paths had crossed yet again, but they still hadn't met.

Jacky was keen to produce her own angel meditations and approached her favourite composer and musician, Llewellyn. Llewellyn and Jacky worked on several angel CDs together, including some meditation CDs.

When Llewellyn and his singer wife Juliana launched their charity Earth Angel, Jacky and her husband John were invited to attend. It was at this point that Jacky discovered that Alicen and her husband Neil were friends of Llewellyn and Juliana, and that they had both been invited. Would they meet at last? Unfortunately, Alicen was unable to attend the launch party but Jacky and her husband John did finally get to meet Neil!

Alicen herself went on to produce several faerie CDs with Llewellyn. As she was his friend, the faerie expert, she was the natural choice. It was Llewellyn who suggested that Alicen and Jacky work on a book of faeries together. Llewellyn approached Jacky with the suggestion and was surprised to hear that Jacky had already begun collecting faerie stories and material for a book – but that it was something she thought might happen in the distant future. With a co-writer, might it be possible to do this now?

Jacky always believed that faeries and angels (her real speciality) were connected, but until Alicen came along she didn't feel that she had enough knowledge to write the book alone. She felt that readers deserved the best possible follow-up book to her work *An Angel Treasury*.

Alicen was the missing piece of the puzzle and it was clear that their paths had crossed (or nearly crossed) several times for a good reason. At the time of writing this, Jacky and Alicen have yet to meet, but netherthless have become firm friends! One day soon perhaps?

A Fairy Treasury has now been born, and Jacky and Alicen would like to thank Llewellyn for his help in bringing this about.

P.S. Jacky and Alicen finally met at the Hay House publishers' 20th anniversary party – once the manuscript was complete!

A Little Note on Our Spelling of 'Faerie'

There are many ways to spell *fairy* and, believe it or not, they are all so commonly and frequently used that they are all considered valid. The spelling of this word, like its namesakes, has gone in and out of fashion throughout the centuries. At the time of writing, *faerie* or *faery* is considered to be the spelling for the serious study of these Otherworldly beings. For this reason and for personal preference we have used *faerie* as our spelling in this book. By the same token, *fairy* is considered to mean the trivial or childlike spelling of the word for these beings, used most commonly in imaginary settings, as in 'fairy tales', for example. In these instances, to make the distinction, we have used this spelling also.

There are also many ways to spell *fey* and *magic*. We have used the spellings shown here for simplicity and clarity. However, throughout the book there are many readers' true faerie experiences, and they all have their own personal preferences for the way that they spell *faerie*, *fey* and *magic*. You will see that we have retained their preferred spellings of these words in these instances as they are, indeed, their personal preferences and we respect this.

Introduction

'Fairy spirits of the breeze, frailer nothing is than these …'
WILLIAM WINTER

Alicen: I am frequently asked the question, 'Why were you drawn to work with the faeries?' People are often puzzled at my answer, which is that I wasn't! The real truth, and I will explain, is that it is really the faeries that persuaded me to work with them.

As a child, as any little girl will probably tell you, I loved the faeries and would immerse myself for hours, looking at pictures of books by the artist Mabel Lucie Attwell. However, I did not give this interest in faeries a second thought as it was a normal part of childhood. I also did not have any special experiences or see faeries as a child, as you would normally expect of an adult like myself, who now lives faeries every day of her life!

It was not until I was 16 years old and I began to develop spiritually and practise meditation that I began to see the faeries. It was then that they told me that I was to work with them. However, at that time I did not know how to work with them. This began a journey of faerie discovery where I searched for many years for how I could know the faeries better and learn their magical secrets. I went down quite a few dead ends in my search, and finally realized that I could not learn their secrets from any book or person – I had to ask the faeries themselves! Of course, how obvious it was once I had found it out, if only I had done that in the first place! However, I had to realize this myself; it was part of the journey I was to take to the faeries' realm. It is for this reason that *A Fairy Treasury* is not a book on how to know the faeries' realm, but more on how to ask the faeries yourself how you can find them.

Faeries, like angels, are known to come closer to the human world at times of crisis in our world. We can see this because we see the faeries more in art, popular culture, music, films and literature right now. The faeries have drawn closer to us and wish to know us more intimately because of the fragile state that our planet is in. Faeries belong to nature and they are the spiritual manifestations of every living thing. If we all get to know the faeries better, then we will automatically find ourselves knowing and loving our natural world in a more wonderful way.

Do not think that the faeries want you to take this serious message in any way seriously! They are beautiful magical beings, and you will quickly find that once you dip a toe into their realm you will begin to see things differently. They will add a little sparkle and magic to your mundane world; a little mischief and imagination. Maybe you will find a little of the magic which you left behind in childhood. We all knew the faeries in childhood, and once you have remembered them I am sure that you will never want to leave them behind again. Let's begin our journey to awaken the magic of the faeries in you once more ...

Jacky: My writing room, a beautiful conservatory which looks out over a small country-style garden, is full of angel memorabilia. In order for me to write about a subject I have to immerse myself fully myself in it. Angels I love, but faeries now have a new place in my heart. The energy of the two is very different, and so I must clear a space for faeries to move in and, for the moment at least, the angels graciously step to one side.

I place rainbow crystals in my window and some large and small pieces of assorted rocks, shells and crystals along my windowsill. I am hoping to entice the faeries in ... First I move the angels out of my immediate vision. A gorgeous, sexy fairy print replaces them on the windowsill in front of me. She looks seductive in her transparent gown of lilac and purple. She has tall gossamer 'insect'-style wings and the mysterious forest around her is shaded in more tones of purple and a magical turquoise colour. Each tree has a nature spirit of its own, a woman standing guard and yet blending into the front of the trunk. The whole picture has sparkles of faerie lights surrounding every plant and tree, protecting, guiding, guarding. It's exactly how I imagine a faerie land might be.

I remove my tablecloth from the waxed-pine working table and put in its place an Indian cotton cloth which has been hand-dyed in yet more shades of purple. The cloth has a pattern of stars and dragonflies. The cloth feels right for the change of energy in my room.

The cushions on my basket chairs – so loved by my cats Tigger and Magik – are replaced with a pair decorated with flower faerie illustrations. 'The willow faerie', based on an illustration by the Victorian painter Cicely Mary Barker, is surrounded by beautiful faerie greens. I place lilac- and lavender-scented candles on my desk and I'm ready to begin. The faeries have filled my working space.

It seems no coincidence that my garden is suddenly filled with butterflies. White ones, red ones … all different colours. Where did they come from? I suddenly spot my neighbour's buddleia shrub (or butterfly plant, as it is sometimes called) which has just now come into flower and is hanging over the fence. Perfect timing! Butterflies are regularly associated with faeries, and their appearance brings a certain magic into my room … the perfect view.

My co-author, Alicen Geddes, and myself have heard that our publishers are interested in our book on the Summer Solstice – a magical day in the faerie calendar. Another coincidence? I doubt it! Every last piece is now in place.

And so I sit now ready to begin a magical journey with nature's mysterious spirit workers, a journey from which I may never return ...

CHAPTER 1

Frequently Asked Faerie Questions

'When thou hast stol'n away from fairy land ...'
WILLIAM SHAKESPEARE

What Is a Faerie?

If angels are the celestial guardians of the universe, then the faeries are the angels of the Earth. They are the spiritual manifestations and magical consciousness of every living thing on our planet. The role of a faerie is many and varied and they come in many different forms, but essentially their function is to guard, guide and nurture the living planet ... and us.

'Fairies are invisible and inaudible like angels.
But their magic sparkles in nature.'
LYNN HOLLAND

Is It True that Faeries Can Look Like Plants, Flowers, Leaves and So On?

As faeries belong to the natural world they can mirror nature in their appearance. This applies to the elemental faeries or *devas* who are the guardians of particular elements and plants. They also take on personality characteristics of the plant they belong to.

Some faeries can 'shapeshift' into different forms at will, so can easily blend into the nature all around them, especially to disguise themselves from human eyes.

'In an opal dream cave I found a fairy;
Her wings were frailer than flower petals, frailer far than snowflakes ...'
KATHERINE MANSFIELD

Are There Different Breeds of Faerie?

Faeries come in many different shapes and sizes and this usually reflects the job that they do. There are known to be four distinct types of faerie, and within these types are hundreds of *fey* belonging to each category.

THE ELEMENTAL FAERIES

These are the spirits of nature and include the winged sylphs of air, the undines and merpeople of water, the salamanders of fire and the dependable gnomes of the Earth. The elemental faeries also include devas who are the spirits of the trees and the plants.

THE FAERIE OR ELFIN FOLK

This is a race of magical hidden people who are often the same size as humans, and they are rarely winged. They dwell in lakes, mounds or enchanted faerie islands, and they are said to be invisible and silent unless they choose otherwise. They are governed by a Faerie King and Queen and they live in organized royal courts. They are also believed to have once been gods and goddesses, but have since been demoted by Christianity and our secular culture.

CREATURES AND DEMONS

These are also part of the faerie race and include such beings as unicorns, the Loch Ness Monster and trolls, for instance.

ENCHANTERS AND ENCHANTRESSES

These are humans with a faerie soul. They are thought to be faeries who have elected to be born into a human body to help the faerie race and humans work more closely together. These people are usually characterized by having faerie features and being sensitive types. After their death, they are thought to return to Faerie Land.

Can a Faerie Be My Spirit Guide?

We all have spirit guides, advanced human souls who steer and protect us, as well as angel guardians. But we also interact with spirits who specialize in a wide range of skills. Faeries can often work with humans who are interested in faeries, gardening and the environment, for example; and also children can have faeries as guides.

If you are interested in 'green issues' and caring for our world, you might want to seek out specific faeries to help you. Faeries are particularly interested in working with humans for anything to do with the protection and care of the planet, which might be why more people seem to be aware of the fey at this moment in time.

One reader told us: 'I talk to my faerie guide a lot. I ask him to show me how he can help me at the moment and how I can enjoy myself more. I ask him to bring me images of things which will help me in my life … although I always expect the images to appear like they do in Harry Potter!'

Modern-day storybooks will certainly help us to open up to the idea of real magic in our lives.

Can Animals See Faeries?

Animals are more readily able to see and sense faeries than humans, as they do not have things like language, technology, negative beliefs and so on to get in the way of being in closer contact with the natural world.

Your pets are quite likely to see faeries in your house, and wild animals are very closely linked to the faeries. Animals and faeries are known to shapeshift (change appearance) with one another. It is often thought that some animals, particularly birds and creatures such as hares, deer, calves, horses and others which are known to be 'faerie favourites', can be faerie messengers to humankind.

Watch out for signs of interest in your own pets. They might help you become aware of the faeries that live in and around your home.

'… In many a nook of the meadows, Fairies may linger and lurk;
Look under the low grass-shadows, Perhaps you'll see them at work …'
'THE WOUNDED DAISY', MENELLA BUTE SMEDLEY

Can Faeries See Us?

Faeries are able to move from their realm, 'Faerie Land', freely to our world, as they inhabit both and so are able to see us as part of their natural world.

'Think of the poor people who can't see the lovely fairies and the spirits …'
THE BOY WHO SAW TRUE

Why Would Faeries Want to Communicate with Humans?

Faeries are guardians of our planet. Presently our natural world is in jeopardy due to the destruction humans have wreaked upon it. This means that the faeries are concerned too for the welfare of the natural world, which is also part of their own world. By communicating with us they hope to help us to heal the Earth. And communicating with them and recognizing the spiritual aspect of the planet may help us to nurture it and take more care of it.

How Can a Faerie Help Me?

Faeries work as our helpers and guides on our spiritual pathway and with any aspect of our lives. If you would like help from your faerie guide – just ask! Write them a wish on a piece of paper, draw them a picture, ask them in a prayer or throw a pebble in a stream and ask your question. Then be prepared for an answer!

> *'... Come little fairies, come if you please,*
> *Nod your heads and ruffle your wings,*
> *Marching in order or standing at ease,*
> *Frolicsome fairies are dear little things ...'*
> 'FEEDING THE FAIRIES', MENELLA BUTE SMEDLEY

Faerie help will come in lots of forms – and usually not in the way that you expected. They colour our dreams and daydreams, send messengers in the form of animals, place clues in the books that you read, the films you watch and radio programmes you listen to. They make life a completely magical experience; so if you ask a faerie for help, do not expect a straightforward reply, and take the time to seek out the magic in your life – you will find it.

Faeries can help with any problem in your life, but first they need to get to know you and build trust with them, as they are sensitive beings who need to know that your intentions come from your heart. Begin to build a relationship with them by connecting with nature more often and helping them to look after your patch of the planet. Show them that you can be trusted with the faerie secrets ...

What Can I Do to Thank a Faerie?

If a faerie has helped you or you have simply felt their presence and want to thank them for being around, then here's how:

1 Rather than thank them directly, which they dislike, leave them a little gift. Their favourite gifts are token amounts of honey, cake, bread, milk or cream.

2 If possible, these should be put into a small natural or biodegradable container such as a sea shell, half a walnut shell or a bowl made from wood or bamboo, for example.

3 Place your gift in a special place in your house that is devoted to the faeries, such as by your hearthside or by a vase of lovely flowers. Even better is to leave your gift outside in a secluded place in your garden or a natural place such as the nook of a tree trunk in a woodland. Perhaps you could create a place especially for this?

4 The faeries do not usually actually take your present. They cannot take a physical thing back to Faerie Land as it does not transfer to their realm, which is a spiritual dimension. However, they take the essence and the love from your gift and this will help you to build a relationship with the faeries.

'I thought I might leave some jam as a little gift for the flower fairies …
That evening, I placed the egg cup underneath a blackberry bush.'
A *FLOWER FAIRIES JOURNAL*, CICELY MARY BARKER

Is It True that Children Can See Faeries When Adults Can't?

Faeries communicate with us partly through our 'imagination', which makes it especially easy for them to connect with young children. Youngsters work well with their imaginations up until early school age when, sadly, logic begins to take over. Using our imagination is a skill that we often lose once we grow into adulthood, although imagination and belief can be reclaimed and nurtured if we wish.

Interestingly enough, it is believed that young children can see a wider range of light than adults. This might account for the child's easy ability to see people and creatures from other worlds, like faeries, angels and deceased loved ones.

*'The fey wonders of the world only exist while there
are those with the sight to see them.'*
CHARLES DE LINT

Would Faeries Be Looking After My Baby Daughter Who Died Shortly After Birth?

Faeries are known to carry the souls of the departed to the afterlife, through the passageway of Faerie Land. Often people see coloured lights around those who are dying, especially babies and children, and these are thought to be the faeries gathering to carry their soul safely to the other realms.

*'The fairies went from the world, dear, Because men's hearts grew cold:
And only the eyes of children see what is hidden from the old ... '*
KATHLEEN FOYLE

There are also faeries whose specific roles are to watch over children (like Faerie Godmothers), and who can check on our little ones both in this realm and their own.

Do All Faeries Have Wings?

Only the faeries belonging to the element of air have wings. Some people believe that these wings are not actual wings, but thought-form energy in the shape of wings carrying the fey through the element of air. Air is meant to represent communication and thought, and the sylph faeries of the air encompass these qualities in the appearance of their wings.

Those lucky enough to see winged faeries suggest the wings look similar to the beautiful wings of birds, butterflies and dragonflies. Although faeries with the traditional gauzy-type wings which we see in pictures did not really start to appear until the 1800s, the winged variety was written about prior to this date.

'…Oh like those fairy things,
Those insects of the East,
That have their beauty in their wings,
And shroud it while at rest …'
'I THINK ON THEE', THOMAS KIBBLE HERVEY (1799–1859)

Have Faeries Always Existed?

Faeries have been around since the birth of the planet, or at least since the birth of humankind. Whether they are here as a connection between humans and the spiritual consciousness of the planet, or here in their own right, is up for debate. As they often appear in humanoid form, we can wonder whether we might have created them with our own consciousness.

There are stories of faeries being around at the time of the creation of the planet. The goddess Lilith was said to be the second wife of Adam, and it is suggested that she gave birth to all of the Faerie Kingdom. And, of course, faerie stories and tales appear in different variations all over the world.

Do Faeries Have Relationships or Partners?

Faeries definitely do have relationships and make life partnerships. Their relationships are not the same as humans'. They are not monogamous and, although they experience love, they are sexually free.

Faeries will not be crossed, but if they are crossed in love, then – according to faerie lore – this is the only thing that can be forgiven.

There is a very good reason for their sexual liberation, as they represent the fecundity of nature. The natural world is continually reproducing and, indeed, this is its purpose: to continue the cycle of life. So for faeries, relationships and love are not exclusive but all-encompassing.

> *'… Fairy lover, when my feet through the tangled woodland go,
> Tis thy sunny fingers fleet, Fleck the fire dews to and fro …'*
> 'ALTER EGO', GEORGE WILLIAM ('A E') RUSSELL

Are Faeries Immortal?

Faeries are not considered to be immortal. We know this because there have been sightings of Faerie Rades, which are faerie funeral processions. Faeries are considered to live much longer than humans, however – especially gnomes, who may live thousands of years.

> *'The fairy creatures were the size and colour of green and grey grasshoppers,
> bearing a body laid out on a rose-leaf, which they buried with songs,
> and then disappeared …'*
> WILLIAM BLAKE

How Do I Know If a Faerie Is with Me? What Signs of Their Presence Should I Look for?

Faeries are always around us, but it is just that we cannot ordinarily see them. If you would like an indication that a faerie is close, ask for proof by way of a sign. Just as our guardian angels will let us know that they are around us by leaving a white feather, the faeries can be even more imaginative.

This will be a subtle communication and often in a way that surprises you; as faeries love the element of surprise!

You may just feel the presence of a faerie, though this requires a quiet time of inner stillness. The sign might be a poke or a prod … be careful what you wish for! They may also show you their presence in many other ways, such as leaving you a faerie gift in the shape of a sea shell, a feather, a special stone or interestingly-shaped stick … although they are more likely to take something than leave something!

A passage from a book may jump out at you, a stranger in a shop may begin a meaningful conversation, a friend may send you a faerie card or you may even have a dream incorporating the faeries. Look for signs and they will find you.

Even if you don't see a faerie you might be able to sense that they are around you. Keep an open mind.

'Blind folk see the fairies. Oh, better far than we,
Who miss the shining of their wings,
Because our eyes are filled with things
We do not wish to see.'
ROSE FYLEMAN

Do Faeries Have a Physical Body?

Faeries belong to our physical world and also their realm too: Faerie Land. As they belong to both realms they do not have a physical body as such, although they do have form. Faerie Land belongs in a realm of its own, existing neither in this world nor the next, but a place hidden within our world, like an invisible bubble. Because faeries can freely visit all these worlds, their form reflects this. Faeries are made up of energy and light, vibrating at a very high frequency. They can slow down these vibrations, so that their bodies can take on a denser form which we are able to see in our physical world – if we are lucky!

Humans sometimes see faeries in their finer vibrational 'bodies', although it is just as common to see them as light forms. Imagine a spinning top, a simple child's toy: once we set the top spinning it gets faster and faster until it almost disappears … or does actually 'disappear' before our very eyes, until it starts to slow down again and we can once again see the toy in front of us. Of course, the spinning top has gone nowhere but our eyes cannot perceive it as it begins to move so fast. So yes, faeries have bodies, but because we live on a different vibration we might not always be able to see them.

One final word here: we are more likely to see faeries when our own vibrational rate has changed (when we are meditating or relaxed, for example). More of this later in the book.

If Faeries Exist, Why Can't We See Them More Often?

Faeries' main purpose is to look after nature, and they naturally work behind the scenes for the benefit of the planet. Indeed, they have been known as the 'hidden people' throughout history.

However, it is generally agreed that faeries were once known to be much more visible to humans in days gone by, and to co-habit with us more freely. It is thought that with industrialization and man's destruction of the environment, the faeries have become wary and distrusting of humans. It is only now when humans are realizing that something has to be done to save our planet that the faeries reach out to us once more and become more visible again in our world.

Hazel understands the difficulties of identifying the faeries – and, worst of all, would anyone believe us anyway? She explains: 'When I was about eight years old, I was in the car in a traffic queue near a supermarket outside York one evening, when a movement caught my eye. I turned and looked, and there was something flying over the roof of the shopping centre. I looked harder, and noticed that it didn't have the shape of a bird, but had a short head and a tubular tail that ended in a spur. Before I could react it was gone. I have never forgotten, and have only told very few people, as I didn't want to be seen as mad or stupid ...'

Faeries do come in all shapes and sizes, so read on and decide this one for yourself! Maybe it's just a matter of knowing where to look!

> '... Were we like the Fays that sweetly nestle in the foxglove bells ...'
> 'WHITHER?' HARTLEY COLERIDGE

Do Faeries Eat?

It is thought that faeries do eat because they are known to have favourite types of food: honey, cake, bread, milk, cream and mead. They are also thought to have all-night revelries where they enjoy lavish fey feasts. However, being not entirely of a physical form, they do not take in their food in the same way that we do, but absorb the food's energy (or essence, as it is known) into their beings.

'… My food the crimson luscious cherry; And the vine's luxurious berry …'
'Fairy Song', Felicia Dorothea Browne-Hemans

Do Faeries Wear Clothes?

Faeries belong to a more liberated society than our own, and because they are also beings of nature, they often do not feel the need to wear clothes. Being from another realm, they do not feel the cold or heat as we do, so clothes for them are merely worn as a form of self-expression.

The materials that their clothes are made from are also different from our own and they reflect the environment in their appearance. For this reason they may wear garments made from leaves, feathers, grasses, seeds or flowers – in fact, anything that can be found in nature. Gossamer is thought to be an extremely special fabric worn only by the faeries. This material is a fine, gauzy fabric which faeries spin to clothe themselves, and is said to be as fine as a spider's thread on a cobweb. It is thought to be the softest fabric known to exist.

Faerie artwork often depicts faeries wearing such things as hats made from seed heads and skirts made from flower petals. Of course, it's likely that these images affect the way we actually 'see' faeries when we encounter them … but who knows?!

*'This place has such a different feel to home.
I'm sure I shall see no end of fairies and gnomes and all that …'*
The Boy Who Saw True

What Is Faerie 'Glamour'?

This is a type of magic worked only by the faeries or those whom the faeries favour. By way of glamour the faeries are able to make things appear to be something that they are not. For example, they can make themselves appear more beautiful and lavishly dressed than they really are, or they can make a handful of buttons appear to be gold coins.

Faeries are also known to work glamour magic in our world too. As everyone knows that riches, fast cars and glamorous lifestyles are a kind of illusion and are not a grounded way of living, we should be wary of faerie glamour in all its forms!

Are Faeries Common to All Cultures?

All cultures across the world recognize faeries in one form or another. Not all countries call them faeries, but 'little people' are part of every culture's folklore. Faeries have been talked about and written about as far back as recorded history.

Can People Be Faeries?

Some people believe that there are humans who have a faerie soul, and because of this they have fey characteristics in their personalities and physical appearance. These people have been called incarnated elementals, enchanters, enchantresses and Faerie Priests/Priestesses.

Jacky: I have a friend who believes that she has lived as a faerie in previous existences. Apart from a love of fine, green gossamer clothing, there are no obvious signs! Some people do seem to reflect this image on the outside, though, and you might have fun spotting potential 'faerie people' at your local 'alternative health' or 'psychic' event!

Where Is the Land of Faerie?

The Land of Faerie is a place not of our world, so it can't be considered to have a physical location on a map. However, there are thought to be special doorways known as 'faerie portals' through which we can reach Faerie Land from our world. There are many famous portals to Faerie Land with wonderful stories surrounding them; these include Glastonbury Tor in Somerset, England and Knockshegouna in County Donegal, Ireland.

People throughout history who have visited the Land of Faerie have reported that it is an exceptionally beautiful place where the light is constantly dusky; a place where the sun never rises or sets but a place of 'in-between', as if it were forever spring. Beware, though: it is easy to get trapped in the Land of Faerie. Read on for ways to protect yourself.

Are Faeries Dangerous?

The term 'faeries' is generic and covers many different types of creature. Some are thought to be very dangerous, whereas others are thought to be not just safe but helpful to humans (see Chapter 3 'Faerie Names A–Z' for more information).

Some of the more dangerous faeries might not have existed at all, not in any real way. Faeries have been blamed for pretty well everything that has gone wrong in the lives of humans for many years, so read carefully and then make up your own mind.

One thing is for sure: if people don't believe in them and don't seek interaction with faeries, many happily go about their lives never seeing or communicating with faeries in any way whatsoever.

CHAPTER 2

The Faeries' Almanac

'Life itself is the most wonderful fairy tale.'
HANS CHRISTIAN ANDERSEN

Helpful Faeries

Despite their mischievous ways, there are many faeries who are willing to help humans. Do beware, though, as there are often conditions attached to their assistance. Remember Cinderella who had to be home by midnight? When she failed to return at the time her Faerie Godmother dictated, all of the magic disappeared and Cinderella was left dressed only in her original rags instead of her beautiful ball gown.

Beware the conditions and consider the following faeries who might help you with your tasks.

Help Needed	Faerie Helper
Children, childcare	Faerie Godmothers, The Gwragedd Annwn (help both mothers and children)
Childbirth/Fertility	Nibelungen (makers of fertility rings)
Fire, creating a hearth fire, lighting candles and barbecues	Salamander
Fortune-telling/fate	Faerie Godmothers and Moerae, especially for the fate of young children
Gardening	Masseriol

Help Needed	Faerie Helper
Housework	Elves (house elves are called Kobolds), Masseriol and Brownies
Mending, sewing, shoe care	Leprechauns
Money/prosperity	Leprechauns (especially associated with gold), Menehunas
Pets/livestock	Masseriol
Spell-casting	Puck, son of Oberon, King of the Faeries
Spiritual guidance	Mother Holle and all Faerie Kings and Queens
Travelling	Menehunas, Murdhuachas (especially if you are lost at sea)

Faeries of Trees

The following is by no means an exclusive list, and you may well find other trees with faerie associations attached to different locations around the world. Use this list to start you off.

Alder

The alder is used in spells to protect against evil fae. The alder is watched over by the water sprite and there is an ancient alder faerie in mythology called *Clethrad*.

Apple

Both the fruit and the bark of the apple tree are used in faerie love spells, and apples are suitable as an offering to faeries as a thank-you gift.

Ash

Traditional faerie lore states that if you place ash-tree berries in a baby's cot it will prevent the fey from taking your baby and trading it in for a 'changeling'. I don't recommend this as suitable for today, though!

To protect yourself from malevolent faeries, stand in the shadow of an ash tree. (See also Hawthorn.)

Birch

There is a Scottish faerie called *Ghillie Ghu* who is said to live in birch thickets.

Dogwood

The fruit of this tree is sometimes called 'Pixie Pears'.

Elder

There is an old English belief that if you place your baby into a cradle made of elder wood, the faeries will pinch him black and blue. The elder tree helps to protect faeries from people and entities which might harm them, especially at night.

Fig

The fig tree has its very own faeries according to Hindu mythology. The fig faeries, known as the *Apsaras*, can bless humankind. You can call upon the fig-tree faeries for good luck and protection.

Hawthorn

Hawthorn is also sometimes known as Faerie Thorn. Along with oak and ash, hawthorn creates the perfect faerie habitat. If you want to have the greatest chance of seeing a faerie, legend suggests you visit a place where these three trees grow together. (See also page 135.)

Holly

Another tree the faeries love.

Nut trees

Nut trees have their very own faeries (or nymphs) called the *Caryatids*.

Oak

Faeries and elves are believed to live in the hollow of old oak trees. When near an oak, turn your coat inside-out to protect yourself from their faerie magic. *Dryads* are the nymphs of oak trees.

Peach tree

The peach is sometimes called a faerie fruit.

Pear tree

In the old 'Language of the Flowers', Japanese pears were known as 'faeries' fire'.

Rowan

If you want to protect your home, plant a rowan tree. As well as protection from faerie spells it will bring you good luck. Rowan was traditionally used in a spell to stop butter being over-churned, and the smoke from a fire made from rowan is used in Scotland to protect cattle.

Thorn trees (blackthorn, hawthorn etc.)

If you want the faeries to bring back a stolen child, then burn a fire on top of a faerie mound. Thorn trees are the meeting places of the faerie folk.

Willow trees

There is a willow faerie called *Heliconian,* although little is known about her.

THE FAERIE AND THE IVY

Margie had an inspirational faerie encounter which she calls her 'one and only':

> About eight years ago when I was 32 years old, I was living on the outskirts of Yuba City, California. Back at my old residence there was an ivy vine that grew wild all the way around the house. I didn't think much of it except that it was difficult to manage, growing as fast as it did. We had a magnificent magnolia tree with huge blossoms out front, and beside that, an apricot tree. Along the front walkway was a hedgerow of white star jasmine with fragrant blooms you

couldn't miss smelling as you walked up to the front door on a sunny afternoon.

On this particular day I decided to take a late-morning nap. The pine headboard of my bed rested against the window that looked out into the front yard where the magnolia and apricot trees stood. I had decorated the headboard with a silk ivy garland, weaving it in and around the bedposts of the headboard. (I've always been an arts-and-crafts kind of person.) I lay down on the bed as I normally would, not seeing anything out of the ordinary, but I did have trouble falling asleep and found myself stuck in a half-awake-half-asleep awareness instead. Immediately I began to 'dream', if that is what you call it when you are not properly asleep ...

I found myself in the middle of a patch of ivy ... but not just a patch! It was all around me, as if the world itself was made of it. I was greeted by a being, a nature spirit, who I can only assume to have been an elf. As best as I can remember, it wasn't a formal 'How do you do?' greeting. But it was pure indescribable joy.

He twirled and jumped around in front of me, swapping from a human-like form to the ivy itself and back again. I clearly remember his shoes! Who would have thought? A nature spirit with shoes? But it was true: just like you would see in a faerie-tale book they were soft like stockings, green, long and pointy, and the tips glowed with a phosphorescent light-green hue. He would not stand still for an instant and was constantly moving, constantly working/playing and constantly joyful! He was free-spirited in every sense of the term. His life was his work, yet it was joyful and unceasingly playful at the same time. He entwined me with himself as he leaped and spun in the ivy and I was captivated by his pure and joyful essence.

And then it ended as I slowly opened my eyes. As I regained focus, the joy was still with me and I remained totally astounded by what I had seen … but the magic hadn't ended yet. As I sat up I noticed a branch of ivy had made its way into the house through a crack in my bedroom window. I was amazed that it was even alive because as I examined the branch I saw that it was severely crushed, yet continued to grow! The remaining portion of the vine had weaved its way through the pine headboard on my bed (through the silk garland) and hung directly over my forehead as I lay sleeping. There at its tip was a newly-formed ivy leaf hanging directly over my forehead. I definitely do not remember seeing this as I lay down to take a nap. Perhaps I just overlooked it, who knows? It was almost as if the branch had grown a foot while I lay resting!

I will never forget that experience for as long as I live. Up until that moment I had considered 'Faeriefolk' to be only make-believe … now I know they are real!

Earth Faeries
MEETING A GNOME, THE GUARDIANS OF THE TREES

Jacky had an Earth-faerie experience of her own … although not as amazing as Margie's!

Walking through the gardens of Chatsworth House, England, a beautiful country property which is open to the public, I spotted an interesting tree. Pushing my way through the shrubbery, I spied the beautiful branches with lovely knots and twists, and immediately wanted to place my hands upon the trunk. Immediately I felt a very strong force, which seemed to stop me in my tracks. Something or someone did not want me to touch this tree after all.

Looking down, I felt and sensed a very old-looking gnome, very much like the gnome statues one would purchase at any garden centre. Wrinkled trousers, baggy top, red pointy hat ... yes, all these, and even a beard. This gnome stood with his arms outstretched as if guarding the tree.

'Please ...' I begged in my mind. I explained that I only wanted to send love to and exchange energy with this magnificent tree. Old trees seem to have a healing energy all of their own, don't they? They hold a kind of comfort about them. Imagine nestling safely amongst the branches in the way that the tree protects a bird nest, keeping it safe and secure. I wanted to fill myself with the ancient wisdom of this beautiful tree, but the gnome was having none of it!

I smiled and he seemed to study me closely. All of a sudden it was as if the force-field had been let down. Whatever it was that was stopping me from approaching the tree had been removed. The gnome moved to one side and I was allowed close. Perhaps I had passed my test! Taking my opportunity, I pressed both hands flat against the tree and, taking one little last look for ants or other unsavoury bugs, I closed my eyes and soaked up the spark of life that lit this tree so brightly in the garden of this grand and beautiful house. Just moments later I stepped back and remembered to say 'Thank you' before I walked away.

I took something of that tree with me that day but I also left a little something of myself behind, as I kissed the trunk.

ASKING PERMISSION FROM THE SPIRIT OF THE TREE

I should have asked permission first of all to approach the tree by communicating with the tree spirit or faerie ... in this case a big fat gnome! Trees give us so much. They help to keep our air fresh and pure, and we use their wood to build our homes and our furniture, amongst other things.

Branches and twigs from faerie trees can also be used for your magical tools, but it's always best to use pieces of wood which have fallen naturally from the tree, if you can. If you have no choice but to cut a piece of wood from a tree, then asking is even more important. Do make sure that you 'feel' your yes answer before removing any part of the tree – and leave an offering in exchange (see page 36 for some suitable faerie gifts).

See Chapter 17 for how to make your own faerie wand.

Flower Faeries

> *'I'll seek a four-leaved shamrock in all thy fairy dells,*
> *And if I find the charmed leaves, oh, how I'll weave my spells!'*
> SAMUEL LOVER

Faeries are of course the guardians of nature, and it's only natural that particular flowers and plants would have associations with faeries. Some people use the term *deva* to refer to these particular types of faerie, the spirit of the flower. Any child knows that faeries live at the bottom of the garden in amongst the wildest of flowers.

In the Balkans, people believe that faeries are actually born in flowers and, as in Romania, each faerie has its own plant insignia or symbol. The Slavonic female faeries called the *Vile* (or *Vily*) are thought to be born from faerie mothers who have been inseminated by dew or, again, actually born from plants.

An active bird population in the garden is often an indication of the abundance of faeries. Faeries, like birds, prefer the quieter parts of your outdoor space.

Jacky says: 'My husband John suggests that by imagining the flower and plant faeries back into existence, it will help clear the spiritual pathway for them to inhabit a garden they have previously left. I know he is right.'

> *'The eglantine perfumes the dell; In richest purple bloom,*
> *a bed of fragrant mountain thyme is spread.'*
> JANET HAMILTON (1704–1754)

PLANT A FAERIE GARDEN

It is believed that by planting certain plants, you can encourage faeries into your garden. There are many plants with faerie-type names too … maybe with good reason.

Faeries particularly love areas with running water. It's no surprise how the saying 'Faeries at the bottom of the garden' came about. Faeries by choice will take the wildest and least disturbed section of your garden, and if that's at the bottom of your garden, then so be it! If you have mature trees, then so much the better.

If you really want to theme your garden, then you can add faerie figurines, pixie homes and faerie doors to your faerie space. A tour around a specialist garden centre, a browse through gardening catalogues or a search on the Internet will find you all sorts of exciting items to 'dress' your space. Try:

- Wind chimes. Look for natural ones made of shells or bamboo. Why not hang several or even make some of your own?

- Bird tables (faeries love birds, and want us to help look after them).

- Bird houses (many different ones are available to buy, or you could design some yourself) or maybe small homes for faeries. (Perhaps you could make and decorate them yourself, too?) Look for unusual designs and hang them in trees and on walls and fences.

- Hang faerie-decorated seed-feeders. It's surprising how many of these you can find in the shops nowadays. Designers, too, seem to associate faeries with gardens!

- Look for strings of bells to hang on trees, or hang small bells on coloured ribbons and decorate trees as you would a Christmas tree. Bells attract the good faeries and scare away the bad ones.

- Hang 'faerie lights' or strings of coloured lights (make sure they are suitable for outdoor use and fitted by a trained electrician).

- Place coloured spotlights to highlight favourite plants or figures. White is pretty, or use different colours to match the flowers in your garden. Green and purple bulbs are especially magical.

- Tea-light holders. (*Jacky:* a friend of mine collects faerie-decorated candle holders at yard sales and jumble sales, and only pays a few pence for them. She lights them on warm evenings to bring a special magic to her garden.)

- Maybe section off a particular part of the garden with a rose arch or gateway if there is room, or a more subtle distinction to mark the faerie-designated area by the way you plant up your space.

- Consider placing a plaque or sign which indicates your faerie garden.

- Remember to include white flowers in your scheme which show up first thing in the morning and last thing at night when the light is dim.

- Consider planting scented plants close to the house so that you can enjoy the scent on warm summer evenings through open windows – if your climate allows.

- Any plant which attracts butterflies is especially suitable. Of course, this will also bring lots of other colour and beauty to your garden. Once you invite the faeries, the butterflies soon appear.

- Include a water feature if you have room. A small pond would work well, or a natural feature which includes rocks, wood or bamboo. Do consider safety when choosing something for your garden, especially if you have young children or pets.

- If you are lucky enough to have trees in your garden, you could make a natural faerie altar from rocks, slate or wood at the base. Or, if not, just find a protected area close by a suitable bush or shrub. Add shells, pretty stones and other natural objects whenever you wish to leave an offering to the faeries. They will soon learn where to find your gifts.

And if you don't attract any real faeries, maybe you could add a faerie figurine or two? Look out for those black-painted silhouette cut-out shapes on plant sticks to pop into tubs and plant hangers. Or pottery glittery faeries which sit on the sides of your plant pots. Try and keep these next to rather than in your pots as the glitter is not terribly environmentally friendly and will shed in time. Try the Internet as well as traditional garden centres and gift shops for these.

Do make sure that you use nothing made of iron or steel, because these metals actually repel faeries and can even be dangerous to them (useful if you want to get rid of naughty faeries, of course!).

FLOWERS, PLANTS AND HERBS YOU CAN GROW IN YOUR OWN GARDEN TO ENCOURAGE FAERIES

'Hand in hand, with fairy grace, Will we sing, and bless this place.'
WILLIAM SHAKESPEARE, *A MIDSUMMER NIGHT'S DREAM*

Here are the more traditional plants and flowers associated with faeries. Do check carefully, because not all of these plants and flowers are suitable for gardens with children, and some may even be poisonous ... but which the faeries seem to like just fine. Just the same, if you have children too, do satisfy yourself as to the suitability of each plant before you consider planting it in your own garden.

Blackberry

In Celtic countries it was forbidden to eat blackberries because they were plants of the faeries (*'à cause des fees'*). Don't you just love blackberry tea ...?

Bluebell

Bluebells are particularly known for their use in faerie magic. They say it is impossible to escape from a bluebell field because you will become impossibly enchanted or charmed by the faeries. If you are unlucky enough to hear a bluebell ringing, then beware, it warns of a malicious faerie. Bluebell woods are particularly beautiful, so it is easy to see how this might come about.

Jacky writes:

When we lived in Birmingham, England as children, we had a very long, traditional English garden. I remember the bluebells growing in abundance along the bottom of the garden. Bluebells are protected flowers here in the UK now, but as children we were allowed to pick them and would bring in handfuls of blooms to place in a glass on the kitchen window. I love bluebells even to this day.

'I do not think I have ever seen anything more beautiful than the bluebell ...'
GERARD MANLEY HOPKINS

Clover

If you find a field of clover, then faeries will probably be close by. Four-leaf clovers are especially helpful in faerie magic as they can be used to protect you against naughty faeries. They are powerful and can be used to break faerie spells performed against humans, and if you wear one in your hat it is said to make invisible faeries visible. You can also make yourself special ointments with four-leaf clovers, or use them to make charms for personal protection.

Cowslip

Do faeries carry cowslips as umbrellas? According to faerie lore they do. Faeries love the lacy heads of the cowslip blossoms. Cowslips can be used in faerie magic, too. They are considered useful for opening secret places and finding faerie treasures and gold.

> 'And I serve the Fairy Queen, To draw her orbs upon the green.
> The cowslips tall her pensioners be ...'
> SHAKESPEARE, *A MIDSUMMER NIGHT'S DREAM*

Daffodil

The daffodil is helpful if you want to invoke the magical faeries and elves to work with you.

Jacky: Even in my garden of specially blended pinks and lilacs I always get a few wild bright yellow daffodils poking their heads through, and messing up my well-designed space. I figure it's a kind of cosmic joke and always let them be. Maybe their appearance around the small tree at the end of my garden is no accident after all.

Daisy

The daisy is another plant (both wild and cultivated) which is used in faerie magic and charms.

Jacky: When we were children we were taught how to make a daisy chain. We would push a fingernail through the daisy stem to make a small slit and then pull another daisy stem right through the hole right up to the head, continuing until we had lengths long enough to hang around our neck as nature's necklaces, or to hang around our wrists as bracelets.

What we didn't realize was that we were following an age-old tradition of hanging daisy chains around a child's neck to prevent the child from being carried away by the faeries!

How many of these magical rituals from childhood do we perform with no knowledge of the origins? A great number, I am sure!

Elecampane (also known as elfwort and elf dock)

Another magical faerie plant whose roots are used in faerie rituals. If you grow the elecampane herb in your garden you will surely attract the faeries in. Placing pieces of the elecampane root around your home is meant to encourage the wee folk to enter.

Evening primrose

See if you can find the fairy fan evening primrose (*Clarkia* of the *Onagraceae* family)! A perfect plant to enhance your faerie garden.

Fern

If you want to find pixies, then search first of all around the ferns in your local wood. Pixies particularly love ferns.

Flax

Another name for purging flax is faerie flax, a plant especially attractive to the faeries, so another great plant to add to your faerie garden at home.

Forget-me-nots

These pretty sprays of fine blue flowers are something I have always grown in my own garden at home. Traditionally they provide protection from the naughty faeries but, perhaps more usefully, they are another flower which helps to unlock faerie treasures and secrets.

Foxgloves

The foxglove is actually a poisonous plant, so needs to be used with care. Foxgloves are often found growing wild in England where I live, especially on the south coast. Their natural pinks and whites stand tall at the back of the borders, but breeders now have produced a wide range of colours including peaches and purples. Faeries seem to like them all.

Old folk names for foxgloves include faerie thimbles (named for the pretty cup-shaped flowers) and faerie gloves, which is a name I remember from childhood. Other names include faerie weed, faerie petticoats and faerie caps. I remember mostly watching the bees visiting the flower heads and seeing them bob in and out. We often wove stories around these flowers as children but, sensibly, my mother warned us that the plant was dangerous.

A friend of mine called Wendy used to giggle at the thought that people might even try and taste them. Wendy used to say, '… remember, never eat the foxgloves … no matter how hungry you are,' and then we would laugh hysterically!

In faerie magic the leaves are used to help release humans from faerie enchantment, although to plant the foxgloves in your garden is also a sign of invitation to the wee folk. If you want to attract faeries to you, then you can always use images of foxgloves in your home or, if you are lucky enough to find a brooch, pin or item of clothing decorated with the foxglove flower, then wear this.

Grass

In traditional tales, faeries are said to use bundles of grass as horses! Imagine them bouncing around on soft mown grass (see also Ragwort).

Before the obsession with crop circles (created by UFOs?), faeries were making impressions upon the grass. Faerie rings were circles of dried or flattened grass which may or may not have had mushrooms as part of their make-up. Some rings have the circle made of darker and more luxurious grass.

For years I was intrigued by a ring in the grass which sat alongside my local fishpond under the shade of the trees. Of course, you always hope it has been made by the faeries ... Other names for the faerie rings include a faerie dance and faerie court.

Hawthorn

Hawthorn is both a bush and a tree. The hawthorn is sometimes known as the faerie thorn and the berries are also called pixie pears. (See also page 17.)

Heather

A good place to start looking for a door to the Faerie Kingdoms or a Faerie Portal is amongst the heather, according to faerie lore. Its stalks are a traditional faerie food. Heather is found in many of the areas around the world where faeries are said to frequent.

Heather has long been mixed up with magical uses. Bunches of white heather are thought to bring good luck and are often sold door-to-door by gypsies.

Holly

This evergreen bush is a favourite of the faeries, especially the bright red berries.

Hollyhock

Pink hollyhocks are the faeries' favourite, and who can blame them for loving these tall, scented beauties?

Jacky: Pink, white, blue ... and yes, I have them at the bottom of my garden!

Beware the slugs who love these too ... the flowers' scent will attract both slugs and snails for miles around, who love to chomp through the new shoots as they push through the earth. The flowers might need a little more care at this early stage but it's worth the effort. Stake them well so that they don't bend and break in the wind. The faeries will appreciate your efforts.

Lavender

Lavender (sometimes known as elf leaf) can be used in cooking as well as magical potions. Lavender is a popular essential oil (aromatherapy oil) and is blended into perfumes and cosmetics as well as air-fresheners for use in the home.

This natural herb can also be used for medicinal purposes and is no longer associated with 'grandmas' as it was when I was a girl. Lavender is a firm faerie favourite.

Lilacs

The scent of lilacs has long been associated with faeries and is meant to draw them into your garden. Angels, too, are said to arrive on the scent of lilacs, so you get double rewards for your efforts ...

Lily

Amongst these stunning beauties are the so-called fairy bells (*Disporum* of the *Liliaceae* family).

Mistletoe

Of course, mistletoe is used in faerie magic. Add mistletoe to your faerie spells; this makes them particularly powerful on Midsummer Night's Eve.

Morning glory

This pretty little flower is a great addition if you want to keep mischievous faeries away from your garden. It seems to repel them in some way.

Mushrooms (and also toadstools)

Jacky: I remember the excitement of seeing my first red-topped toadstool in the woods of Sutton Park in England. I immediately thought of the pictures of faerie toadstools in my childhood books of faerie tales. Those mushrooms and toadstools with the bumpy tops are those traditionally seen as faerie furniture ... or umbrellas.

Faerie rings or circles (made of grass) can also be created with circles of mushrooms. There are some fun faerie mushroom names including pixie hood, dryad's saddle, elf's stool, elf cap and fairy club.

Orchid

I love the exotic blooms of the orchid plant and have quite a collection at home along my conservatory windowsill. Perhaps like other flowers, their flower heads remind some of the delightful designs of faerie attire.

Orchid names include the green fairy orchid (*Hammarbya paludosa*), and the tiny flowering fairy slipper orchid (*Calypso bulbosa*). Interestingly, many healing flower essences combine the names 'orchid' and 'fairy'!

Pansy

The pansy's claim to fame? Shakespeare's Oberon, the Faerie King, added pansies to his love potion (in *A Midsummer Night's Dream*) to help both man and woman 'dote upon each other'… Although it's not strictly ethical to bend the free will of another, I guess the same rules don't apply to faeries!

Peony

If you want to dream about the faeries or interact with them whilst you sleep, plant peonies in your garden, or bring their blooms into the house. Stake them well because they soon drop.

Jacky: I have several of these and they can be quite hard to grow and they hate to be moved. Once they get going they are well worth the effort. Their rose-like blooms can be breathtaking.

Poppy

Look out in particular for the fairy poppy. Poppies again are seen as faerie clothing, particularly skirts.

Primrose

The lore surrounding primroses is quite specific. If you want to invite faeries into your home you hang primroses on your door, but if you throw the petals along your boundaries it acts as a magical obstacle which stops the faeries crossing over.

Faeries are said to be attracted to the blossoms growing in your garden, but make sure you take care of the primroses or you'll upset the faeries for sure.

Ragwort

Faeries use the stems of ragwort as transport or 'horses' (see also Grass), according to legend. They also use them to fly on, like broomsticks.

Rose

The faeries are attracted to the exquisite scent and prettiness of the blooms, and so rose petals are useful in magical concoctions. Roses have long been associated with love, especially the red blooms. Work with the faeries to create love spells.

Rosemary

Jacky: I have always found myself attracted to rosemary, an easy-to-grow scented herb. The plant can grow fairly large, so it's easier to contain in a large pot and grow it on your patio or by your door. You can hang bunches of rosemary on your front and back doors to keep away malicious faeries, or use rosemary oil (which has quite a strong smell) or rosemary incense to attract faeries.

St John's wort

St John's wort is used to protect you from faerie spells and enchantments.

Thistle

Pixies love thistles, which are also called pixies' gloves.

Thyme

Wearing bunches of wild thyme is said to be helpful in opening your faerie eyes. Tradition says that if you place a sprig of thyme over your eyes whilst you lie on a faerie mound (of course, you have to find a faerie mound first) then you are sure to see faeries … an exciting thought.

Lay the dried herb along the entrances to your home to invite these magical creatures in. You can also use thyme in faerie magic.

Violet

Violets are the flowers of the Faerie Queen and you can use this plant in your faerie spells.

Wood sorrel

If you've trouble with some pesky elves, then wood sorrel acts like a magical detergent. It cleans and clears them out!

Of course, all this information is traditional faerie lore, so you'll have to use your own best judgement as to whether any of it is appropriate for today's world. Let us know if you have success with any of these!

Attracting and Repelling Faeries – Quick List

Type of flower/ plant/herb	Attracts faeries	Repels faeries	Useful in spells	Protects faeries
Blackberry	🌹	🌹		
Clover	🌹			🌹
Cowslip	🌹		🌹	
Daffodil			🌹	
Daisy		🌹	🌹	
Elecampane	🌹		🌹	
Evening primrose	🌹			
Fern	🌹			
Flax	🌹			
Forget-me-nots	🌹			
Foxglove	🌹			
Grass	🌹			
Hawthorn	🌹		🌹	
Heather	🌹		🌹	
Holly	🌹			
Hollyhock	🌹			
Lavender	🌹		🌹	
Lilac	🌹			
Lily	🌹			
Mistletoe			🌹	
Morning glory		🌹		
Mushrooms (and toadstools)	🌹			
Orchid	🌹			
Pansy			🌹	🌹
Peony	🌹			
Poppy	🌹			
Primrose	🌹	🌹		
Ragwort	🌹			
Rose	🌹		🌹	
Rosemary	🌹	🌹		
St John's wort		🌹	🌹	
Thyme	🌹			
Violet			🌹	🌹
Wood sorrel			🌹	

OTHER WAYS OF USING FLOWER ENERGY TO ENCOURAGE OR DISCOURAGE FAERIES

Of course, if you don't have a garden space … or even a window box, you can always fill a pot with flowers and place it on your kitchen windowsill. Look for a longer box shape so that you can fit in more plants along your narrow window ledge. Decorate with a tree branch, shells, crystals and faerie plant sticks. Don't forget to ask permission from the faeries before taking anything from nature. Or place several pots closely together and arrange them on a tray alongside a faerie figurine and light them with tiny indoor faerie lights. Atmosphere is everything!

Remember to add both plants that encourage faeries into your space and those that repel the naughty faeries!

You can also use the essence of the flowers in aromatherapy oils (oils which use the real plant rather than synthetic oils, which do not hold the imprint of the plant), bring cut flowers into the home, or use the dried petals in potpourri.

Look for scented candles and soaps which use the natural flower oils, and learn about flower essences, and herb and fruit teas which have a faerie connection, using the chart as a guide. You might find other plants of your own which have traditional faerie associations too.

Faerie Food

Faeries are attracted to a wide variety of human foods but particularly those that are unavailable in their own realms. They especially like sweet things!

Gifts of food are appropriate as thank-yous and include:

- honey
- milk and cream
- butter
- bread or freshly baked cake
- mead
- fruit – especially berries.

THE BLOSSOM FAERIE

OK, it's time for a story – Carol saw a 'blossom faerie'.

When I was five years old, I lived in upstate New York with my family. We were just a block from Lake Ontario, and lived in a lovely home. In a corner of the yard grew a beautiful ornamental cherry tree and every Spring it bloomed the most gorgeous fluffy pink blossoms ... so abundant! I always felt that it looked like a giant cone of cotton candy and it was at all times my favourite place to be. I called it my dreaming spot.

I'd lie beneath that tree on a blanket to think, read, play and be cool in the afternoon shade. One day as I lay beneath my beautiful tree, a faerie appeared, flitting about the blossoms, much as one would expect to see a humming bird. I couldn't believe my eyes and recall sucking in my breath, afraid that even breathing might frighten it away. I was frozen in surprise. It continued to flit about for a few moments, then looked over as if it suddenly noticed me staring. Then, as quickly as it appeared, it simply darted off.

I ran out from beneath the tree to see where it went, but it had simply disappeared. Breathless with excitement, I sat back beneath the tree thinking, 'It's TRUE! It's TRUE! They DO exist!' I was ecstatic and overwhelmed! I sat for a moment trying to decide whether to tell anyone or not, imagining my brothers laughing at me ... but I did choose to run and tell my mother. She listened intently to my report and assured me that if I saw a faerie, then indeed they MUST exist!

It then became my quest to see that faerie again and I literally camped out under that cherry tree waiting and waiting. At night, I would sneak out of the house because I'd read somewhere that faeries love the evenings. I brought my Brownie camera, a flashlight, and a jar ... just in case.

I tried everything, even hiding the camera and recreating the events that led to the first sighting, but nothing appeared and I never did see that faerie again!

But I never stopped knowing what I DID see that day, and wanting to see it again. I'm a middle-aged woman now and still hold out hope of faeries appearing to me again. In the meantime, I paint them!

We love Carol's delightful story. Of course the secret is in the dreaming. Relaxing in quiet bliss helps to transport us to the realms of 'daydreaming', which opens the portal to the faerie-side! It sounds simple – sadly it's not as easy as all that, which is a shame!

Flower Faerie Painters
CICELY MARY BARKER

For many years faeries have been thought to hold guardianship over specific trees and flowers. The Victorian artist Cicely Mary Barker (1895–1973) further encouraged this thought in the public mind by producing her stunning *Flower Fairies* books which were illustrated by her own paintings. Her first book, *Flower Fairies of Spring*, was published in 1923; over the next 25 years she created a further six *Flower Fairies* books, which included faeries painted with plants, flowers and trees.

Her plant illustrations were perfectly accurate and she even called upon the staff at Kew Gardens to find specific plants for her paintings. Her sister Dorothy worked at a kindergarten and Cicely found the children a great inspiration in her work, often sketching them and using them in her pictures, adapting them into the faeries she adored.

Cicely's fairy images were beautiful interpretations of childlike figures dressed in leaves and flowers with delicate butterfly-style wings. Cicely's images were often accompanied by her simple lines of prose and botanical information.

Her pretty figures often wore hats made from leaves or flowers. She was inspired by everything in nature, and even a simple seed head would become a little bonnet, or a bunch of leaves a skirt.

Some of the fairies were barefoot and others wore little stockings. Her fairies always blended in with their surroundings and matched perfectly the flower or plant which they protected.

Her paintings have remained popular and today you can buy many items with her illustrations including tins, trays, badges and even clothing. Her books have become classics amongst children's literature, and naturally appeal to adults too.

Jacky: One of the flower faeries painted by Cecily Mary Barker was a willow faerie ... I have this illustration of Cecily's on cushions in my writing room ...

Lizzy van Leeuwen from Holland says she has seen a willow faerie, and she told us all about her encounter:

I was walking in the park with my husband when a young willow drew my attention. It wanted to play with me! I headed over to the tree and touched the bark to greet and make contact and I felt the spirit of the willow had invited me to dance around the tree!

While I was dancing and hopping around the willow, I heard a lot of giggling and laughter around me and was pushed (in a friendly way) a couple of times! I stopped because I got dizzy and then the nymph of the willow appeared in front of me. She was a beautiful, young, feminine spirit of nature. She was about one metre tall, very slim and feminine. Her long hair was green and was adorned with willow leaves. She wore a white transparent dress.

Her face was cute with a small nose and mouth and a green complexion with a translucent skin. She had a childlike character and was playful.

Lizzy paints faeries herself, inspired by the many experiences she's had. One day she came across the Moss Lady, who even left her a beautiful gift:

> She was a soft, friendly and feminine entity, transparent and ethereal. She invited me in, granting my request to come closer. The place was covered with lovely, rich moss, in bright and deep green tones. I could sense her breath all over the place.
>
> I asked her if she could guide me to a place where I could give my libation to her. She guided me to a beautiful spot near a tree trunk. Out of gratitude and with deep respect and honour, I offered three small chocolate eggs at that spot. She whirled all around me in a flowing green spiral. She suddenly stood behind me and she lovingly draped a beautiful coat, made out of moss, on me! I felt very honoured and intensely safe.
>
> I said goodbye and walked towards the exit. I still felt the coat around me and suddenly, in front of my feet, I saw a small branch, richly covered in moss, lying on the path. It was a goodbye gift from the lady herself! After asking permission, I picked it up and cherished it.
>
> Back home I placed it on my table. Together with two pieces of rose quartz, a small candle in a little green glass and lavender incense I made an altar in honour of the Moss Lady. I put on the CD *Journey to the Faeries* by Llewellyn and started to paint the Moss Lady.

Faerie Times and Faerie Dates

There are important dates in the faeries' year. Shakespeare (in his play *A Midsummer Night's Dream*) and Kipling have firmly associated Midsummer Night as a great time to see faeries! In Sussex, England, all ancient Hill Forts are said to be haunted by the faeries at midnight on Midsummer Night. If there is a full moon on Midsummer's Eve then so much the better – it means you are more likely to actually see a faerie.

March 15	Festival of river nymphs and water faeries, a dangerous day for swimming
April 30/May 1 (Beltaine/May Day)	Faeries ride out from their hills to celebrate Beltaine on May Day Eve
June 21	World Fairy Day (see Faerie Resources Directory for more details)
August 7	Faerie hills and dwellings are revealed on this day
September 29	Doors open between our world and the faerie realm
November 8	Another day when it is possible to catch a glimpse of Faerie Land
November 11	Festival of the blackthorn faeries

For more important faerie days of celebration and significance, see Chapter 10.

Faeries of Mischief and Misrule

Faeries are traditionally mischief-makers, and many things that go wrong are blamed on the faeries. Those tangled knots which you find in your hair when you wake up in the morning are called 'elf-locks', for example, and there is an old saying, 'Any man can lose his hat in a faerie wind!'

THE FAE STEAL MY SHIRT

There are plenty of fun stories of naughty faeries. This is one of our favourites, sent by Christina from the US.

My husband and I were living and working at a Renaissance Festival (where people dress up like they're in the Middle Ages and play around all weekend). We were packing for a few days at a family reunion and I tried on one shirt, took it off and placed it on the bed, tried another one, decided on the first, and when I turned back to the bed where it had been set, it was gone!

I blamed my husband, of course, but he denied it and I realized he hadn't even been near the bed. I looked for the shirt EVERYWHERE. It was nowhere to be seen. I knew then that we were experiencing a bit of faerie mischief, so as we left we placed a few bits of chocolate on our table and said aloud, 'I would like my shirt back sometime because I really like that shirt … and I've left you some chocolate to exchange for it.'

We left a while later, pondering the likelihood of my shirt ever returning. We arrived at the reunion, set up our tent and sleeping bags, chatted with family and, no more than two hours later, I went into the tent to finish setting things up inside. Lo and behold, my shirt was sitting on top of my clothes bag, gently placed there. I thanked them, of course, for returning it and brought it out to show my husband, who was utterly perplexed.

Different Names/Spellings for the Word 'Faerie'
Faeries are called many things the world over. In some cultures
it was thought of as bad luck to mention their names at all –
hence the phrases 'the little people' and so on. Here are a few
of the more common ones.

- Fairy
- Faerie/Faery/Fairye/Fayerye/Feri/Frairie
- Pixie (sometimes interchangeable with the word 'Faerie')
- Fay/Fey/Fae
- Fee
- Elf (also interchangeable with 'Faerie')
- Elfin/Elven
- God's People
- Little People
- The Hidden Ones
- The Strangers
- The Wee Ones
- The Good Neighbours
- Men of peace
- The Lovers
- Little Darlings
- The Fair Folk
- The Good People
- The Secret People

Names for the Land of Faerie
- Faerie Land/The Land of Faerie/Fairyland
- Elphame
- Annwn
- Tir na n-og/The Land of Youth
- Otherworld
- The Underground Country
- Gimlé

Water Faeries

Many faeries come under this category including, not surprisingly, mermaids. These creatures have been spotted for years by sailors out at sea. Some say that the sightings of half-human/half-fish are just wishful thinking by lonely seamen, especially sightings of the more typical beautiful female mermaids who are said to be occupied in brushing their hair and looking at their reflection in a mirror. Yet tales persist around the world and, although less common, mermen, the male version of this being, are occasionally sighted too. Alicen had her own experience.

MAGICAL SECRET OF THE SEA

It was the year 2002 and we were on a family holiday to the remote Scottish island of Raasay in the Western Isles. It was the first day of our holiday and we were eager to explore the island. We came across a lovely little cove of a beach which overlooked the Isle of Skye and it was completely deserted apart from a friendly sheepdog who wanted to play. The children and Neil decided to explore the beach with the lively dog. I, however, felt instantly mesmerized by the sea. I felt compelled to look out at the calm water and I felt rooted to the spot. It was as if nothing else existed for me at the time, except for the sea. The gentle sound of the waves running over the sand seemed to be accentuated and everything else seemed to fade into insignificance. The sea was holding my focus as if it was a being asking for my undivided attention.

Carried on the waves I began to hear music and singing. It was the sound of a beautiful female voice and by now I felt as if I was completely belonging to the world of the sea. Everything had taken on a heightened quality, appearing magical and more beautiful. The enchanting singing held my attention and I felt in a blissful state of being. I was utterly 'existing in the moment' and time was dreamlike and immeasurable.

At the deepest moment of the immersing sea experience, I briefly saw quite close to the shore a female figure. Then I saw her disappear beneath the waves. As she disappeared a large tail fin, as large as a whale's, flipped up and splashed the surface of the glittering water; it was a magical and captivating moment. Then it was gone and with it the music and singing ceased too, as if a spell had been broken. All of a sudden everything came back to normality; I could hear the children laughing and the sheepdog barking. Neil came up to me and put his arms around me and I said to him, 'I've just seen a mermaid.'

CHAPTER 3

Faerie Names A-Z

'What name weareth she? Tell us it is true;
Whisper it low to the fairy crew.'
EDWIN ARNOLD (1852–1904)

Faeries are part of the ancient culture of countries all over the world. Despite the fact that different countries have varying names for the faerie folk, the similarities are often surprising. Some of the faeries on our A–Z are a general term for a 'type' or 'breed' of faerie, while others are names for a single or 'one-off' faerie.

Here is a quick reference for you:

A

Alven	A water faerie
Ankou	An Irish 'death faerie'
Apsaras	Fig faerie
Attorcroppe	Poisonous serpent-like creature

B

Banshee	See *Beansidhe*
Basilisk	The basilisk has the head and body of a snake with human-type arms. Considered very deadly.
Bean Fionn	A water faerie who was thought to drown children

Beansidhe	A female faerie known for her death wail
Bean Tighe	Faerie housekeeper with the appearance of an old woman
Bocan	A type of hobgoblin blamed for road attacks in the 19th century
Boggart	A type of wood-eating dwarf faerie
Brownie	A friendly house faerie
Buachailleen	Lives amongst livestock … teasing animals
Buggars	Shapeshifting and dangerous goblins
Bunyips	Swamp faeries
Bwbacks	House faeries
Bwciod	Fire goblins

C

Cailleac Bhuer	This 'blue hag' walks through the Scottish Highlands with her walking stick
Callicantzaroi	A trooping faerie
Caryatids	Nut-tree faeries
Churichaun	This leprechaun type of faerie is most usually found around alcohol stores
Corrigan	A beauty by night, ugly by day

D

Devas	Commonly-seen glowing balls of light (orbs). Nature spirits.
Djnn	A faerie of the lamp (genie) of Middle Eastern origin
Dracs	Water-floating faeries sometimes seen as human females
Drakes	These faeries are best known for their foul-smelling odour
Dryads	Every tree and bush is said to have its own dryad or spirit
Duergarr	A troll-type faerie

Dwarf	Small people with shrivelled faces who work with metals and magical jewellery. Dwarves live to an old age and can be invisible to humans.

E

Ellyllons	Lake faeries who ride on eggshells. Of Welsh origin.
Elves	These creatures live both inside and outside. Found in many nursery rhymes and fairytales, often disguised as mice. The elf is responsible for the care of deer, amongst other things. Originally of Scandinavian/Saxon origin, they also dwell in Britain and are a magical race of people. There are white or light-shining elves who are good, and dark elves who are malevolent. J R R Tolkein took his inspiration for the elves in *Lord of the Rings* from the Icelandic elven sagas.

F

Fachans	Ugly and unfriendly faeries
Fairshee (Fair Sidhe)	Known as the fairymen of the hill. Fairshee are tall in faerie terms and visit humans in their sleep. Although they are shapeshifters, they appear regularly as handsome males with great desire for human females.
Faerie Queens	Every district has its own Faerie Queen who rules over her royal fey court with her Faerie King. There are many Faerie Queens and The Queen of All Faerie in Britain is said to be Queen Mab, who is of Welsh and English origin.
Faerie Godmothers	Originally derived from the Fates, powerful goddesses now demoted to fairytale beings whose role is to watch over children.

Fenshee (Fen Sidhe)	Fenshees are related to the Fairshee. They are particularly good at playing music … but don't go following that faerie music unless you want to get hopelessly lost.
Fetch	A faerie double or 'co-walker' – your human likeness in faerie form. If you should meet this faerie double, tradition states it's a sign of your passing, although this has not been proven. Your 'fetch' could be useful for magical means.
Fir Darrigs	Fat and dangerous faeries
Fireesin	Naked, hairy creatures, mostly found in agricultural settings
Fire fay	These tiny little red fire faeries are relatives of the salamanders. The fire fay have a human-like appearance and can be found around all fire sources like bonfires, home fires, hot springs and volcanos.
Fisher King, The	Another faerie-connected being from the time of Arthurian legend, who is associated with the Grail
Flower faeries Flower fay	Made popular by the artist Cicely Mary Barker. Each flower is said to have its own faerie guardian, and the faerie echoes the shape and colour of the flower it represents. However, these are fictional faeries; the true flower spirits are the *devas*.
Folletti	Tiny fey with unusual backward-facing feet
Formorians	Sea monsters
Fossegrim	Waterfall guardians
Fylgiar	Faerie companions, who rather frighteningly announce an individual's death

G

Gancanagh	A pipe-smoking Irish faerie
Gandharvas	The Gandharvas are musical, underground faeries

Gans	The Native Americans called these the Apaches; they are mountain spirits
Geancanach	Characterized by their large eyes and ears, and usually found around the hearth
Genie	See Djnn
Ghillie Dhu	Scottish tree spirits
Giants	Legends exist all over the world of these very tall and often unattractive (half-faerie, half-human) creatures. Although they are not thought to be terribly bright, they are considered kindly.
Gitto	Beware, farmers, this pesky faerie likes to mess with your crops
Glashtin	Storm faerie
Glaistig	Part human female, part animal, this faerie is particularly interested in the human male … but not in a good way. This blood-sucking faerie is considered very dangerous.
Gnomes	These Earth faeries are one of the more well-known of the faerie folk. Gnomes are the elementals of the Earth.
Goblin	Malevolent and mischievous faeries. A general term given to any evil fey. See also Boggarts.
Golem	A faerie with a human-type appearance and robotic-like reactions
Green Man, The	Also known as a pagan god. His face is created in leaves and branches and his role is that of father of all living creatures.
Gremlin	Sometimes called sky boogies and seen flying alongside aeroplane wings during the Second World War, usually causing damage to aircraft
Gruagach	Female cattle guardians who enjoy human contact
Gwragedd Annwn	Dancing water faeries with a childlike appearance
Gwyllions	Welsh mountain faeries who love gold teeth and earrings!

H

Hamadryadniks	Tree spirits
Hearth fey	Relatives of the house brownies, they also have a lot in common with the salamanders. Usually found around the home fire or cooker.
Hobgoblins	A generic term for evil faeries. Lazy trouble-makers but, surprisingly, it is suggested that they love the humans they play tricks on!
Huldrafolk	Mountain-dwellers, and thought to be dangerous to humans
Hyldermoder	Scandinavian tree faeries
Hyters	Faeries who show themselves as birds

I

Ieles	Cat-like blood-sucking fey
Imp	Imps are invisible but great friends of witches. You can catch an imp in a bottle of water sealed with a cork, where it is said to live quite happily. They are harmless but like fancy clothes.

J

Jack Frost	Faerie of the ice/snow and the Snow Queen's magical consort
Jimaniños	Prank-playing trooping faeries with a childlike appearance
Jinn	See Djnn

K

Kelpies	Bad-tempered water faeries who are thought to be dangerous to humans and animals. They take on the appearance of horses riding the waves.
Klaboutermannikins	Best known for their invisibility
Knockers	These Cornish faeries live underground, famously in mines, and warn miners of underground danger by making knocking noises

Kolbald	Another pipe-smoking dwarf, sometimes blamed for poltergeist activity (poltergeist translates as 'noisy ghost')

L

Leprechauns	These male faeries of Irish origin are the shoemakers of legend and fairytale
Lesidhe	Search deep amongst the woodland trees and plants to find these faeries, who like to disguise themselves amongst the greenery
Lob	A goblin attracted to negative human emotions
Lorelei	Lorelei gets blamed for luring sailors to their deaths on the rocks below the clifftops where this alluring lady sits and sings
Lunantisidhe	Blackthorn-tree guardian and moon-worshipping faerie
Lutins	Another shapeshifting faerie with unpredictable moods

M

Mal-de-Mer	Dangerous sea monster
Masseriol	*Masseriol* means 'little farmer'. As the name suggests, they can be helpful around livestock and crops, even helping in the house occasionally.
Mazikeen	Angel-like winged faeries who can't be trusted around the home
Menehumas	Help lost travellers and guard money
Merlin	A solitary magician with faerie connections, known as the Master Wizard, and King Arthur's counsellor. It was said that his mother was a nun and his father an angel.
Merpeople/mermaids and mermen	Water creatures with human bodies and fish tails recorded by sailors over many generations

Moerae	An aspect of the triple goddess (maiden, mother and crone or wise woman), thought to watch over the life-path of humankind
Monaciello	Watch out for your liquor cabinet as this is another wine-loving faerie
Morgan Le Fay (Lady of the Lake)	A solitary faerie/witch woman well-known from tales of Arthurian legend. Legend suggests she is a water nymph and daughter of King Avallach (ruler of the Isle of Avalon). Her name translates literally as 'Morgan the faerie'.
Mother Holle	A friendly faerie of Germanic origin who loves working on her spinning wheel, sometimes considered a goddess and interchangeable with an aspect of the Snow Queen Faerie/Holda
Muireartach	This one and only faerie is sometimes considered to be a crone goddess who is associated with sea storms
Murdhuachas	Sea faeries, a little like Merpeople

N

Neck/Necker	An attractive, musical, shapeshifting water faerie
Nereides	Considered dangerous to children, these faeries are usually found around the sea
Nibelungen	Dwarf faeries found in woodlands, hidden crystal realms and the elusive fertility rings they are known to create out of gold
Nicker	See Kelpie
Nixen	Male and female water sprites, considered dangerous to swimmers
Nokkes	Singing water faeries found in rivers
Nucklelavees/nuchlavis	Half-human and half-horse, these shapeshifting faeries smell pretty bad
Nymphs	Pretty female faeries known for their sexual longings. A nymph is a type of faerie rather than an individual name. Witch faeries.

O

Ogres	See also Giants. Unpleasant creatures known for their habit of eating animals and humans. Thought to live in the clouds (like in the fairytale *Jack and the Beanstalk*).

P

Pan	Male nature faerie associated with goats
Puck	An English wood faerie known for his pipe music. He has horns on his head. In ancient times he was considered a demon. He appears in Shakespeare's *A Midsummer Night's Dream*.
Phookas	These Irish faeries have horse-like bodies with male heads. These faeries do like to annoy humans, especially children, so contact is not suggested.
Pillywiggins	Spring flower faeries
Pixies/piskies	These familiar large-headed faeries also have pointy ears and wings. Pixies are fun-loving faeries and have been known to help humans.

Q, R

Red Caps	The Red Caps are usually friendly folk, but there are legends of cannibalistic behaviour both amongst their own kind and other faeries, so beware!
Robin Goodfellow	This woodland faerie has the ability to transform himself into a horse at will and can also transform himself into fire.

S

Santa Claus	Believe it or not, Santa is an elf, well known of course for distributing presents at Christmas
Salamanders	Fire elementals with a lizard-like appearance, and larger than their cousins the fire fay. Red and yellow in colour.

Selkies	Beautiful sea faeries from Scotland and Ireland who can appear in human or seal form. They were believed to control storms and the sea. These beautiful, both male and female, faeries can be found along the coastline.
Servan	These Swiss faerie folk are unseen by the human eye but are known to exist because they leave footprints behind
Shellycoats	Shellycoats are from Scotland, but faeries of a similar nature are found all around Europe. They are water faeries with round bodies who can be pranksters.
Shopiltees	'Water horses' who might be extinct, certainly from our own realms
Silvani	Transparent wood nymphs usually seen wearing animal skins, but they also wear red. Half-man, half-goat.
Snow faeries	Seen as small white sprites or 'trooping faeries' believed to bring on frost and snow. They follow and are illuminated in the wake of the Snow Queen Faerie.
Snow Queen	Queen of the snow faeries and all of winter. She is of Germanic and Scandinavian origin. Bewitchingly beautiful sometimes and, at others, a hideous hag faerie.
Spriggans	These 'rock-like' faeries can be dangerous and are believed to be found around the UK, especially in Cornwall
Sylphs	These tiny flying faeries are fairly transparent and appear at various places around the world. Elementals of the air.
Sylvans	Woodland faeries who are believed to be malevolent, particularly dangerous to human men

T

Tighe	Sometimes called Bean-Tighe. They are believed to assist in household tasks ... but not if you have a cat!
Trolls	One of the more well-known faeries, appearing in fairytales where they eat humans and animals. They are unattractive in appearance but find humans ugly, apparently! Luckily they don't enter human homes.

U,V

Undine	Undines are spirits of fresh water and are usually depicted as slender and beautiful young women with exceptionally long and lustrous hair. They are the guardians of wells, rivers, streams and lakes and will lure men to their deaths with their haunting song.

W

War faeries	War faeries wear their battle clothes of red, blue and white with fancy headdresses covered in feathers and bull horns. Part of their role is to send their enemies 'fetch' to announce impending death.
Well faeries/water sprites	These faeries are water guardians and the spirits we send our requests to when throwing coins into a fountain or water well to make a wish
Wiskie	Small black faeries with silver wings found mostly in woods and forests. Look for them in shafts of sunlight and you will see these pretty faeries with their cat-like eyes.
Will o' the wisp	Popular in England, these faeries often appear as orbs of light around bogs. They are blamed for leading humans to their death through dangerous woodland paths.

Yeti	Is the Yeti, or Bigfoot as he is known in some parts of the world, a faerie being at all? Tall and hairy, this creature is still seen from time to time in remote areas but never caught ...

Faeries of the Seasons

Faeries are sometimes seen around or are associated with the different seasons of the year. Some faeries, for example, appear during the harvests either to help or harm ... it might initially be difficult to tell which!

Season	Faeries
Winter	Jack Frost, Snow Faeries, The Snow Queen
Spring	Devas Pillywiggans Flower faeries (If you live in a part of the world where frost is common in spring, the winter faeries may appear as well)
Autumn/fall	Morgan le Fay, Faerie Queen of the Apple Isle
Summer	Will o' the wisp, wiskies

Weather Faeries/Weather Associations

Although faeries are not 'in charge' of wind directions like the angels are, there are several that are associated with weather. Faeries seem to get the blame in nature. If something goes wrong, there seems to be a faerie at fault!

'Into something rich and strange. Sea-nymphs hourly ring his knell ...'
WILLIAM SHAKESPEARE, *THE TEMPEST*

Here are some of the common ones.

Weather	Faeries
Winds	Glashtin – This faerie is active during storms and has been seen 'riding the winds', according to Edain McCoy, author of the excellent *A Witch's Guide to Faery Folk*. In fact, the Manx used to believe that the Glashtin actually caused the storm in the first place … maybe they are right. Sylphs are also known as 'wind singers'.
Storms	Gwyllions – Faeries who fear storms. Muireartach – Especially relating to sea storms. Their name means 'one of the sea'. Selkies – Scottish faeries who are also thought to have some control over sea storms.
Snow/frost	Jack Frost/snow faeries – These faeries were thought to bring a frozen death to unwary travellers. Other names include Old Man Winter and The Frost King/Snow Queen.
Sun	Limniades – Greek sun gods. Wiskies – find them in shafts of sunlight.
Moon	Lunantisidhe – Meaning 'moon faerie'. The lunantisidhe worship the moon goddess.

ENCOUNTER WITH THE SNOW QUEEN

Lizzy encountered the Snow Queen. She told us:

> She was exceptionally warm with a soft feminine appearance. She seems aristocratic but strangely helpful. Her hair was long and dark brown to black and she wore a crown of light and a snow-white fur coat. Though her aura felt icy and cold, her character wasn't!

Faeries of the Zodiac

It's fun to work with the faeries associated with your birth sign. Each zodiac sign has related symbols and elements which influence it, and these give us clues to the faerie signs. We also have to consider which faerie personality traits best match those of the birth sign. Here are some faeries for each sign of the zodiac. You can adopt these for magical or spell use if you wish.

Zodiac sign	Symbol	Element association	Faerie association
Capricorn	Goat	Earth	Gnomes, gwyllions
Aquarius	Water-bearer	Air	Sylphs, water sprites
Pisces	Fish	Water	Nymphs, selkies
Aries	Ram	Fire	Salamanders, pan, silvani, fire fay
Taurus	Bull	Earth	Gnome, gruagach
Gemini	Twins	Air	Fetch, sylphs
Cancer	Crab	Water	Water sprites, merpeople
Leo	Lion	Fire	Salamanders, Robin Goodfellow – also, faeries are said to sometimes turn themselves into cats!
Virgo	Virgin	Earth	Gnome, leprechaun
Libra	Scales	Air	Deva, sylphs
Scorpio	Scorpion	Water	Merpeople (mermaids), muireartach
Sagittarius	Archer	Fire	Salamanders. Many faeries are archers including Puck (from Shakespeare), Robin Goodfellow and spiggans

Faeries and Their Crystal and Element Associations

Here is a list of some of the more used associations between the elements, the types of faeries and their crystal associations. This is just a guide, and we like to think that at all times if you feel another crystal will work better, then go with your own instincts – empower yourself!

Element	Type of faerie/association	Crystal association
Air	Sylphs	Agate, citrine, lapis
Water	Undines/nereids/merpeople	Amethyst, moonstone, pearl
Earth	Gnomes	Emerald, jet, onyx
Fire	Salamanders	Amber, diamond, ruby

Faeries of the Zodiac/Crystal/Flower (see also Faerie Crystal Association)

You might find these associations useful for your faerie spell work, but if your natural intuition tells you differently, then work with what feels right to you.

Zodiac sign	Type of faerie	Flower	Crystal
Capricorn	Gnomes	Snow Drop	Garnet
Aquarius	Domovoy	Primrose	Amethyst
Pisces	Merpeople	Daffodil	Aquamarine
Aries	Brownies	Sweetpea	Ruby
Taurus	Faeries/elves	Foxglove	Emerald/amber
Gemini	Sylphs/zephyrs	Lavender	Topaz
Cancer	Hobgoblins	Jasmine	Moonstone
Leo	Dryads	Marigold	Jasper
Virgo	Trooping faeries	Lily	Citrine
Libra	Barbegazi (frost faeries)	Cosmos	Opal
Scorpio	Subterranean faeries	Cacti	Topaz
Sagittarius	Uldra (snow faeries)	Poinsettia	Peridot

CHAPTER 4

The Meanings of Faerie Names

'When the first baby laughed for the first time,
the laugh broke into a thousand pieces,
and they all went skipping about,
and that was the beginning of fairies ...'
J M BARRIE

There is an old belief that says if you name something you invoke it, or bring it about. According to folklore, to protect yourself from negative faerie energies, faeries were rarely referred to by name and often given some general name like the 'wee folk' or the 'good neighbours'.

In many cultures, the naming of a child is carried out in a ceremonial rite. A name is very important and ancient beliefs suggest that the child takes on the meaning of the name in some way.

Children who hadn't been named or baptized were thought to be at risk of the faeries stealing them away. At the very least, in some cultures the child's real name was kept a secret until such time as an official naming ceremony could take place, so as to protect the child from those who wished the child harm. It was believed that the person holding the child's name had a special hold over the soul or spirit of the child.

The 'secret name' is a belief that is carried over into several fairy tales. Once the name of the faerie is discovered, the faerie loses some or all of his or her power. Rumpelstiltskin was one of these, and the faerie Puddlefoot was said to have 'disappeared in a huff' when given a name!

Meanings of names can vary from place to place, and there are always variations of each name (different spellings and so on). You might find this list useful if looking for a magical name for your own child, or a pet.

See, too, the main list of faerie names (A–Z in Chapter 3) – and for more modern faerie names you might enjoy checking out the names used by Disney in its animations (Chapter 9).

Female Names

Name	Country of origin/ derivation	Meanings	Other names/ variations
Afreda	Not known	Elf power or elf counsellor	(Masculine) Fred Freddie, also Frieda, Alfried and Elva
Alvara	Germany	Elf army or elf friends	Alva, Alvie, Aethelwyne
Arethusa	Not known	Nymph	None
Blossom	English	Like the flower or bloom	None
Breena	Gaelic/Celtic	Faerie Land	None
Brucie	French	Sprite of the forest	None
Carling	Old English	Witch Hill	None
Diana	Roman	Named for the goddess of hunting	Diane, Dianne
Donella	Celtic	Elfin girl with the dark hair	Donna
Dulcina	Latin	Rose (named for the plant)	Dulcie
Eglantine	French	A wild rose	Eglantina
Elga	Anglo-Saxon	An elfin spear	Elgar
Ella	Anglo-Saxon	Elfin, of the elf people	None

Name	Country of origin/ derivation	Meanings	Other names/ variations
Ellette	English	The little elf	None
Elfie	Not known	The good elf	Elva, Elivina, Elvena
Eolande	Gaelic/Celtic	The violet flower	None
Erline	Anglo-Saxon	Elfin	Erlina
Faerydae	Not known	Gift from the faeries	None
Faylinn	English	The Faerie Kingdom	Faylynne
Fay	French	A faerie or elf	Faye
Fayette	French	Little faerie	None
Gelsey	English	Jasmine (the plant)	None
Gullveig	Norse	A witch	None
Laila	A biblical name	The name of an angel said to watch over spirits of the newborn	Layla
Liliana	Latin	Lily flower	Lily, Lilly, Lilli
Louella	Not known	A famous elf	Luel, Luella
Marigold	English	From the golden flower	None None
Maurelle	French	Elfin (dark)	Maurele
Naida	Not known	A water nymph	Nayida
Nixie	German	Water sprite	Nyx, Nix
Ordalf	German	An elf spear	Odile, Odelina, Ordella, Odete, Oda
Radella	Not known	An elf counsellor	Raedself
Raisa	Russian/Celtic/ Gaelic	Rose	Raisie
Rhiannon	Welsh	Witch or goddess, queen, nymph	Rhian, Rhianon, Rhiana, Rhyannon
Rhoslyn	Welsh	Rose	Rhslyn, Rhoslynne, Rhoswen, Rhosilyn
Rosa	Latin	Pink rose, little rose, white rose	Rose, Rosie, Rosalie, Rosalia, Rozalia, Rosetta, Rosina

Name	Country of origin/ derivation	Meanings	Other names/ variations
Rossa	Latin	Beautiful flower	None
Roxanne	Latin	Graceful rose	None
Rusalka	Czech	Mermaid, water sprite, wood sprite	None
Sebille	English	A faerie	None
Shaylee	Celtic/Gaelic	A faerie princess of the field	Shayleigh
Shea	Irish	Faerie palace	Sheah
Susan	Celtic/Gaelic/ French/Latin/ English	Lily	Suisan, Susane, Susanna, Suzanne, Suzette
Tana	Slavic, Russian	Faerie Queen	Tania, Tanya, Tatiana, Tianna
Titania	Greek	Faerie Queen (from Shakespeare)	None
Tenanye	Not known	Cheerful Faerie Queen	None
Xantho	Not known	The golden-haired sea nymph	None
Zanna	Latin	Lily	Zana
Zuzana	Slavic	Rose	None

Male Names

Aelfdane	Denmark	Danish elf	None
Aelfdene	Denmark	Coming from the Elf Valley	None
Alberich	Norse	Mythological name – A famous dwarf	Alfrigg
Alston	Old English	From the elf's house	None
Alvin	Old English	Elf wine	None
Avery	Not known	Elf King	Aelfric, Aubrey
Brokk	Norse	Mythological name – A famous dwarf	None

Name	Country of origin/ derivation	Meanings	Other names/ variations
Dain	Norse	Mythological name – A famous dwarf	None
Drake	English	Dragon	None
Durin	German	Mythological name - A famous dwarf	None
Eitri	Norse	Mythological name – A famous dwarf	None
Elden	Not known	From the valley of the elves	Eldan, Eldon
Elvin	Celtic/Gaelic	Friend of the elves	None
Elvy	Not known	A warrior	Elvey
Genius	Not known	Mythological name meaning 'guardian spirit'	None
Hefeydd	Celtic	Mythological name (father of Rhiannon)	None
Hreidmar	Norse	Mythological name (dwarf king)	None
Kallan	Irish	Warrior	Kalen, Kailen, Kennen
Nidhug	Norse	Mythological name meaning 'dragon'	Nidhogg
Oberon	From Shakespeare	King of the Faeries	None
Orin	Irish	Pale-skinned faerie	Oren
Puck	English – from Shakespeare	Mischievous	Puk
Sindri	Norse	Rose field	None
Suelita	Spanish	Mythological name (a dwarf)	None
Warren	German	Gamekeeper or watchman	None

CHAPTER 5

The Hierarchy of Faerie

'Faerie is a perilous land, and in it are pitfalls for the unwary,
and dungeons for the overbold.'
J R R TOLKEIN

Once Upon a Time …

What little girl doesn't dream of becoming a faerie princess? It seems that the hierarchy of Faerie has already been woven into our lives from childhood, and most of us realize that the fey have kings and queens, if only from references in fairy stories and literature. This is part of the faeries' power, as by belonging to our imaginations in childhood they eventually shape who we are as adults, if only in a small way.

To some of us it is a radical connection to how we perceive the fey as adults. The faeries are able to come to us through our imaginations, and the more we embellish this vision of them, the more they are able to become real in our lives. The faeries begin first of all in our 'imagination' or the higher creative mind; but don't think for a minute that we are 'making them up'. Faeries are real!

Here we explain about how the faeries live in their societies, and you will see that the storytellers didn't get it far wrong after all. This is because the faeries are able to influence and colour the work of writers, artists, musicians etc. through their imaginations. It makes you think, doesn't it …?

Gimli: [about to fight all of Mordor] I never thought I'd die fighting side by side with an elf.

Legolas: How about side by side with a friend?

Gimli: [pause] Aye. I could do that.

JRR Tolkien, from *Lord of the Rings: The Return of the King*

The Trooping Faeries

These are also known as the Aristocratic or Heroic Faeries. They gained this name because they are the aristocratic class of the faerie race. The Trooping comes from their famous pursuit of riding out in magnificent processions known as Faerie Rades.

When the author Tolkien wrote in *Lord of the Rings* about the elves, and in the way that he described them as the '… fairest folk' who walked with '… starlight shimmering on their hair and in their eyes. They bore no lights, yet as they walked a shimmer, like the light of the moon … seemed to fall about their feet … and passed like shadows and faint lights: for Elves … could walk when they wished without sound or footfall,' we have an example of how a fiction writer has accurately described the way of the real faeries. It also illustrates the nature of the Trooping Faeries, who are known as the Elven or Faerie race: a magical tribe of people. These faeries, often referred to as elves, do not have any wings and are thought to stand at the same height as humans, some say taller. They are similar to humans in appearance, but with a magical elfin dimension, such as luxuriant long hair, large slanting eyes and pointed ears. They have sylph-like bodies, delicate features and they are exceptionally beautiful in an Otherworldly way. They are also said to have a breed of horse that is kept only by them, a highly-strung breed of faerie horse which they have shod with silver shoes and adorned with golden bridles and jingling bells in their manes. These horses are meant to have bodies of fire, flame and ether, with large eyes, and are the fastest and most spirited of steeds, reputed to live over a hundred years.

The Trooping Faeries live in organized royal courts, presided over by a faerie/elven King and Queen. In fey society the Faerie Queen is always the one who has slight dominance in the kingdom in honour and respect of the female influence in (mother) nature, above the Faerie King. These courts possess members as any human court would do, such as knights, princesses, lords and ladies etc.

The Trooping faeries are mostly found in countries that also have an aristocratic or royal history, such as the United Kingdom, Ireland, Russia, all northern European cultures and Scandinavian countries. Other countries and continents which do not have such a history, such as the United States and Australia, have developed faeries in different ways with predominantly Solitary Faeries (which we will explain further in this chapter).

There are many famous faerie courts, most notably the Irish courts of the Tuatha de Danann (pronounced *Tootha day danan*) and the Daoine Sidhe (*Theena Shee*). In Scotland the most famous faerie courts are The Seelie Court (composed of benevolent fey) and The UnSeelie Court (known to be a kingdom of evil faeries).

However, although there are notorious and celebrated faerie courts, it seems that each locality may have a Faerie King and Queen with their own court. The United Kingdom and Ireland are most known for this phenomenon.

Alicen: I put this theory to the test when I moved to a new location in 2004. Living previously in England I was used to the energy of the English faeries, which now in hindsight seems more sedate and gentler than that of their Scottish counterparts! This is of course in keeping with their environment, as the Scottish landscape is much wilder and untamed. I moved with my family to one of the Orkney Islands, Westray.

Before we moved there I knew nothing of the local faerie traditions or even if there were any. By strange 'coincidence' we ended up living in a house which is opposite an ancient faerie mound known locally as the Mound of Skelwick or Old Kirkhouse and thought to be the site of archaeological deposits and possibly a 13th-century chapel. I asked the faeries of Skelwick to contact me and I began to have strange and vivid dreams which all featured the faerie mound.

This culminated in January 2005 when I was sitting at my writing desk on a wild, windy day by seeing with my clairvoyant eyes the Faerie King and Queen whom I felt belonged to the mound. They did not look at all like any other Faerie King and Queen I had ever seen. They arrived on a wave (the mound is right next to the sea) hand-in-hand and alighted on the faerie mound. They were Norse in appearance and I later concluded that because of Orkney's Viking history, this may have been why. It was such a profound and intense experience that I immediately felt inspired to write a short story about it. Here is a short extract for you:

'Hand-in-hand on the white foaming wave of a memory, the sea crashes in between two islands, the faerie isle … Wild white horses plunge in rearing at the sea wall and dissolving back to the deep. They come on a January storm, belonging to the sea, the sky, the Earth. They appear as shimmering orbs of luminary light, shining through the sea spray. The King and Queen of the Skello faeries emerge from a sea that had journeyed them …'

Magic All Around You

If you would like to try tuning in and discovering the Faerie King and Queen of your own locality, you may like to try this exercise.

Seek out a place in nature that is in your locality. This may only be a park, as even London parks often have faerie court connections, such as Greenwich Park for example. Try to visit that place often for a few weeks and get to know the feel of the place. Take a small present for the faeries which live there such as honey in a walnut-shell container. Anything that will not create unnatural litter and can be placed discreetly under a bush or in the nook of a tree etc. When you visit, mentally ask the faeries of that locality to reach out to you and connect with you. This process takes time and you also have to remember that the fey will gradually need to gain their trust of you.

Once you have taken a few weeks (at least a month would be good) over this process, then actively tune in to the fey. Take a blanket to sit on and simply sit with your eyes closed in your chosen locality, requesting that the benevolent fey court of that place make themselves known to you. Make sure that you request the protection of your guardian angel or similar deity … whomever you are used to working with.

At the first attempt you may very well get no results, but keep trying and the faerie door to their court may be opened ever so slightly for you. Look out for images in your mind as you tune in that could be faerie impressions and not your own thoughts; listen to the breeze and also your perceptions of how time is moving. All these are indicators that you are becoming close to their realm.

Watch out for signs in your daily life and dreams, such as references to faerie monarchs in films, books, paintings, TV programmes, radio programmes and conversations at bus stops! The faeries weave their magical signs into all aspects of our lives, not just into meditations, and recognize that all of life is a magical process. So keep your pointy faerie ears pricked up and magic will come to you … You may want to keep some notes in a special book that you keep for the purpose, sketching in any images which also come to mind.

The Solitary Faeries

If a faerie being does not belong to a faerie court, then he or she is known as a Solitary Faerie. These faeries, as their name suggests, mostly live alone and their nature is wilder and less refined than that of the Trooping Faeries. They are more likely to be the type of faerie that is the guardian of a tree, for example, or a particular wild place in nature. They are mostly unkempt in appearance and will display aspects of nature within their appearance such as twigs in their knotted hair, leaves as garments and brown, earthy-coloured skin. They are wilder in character and are equivalent to the country dwellers of the faerie realm.

The Queen of All Faerie

All faeries, no matter whether they are Solitary or Trooping, are governed by the Queen of All Faerie who governs over all Faerie Land. She is popularly known in England and Wales as Queen Mab, but has other names in other cultures. In 16th- and 17th-century literature, Mab was known as the midwife of the faeries, although this might be because of the magic (rather than the babies) she gave birth to! Shakespeare called her 'the midwife of dreams' in his play *Romeo and Juliet*.

All fey are bound to obey her and her word is final. No faerie would ever like to disobey the wrath of the Queen of All Faerie. She is a powerful monarch with goddess-like status, revered among faeries and capturing the imaginations of humans.

Imagine …

If the Solitary or Trooping Faeries have captured your imagination or rekindled a spark of childhood memory, this could be the first step for your connection with the fey. Imagination is one way in which they reach you. What better place to start than where you left off when you waved childhood goodbye?!

For more about Faerie Kings and Queens, see the next chapter.

CHAPTER 6

The King and Queen of Faerie

'I met a Lady in the Meads, Full beautiful – a faery's child,
Her hair was long, her foot was light, And her eyes were wild.'
JOHN KEATS, *'LA BELLE DAME SANS MERCI'*

The Hidden Knowing

We invite you to follow us on a journey, to uncover what we have
lost within ourselves; to remember the King and Queen of Faerie.
The faerie monarchs are waiting to be rediscovered. We knew
them once, but, like our ancestors, they have become buried
beneath the earth, along with the knowledge to work with them
and their kind. The King and Queen of Faerie in their many
guises have impressed their messages in these pages and are
reaching out to form a spiritual relationship with humankind.

The King and Queen of Faerie are the secret knowledge to the
mysteries of natural magic, the consciousness of our environment
and also the keys to existing in harmony with the tides and cycles
of the Earth and, in so doing, the natural condition of ourselves.
The Earth mirrors our own wellbeing as a race and, if we are
not in tune with this aspect of the divine both practically and
spiritually, then we will see the effects in ourselves.

Who Are the Faerie Kings and Queens?

Faeries in all their guises are the spiritual embodiments of the consciousness of the planet Earth. They are beings who belong neither to this world or the next, but exist in a realm of in-between. They are connected by nature to us and this is the magical window upon which we may communicate with them and vice-versa.

Faeries live in societies similar to our own and often mirror the culture and hierarchy of our own country. As mentioned in the last chapter, every culture across the globe has its legends of their Little People, and with them their own fey king and queen. Northern European and Scandinavian countries, together with Russia, have the most documented evidence regarding fey monarchs. This is of course in line with the tradition of monarchies that once existed or are still present today in these human societies.

Faerie kings and queens in other continents such as the United States do exist, yet they are much scarcer in their documentation and are likely to preside over the elemental faeries rather than one of the magical races of faerie people. One example in the US is the Faerie 'Queen Summer', who rules over the Elves of Light (Native American faeries). Similar instances occur in South Africa and Australia with their Aboriginal elementals.

Therefore the faerie monarchs can be placed into two distinct types: those of the elemental faeries and those of the aristocratic faeries.

Elemental Faerie Monarchs

The elemental faeries are essentially the spirits of nature which inhabit every single natural feature upon the Earth. These faeries have been categorized as the sylphs of air, the salamanders of fire, the undines of water and the gnomes of the Earth. Within these four main types there are thousands of different varieties of elementals, all of which belong to their own aspect of nature, such as a species of tree or flower. They also take on the indigenous characteristics of the location in which they dwell.

Alicen: My own experience of meeting an elemental king is with the Cornish Knocker Faeries. In the year 2000 my family and I were on holiday near St Austell in Cornwall. From the moment we set foot in the chalet I had an uneasy feeling that we were not altogether welcome. I had tried my best to ignore these feelings and get on with the holiday. However, throughout the course of the week the rest of the family began to have strange dreams and we would all repeatedly wake up in the night.

Towards the end of the holiday, during a particularly disrupted night, Neil – who's usually less sensitive at picking up these vibes – said to me, 'Tomorrow morning as soon as the shops are open, I'm going to buy a big tub of salt and you can sort this out, because it's definitely not normal!'

Sort it out I did. At this point in the holiday I was unaware of what kind of faerie being I was dealing with, so I tuned in and asked. At once an extremely angry elemental, about three feet tall, appeared from beneath the floor and was standing within my circle of salt. He was a little grey-bearded man who looked very like a miniature wizard to me. He told me that he was the King of the Knocker Faeries and this chalet had been built on the site of a mine – his mine, to be precise, and his home. In fact he was in a dreadful rage and stamped his feet and staff upon the floor.

Undeterred by his rampaging about, I tried to explain to him as calmly as I could that, although I sympathized with him, he couldn't continue to sabotage our dreams and cause general mischief. He definitely wasn't happy about this, but I was very firm with my request and, in an incensed fury, he disappeared into the ground from whence he came in a whirl of salt and dust. After this we did not have any further problems with sleeping.

Knocker Faeries are the guardians of the tin mines of Devon and Cornwall. They take their name from the help they give to miners by knocking on the walls of the mine to herald danger while the miners are working. This particular Knocker Faerie will remain in my memory forever, and of course he was perfectly justified to be angry at his home being violated. The force of his anger will always stay with me, too, and it is no wonder that faeries are sometimes remote from humans, as we have been responsible for the rape of the Earth. Now is the time to turn the tide and win back that trust which has been lost.

Incidentally, at the end of the holiday Neil went to the site office to settle our bill. He casually happened to mention strange vibes in the chalet and the lady instantly became uneasy. She told him that lots of people mentioned it after staying in that chalet. She also told him that the whole site was built on the location of an old disused tin mine. Everything now made perfect sense.

THE ELEMENTAL KINGS

The four elemental kings originally had little form. However, occult practitioners of many traditions have, over the centuries, imprinted their own visualizations around them, using knowledge of magical correspondences. These images of the four kings now have universal recognition, and the kings themselves have evolved into separate beings in their own right. Such is the power of thought.

Here are simple descriptions of the elemental kings to help you visualize them. (We have also listed their Greek names in brackets, if you feel you are more drawn to work with this aspect.)

King Paralda (Eurius)

Paralda is the Lord of Air and commands the winged sylphs. He is typically visualized as a young man with long flowing fair hair. He is clad in clothes of a light and gauzy material in a pale blue, representing the sky in springtime.

King Djinn (Notus)

Djinn is Lord of Fire and governs his flickering salamanders. He can be visualized as a man in his twenties or thirties with vibrant golden hair. His clothes are red, representing the heat of the summer sun.

King Nixsa (Zephyrus)

Nixsa is Lord of Water and rules over his undines. He can be seen as a middle-aged man with red hair, which represents autumn. His clothes are in a flowing material, mirroring the green hues of the sea.

King Ghobe (Boreas)

Ghobe is Lord of the Earth and reigns over his gnomes. He appears as a distinguished and powerful old man with iron-grey hair. He wears robes of a heavy warm material in black, to represent the season of winter.

If you would like to visualize the kings in their less traditional sense, you can imagine them closer to their natural form. For example, King Paralda, Lord of Air, can be pictured as made up of the element he represents. You may like to see a whirl of air, like a whirlwind with gossamer wings.

This approach relies more on your imagination to conjure your desired image, and therefore may bring stronger associations with the elemental kings. Do not worry that you are visualizing these kings incorrectly, for as long as you stay within their own element, your vision cannot be wrong. The elemental kings are mutable beings, governed by the force of nature and their element, not the form they take, which is only for our purposes. They do not need a physical form to govern their element, and it is only human beings who have given them these names, characteristics and human forms.

These elemental kings are the overseers of all the elementals belonging to their spiritual sphere. However, within these we also have kings and queens of the many elemental faeries in those realms. For example there is Ran, Queen of the Mermaids and Water Faeries, and the King of the Knocker Faeries mentioned earlier.

The Aristocratic Faerie Monarchs

The aristocratic faeries are quite different from the elementals. They are believed to be a race of magical people descended from the gods. These faeries very often appear as the same size as humans and in human form, but with an extra magical dimension to their being.

> '...*Her eyes were blue, and her fine curling hair,*
> *Of the lightest of browns, her complexion more fair...*'
> THE FAIRY, CHARLES LAMB (1775–1834)

The aristocratic faeries, the hidden folk, have been known throughout history to intermingle with humans, to assist them and even to marry them. There are many famous courts of the aristocratic faeries, among them the Seelie Court, which means the Blessed Court. The Seelie Court are known to be good faeries that reside in the Highlands of Scotland. Their malevolent Scottish counterparts are known as the UnSeelie Court, which means the Unblessed or Uncanny Court.

The most legendary faerie court is that of the Irish Tuatha De Danann, which means 'People of the Goddess Danu'. This race of magical people came to Ireland and ruled for many centuries. However, the invading Milesians defeated them and so the Tuatha De Danann retreated to the Hollow Hills (mounds, raths, or sidhes) of Ireland.

Some say that with the rise of Christianity they actually diminished in size as a race because they were seen as less important by humans. This is how they became The Little People or The People of the Sidhe. The Tuatha De Danann dwell in Tir na n-og, which means 'The Land of Eternal Youth'. There are numerous faerie kings and queens of the Tuatha De Danann, and just as many legends belonging to them.

In this chapter we will be focusing mainly on monarchs of the aristocratic faeries, as these are well-documented in history and legend.

The Lost Gods and Goddesses

There is a belief that the King and Queen of Faerie wish to embrace their status as deities once more. Faeries are making a spiritual comeback around the world, with many people feeling drawn to work with them. As we form a closer relationship with our planet and wish to heal it, then this is a natural occurrence, as of course the fey are the spiritual consciousness of nature. The King and Queen of Faerie, being the purest energies expressing this, become our primary focus once more, along with the already existing gods and goddesses around the world.

The King and Queen of Faerie were once lost, but now that we have rediscovered them, by working with them and honouring them we may return to them the dignity and importance that they deserve. Their magic has been hidden from us by religion (post-Christianity) and science. Now is their time to return and for us to give them back their power – and for them in turn to empower us.

The Sparkling Faerie Queens

All faerie queens are aspects of the goddess and are relevant to a spiritual pathway trodden in the 21st century. Although in history, legend and literature they are often portrayed in romantic and poetic terms, they still bring to us very modern values. They are feisty women, strong and formidable yet beautiful, loving and caring. We can see them as fantastic role models as they embrace in all their guises the matriarch, mother and maiden aspects of the goddess and women. They also encompass all of our life phases as women, reinforcing the belief that we can be beautiful, desirable and sexy without having to be submissive. Of course we cannot be faerie queens, but we can call upon them to bring magic and perspective into our lives, as they can be our mentors.

The faerie queens are just as relevant to the male faerie-seekers among us. A faerie queen can help you to bring out the anima in you (your female side). Those qualities may be sensitivity, psychic and magical ability, the creative arts, nurturing and caring. A faerie queen can also help men to understand relationships with women more fully and the female condition in general. If you choose to work closely with a faerie queen as a man, she will be your mentor and spiritual fey guardian, just as a faerie king would do if you chose to work with one of them.

A CLOSE ENCOUNTER OF THE FAERIE QUEEN KIND

Lizzy van Leeuwen had an encounter with a faerie queen. Her message reflects our own beliefs as to why faeries are visiting us at this time.

I woke up scared and felt myself being pulled into something unknown. I was aware of shadows which played before me whilst my eyes were tightly closed. In front of me a kind of portal opened and I felt one or more presences slide by. I was aware of giggling (like a child), and saw a golden glow turning into an aura of soft pink, green, gold and neon-blue colours. Telepathically I saw a waxing moon.

In front of me appeared the Royal Court of Faeries. They were about two metres tall with long beautiful faces, and again had the light-blue neon glow about them as they stood by my bedside.

The beautiful Faerie Queen sat on a bright white faerie horse and had a gracious look on her face, just like those accompanying her. She was a Faerie Queen of the highest rank with an aristocratic appearance of blue translucent skin and black, rather small, almond-shaped eyes. She was wise, serious, feminine and magical. Around her were tiny light orbs, which were actually little flying faeries!

The Faerie Queen had caught my attention and I received images and messages from her: 'Take care of birds, feed them birdseed whenever you can, especially during these cold days, and use the seed in rituals.' I was told, through images, how to do all of this. She said the birds need to be taken care of and protected by humans in order to evolve into the creatures they truly are. I decided to go out and buy birdseed the next morning and to dedicate myself to the task I was given. Suddenly something brushed past my head. I had to smile because I knew it was a winged fae! It was about three to four cm and was almost completely made of light.

After my 'conversation' with the Royal Court I enjoyed their company for a while (the room was full of them now!) and after a while it became silent ... Not for long, though ... After a short period I felt a feminine presence with a healing character. She sat next to my left ear (which was buzzing and bugging me) and brushed it, saying, in a soft voice, she was healing me from the inside.

I thanked the faeries deeply for this encounter. I received one final message from the Faerie Queen: 'Don't be afraid of us, your fear distorts our connection, lose your fear, lose it ...' And then it became real quiet.

I was filled up with energy and felt positive. I went out of the bed and decided to write this down. When I checked the clock, I saw it was four minutes past five in the morning!

The Shining Faerie Kings

As with their female counterparts, the faerie kings are all aspects of the God.

They are the original 'New Men', combining strong leadership qualities with the more feminine traits of spirituality and sensitivity. They too are positive role models in their many different kingly aspects. The faerie kings demonstrate to us that they can be sensitive, caring and protective of their families and other people as well as being brave, loyal, heroic and determined. They lose none of their masculine qualities by displaying some feminine traits.

Being a woman does not stop you from contacting the faerie kings. They will help to bring out the animus in you (your masculine side). As a woman this can be particularly helpful if you are involved in business, often considered a man's world. They can be your spiritual mentor just as well as any of the faerie queens would be.

The faerie kings and queens can be there for us in all our life phases; this chapter can help you to begin a relationship with them and learn how best to contact them.

The Glamour of the Faerie Monarchs

The sexual pull of the faerie kings and queens is legendary and they can appear to us as alluring, beautiful, bewitching and powerful beings. For many of us the initial attraction of working with a faerie monarch is the sexual attraction. This aspect of working with them is common, but not universal, and is entirely expected if this is the way in which you experience them. This does not make them less spiritual beings to work with because they function on this energy level.

The faerie realm, being one with nature, also takes on its traits as an intrinsic aspect. Nature is continually reproducing itself and this is its driving force, to of course create life in all its forms, be they plant, animal, mineral or human. Faeries personify this vital life force in a magical fecundity. Faerie kings and queens are the most potent possessors of this life force and cannot help transmitting this to you when you connect with them. Sex to faeries is seen as natural, sacred and god-given and they are not ashamed of it in any way. It is this blessed energy force which brings life, the most wonderful gift to have bestowed upon any being. Therefore sex and sexual attractiveness are revered among faeries.

'Glamour' is the name given to faerie magic which brings them to appear in our world, enhancing their already natural beauty. It is a shimmering faerie cloak of illusion. When working with the realms of fey, we should always remind ourselves that glamour is their magic and it is not real in our world. We may be attracted to a faerie king or queen, and that will sometimes be the factor that draws us to work with them; however we cannot act upon this magnetic pull. It can only exist in Faerie Land and we should not focus upon this as the only attribute a faerie monarch can bring to our lives.

Contacting the Faerie Monarchs

Beginning contact with the faerie monarchs is to start a very magical and celestial relationship. If you listen carefully, they will be the best spiritual guide and will surpass any mortal teacher. At this moment you may be wondering if there really is a faerie king or queen out there to guide you on your pathway. You will know when your faerie monarch has found you. You may think that it is you who does the choosing, but your special fey monarch knows who you are already. Finding out who they are is all part of the sparkling journey of discovery.

When you make contact with a faerie king or queen, you are forming an alliance with the purest faerie power. Working with the faerie monarchs is equivalent to contacting a god or goddess. These monarchs were once considered to be of the gods themselves and have only been demoted in the eyes of Christian cultures that they herald from.

To work with a faerie king or queen you need unwavering belief and desire; everything else is a technicality. No book can help you to find the belief and the desire which must come from your heart. If you have these two fundamental ingredients, then you can be successful when working with the fey monarchs.

We have chosen an example of a faerie king and queen for you and ways to connect with them if you choose. Later on in the chapter is a list of many faerie kings and queens, each with a simple introduction, to inspire you if you should choose to work with a faerie monarch. If you already have experience in working with gods and goddesses, then transferring this to working with the fey monarchs should be a very natural process.

All the kings and queens of Elf Land await you ...

KING SIL: THE SECRET MONARCH

*'They were the ones who would carry the king and queen to this in-between place; an eclipse with our time and the Land of Elves...
The Priestess of Elphame spoke her words of invocation to King Sil in a felicitous state of peace and equanimity. Her Priest became enveloped within a radiant golden light and a tingling sensation poured through him as he received the presence of King Sil.'*
ALICEN GEDDES, *THE ELFIN ECLIPSE*

The time has come for this mysterious, ancient and mainly forgotten king to emerge. His secrets as a monarch, like those of the faerie mound he guards, remain shrouded in mystery to historians and spiritual seekers alike. Let us now unearth the enigma of King Sil.

King of Hearts

The most significant element regarding King Sil is that he is fundamentally associated with Silbury Hill at the World Heritage Site in Avebury, Wiltshire. According to legend the hill is named after King Sil, whose name means 'great'. Some sources say that Silbury could then mean 'great hill'. However, other authorities theorize that *Sil* has many other possible meanings, maybe deriving from the Old Norse word *silga* which means 'landmark', or that *Sil* relates to the time of the first harvest. Whatever the origins of the name, no one disputes King Sil's essential connection to Silbury Hill.

By learning about Silbury Hill we can derive a greater understanding of the king himself, as in many instances he takes on traits of the site's characteristics. The site is the largest artificial mound in Europe and extends over five acres. If you have ever visited Silbury Hill, you will know of its imposing presence on the landscape surrounding it. This great monument leaves you in spellbound awe, just at the sheer size of it, as it dominates the countryside around. At a height of 130 feet we can see why Silbury Hill is considered to be the centre of Avebury and even thought to be the spiritual heart of Britain. The site was built on a ley line and is also aligned with the solstices. It is also claimed that the hill has lunar and solar associations, as when the moon is full and the midday sun is present, they both align themselves to this ley line.

Historians still have no solid conclusions about the real purpose of Silbury Hill; similarly, no facts exist about the life of the king. We do know that Silbury Hill was built around late July or August approximately 2900–2500 BC. Some theorize that the mound may have been constructed as a burial chamber for the king. Legend tells us that he is buried in a golden coffin within the mound. Other accounts tell us that he resides within Silbury, buried upright upon the saddle of his golden horse.

How the communities viewed life at the time Silbury Hill was created can help us see the significance of these legends. The Earth was seen by these essentially pagan peoples as being a sacred mother who emerged from it; when death came to us, the Earth embraced us once again, transporting us to the afterlife and eventual rebirth. Silbury Hill can be seen within the landscape as a pregnant mother, the womb within the Earth. Sil within his mound is also thought to have powers over death, the passage to the afterlife and rebirth. Legend says that he waits on his horse, ready to return one day to uphold his mission to save Britain, the island he serves. In this way he is likened to King Arthur, who is also said to await rebirth to save his land and is similarly connected to Silbury Hill, as is the Faerie God Bran; all three share similar traits.

The Road to Faerie Land

King Sil's connections to Faerie are many. Silbury Hill is also considered to be a portal to Faerie Land, of which Sil guards the entrance and admits safe passage. Robert Graves in *The White Goddess* regards '... Silbury to be the original Spiral Castle of Britain'. This makes Silbury Hill an immense site of faerie power and significance, as the spiral '... represents the journey through the labyrinth that the soul travels into death and the Underworld and outward to rebirth,' says Anna Franklin in *The Illustrated Encyclopaedia of Faeries*.

The Spiral Castle is also integral to those who follow Faeriecraft, as this is the imagery we can use to visit Faerie Land when in ritual or meditation. King Sil, the host and keeper of the spiral, is a magic spinner to the Otherworlds, able to command the power of the threads of life itself.

How to Work with King Sil

The optimum time to connect with King Sil is on the night of the full moon, as local folklore says that he still rides the perimeter of the hill on moonlit nights, wearing his golden armour and upon his golden horse. The festivals of the midwinter and summer solstices are also special times for Silbury Hill and therefore for its king.

If you would like to contact him by leaving a gift on your faerie altar, you could place a token of something gold upon your altar, also the golden elixir food of honey.

Once you have nurtured a relationship with this king he can be contacted for help with all the major life transitions: conception, birth, death and crossing over to the afterlife. You can also work with him if you wish to visit Faerie Land and he will act as your guardian if you wish to travel with him.

King Sil's Message

It is a belief that King Sil's time is about to come for him to reign again as a spiritual monarch. This can only be achieved by working with him and connecting with the mound that he inhabits. By journeying with King Sil we awake the spiritual consciousness of the land and unearth the passage to Faerie Land that lies forgotten. This is an immensely powerful king who should be approached with respect, for he has much to impart to us.

We connected with King Sil to bring you a pathworking, to help you begin your journeying.

TREADING THE SPIRAL OF SIL

Alicen: This meditation was received on a beautiful spring evening in late April on the night of a full moon. According to my magical diary this particular moon is called a wishing moon and is favourable for rebirth and initiation. I felt that it was especially poignant to be meditating on King Sil, the faerie king of rebirth on this night. In honour of Sil I lit a gold candle; you may like to do the same. I asked him to bring a meditation journey for you to experience him. The following is what I received.

Visualize yourself on a clear moonlit light in the meadow that surrounds Silbury Hill. From an entrance in the side of the mound, that does not ordinarily exist, you hear the sound of a horse's hooves. Riding calmly and serenely out of the mound is a figure that you begin to see forming, almost as if it is made out of a cluster of golden lights or fireflies. As the horse comes nearer to you, the lights appear to have taken shape in the form of a man wearing golden armour, of a brilliance you have never seen before. The magnificent horse halts before you, so close that you can feel its warm breath upon you. King Sil says nothing, but his presence is quite electrifying.

Take a moment to adjust to the immense energy of his being. Do not rush; he knows why you are here and can wait as long as you need.

* * * *

When you are ready to continue, King Sil holds out his hand to you; he wants you to ride with him around Silbury Hill. You stand on a tree stump and climb up behind King Sil on his beautiful horse. As soon as you are upon the horse, it feels like nothing you have ever experienced before. You almost feel as if you are floating upon an invisible force. You feel not just held by the horse's own body, but carried by the consciousness of the universe. It is a wonderfully safe and all-encompassing feeling and you may even feel the sensation of being held by God or angels upon the horse.

This is no ordinary horse, but a faerie steed of great power that has carried this monarch over many centuries and through many realms. He wields the power of the universe in his limbs and is a noble creature to behold.

King Sil now takes off his golden helmet and carries it underneath his arm. You see a middle-aged, attractive man with a dark beard and flowing dark hair. He smiles and then urges his horse forward. As you are carried around the perimeter of the hill, your perceptions change. You notice that the horse leaves a beautiful trail of shimmering golden lights behind you as he walks. This lights up the mound and gives it a magical glow. It begins to feel as if nothing else exists but this experience. You hear the soft breath of the horse and the sounds of the hooves upon the long grass.

You smell the metal and oil of Sil's armour so close to you and the fragrance of the cool night air fills your being. Your senses are being awakened and with them your experience is deepened.

It is as if Sil's horse is walking a magic circle around the hill, for now you are within it; and the world outside, along with your life's burdens and any worries you may have, are far behind. Sil has taken you to a magical mind-place where your spirit can really be free. As the horse walks, you look up at the full moon and the stars.

Make this your wishing moon, too, and pledge one wish upon the moon. Once you have made your wish, you notice that the horse has started to climb the mound. You take the liberty of holding onto Sil now, as it is a steep climb. Relax and enjoy the sensations of the heightened awareness you have of everything around you. Make this journey of mind and spirit whatever you want it to be.

Soon the horse reaches the top of the mound and instead of seeing the landscape of Avebury and the surrounding Wiltshire countryside, you see the land full of grassy mounds. 'The city of faerie mounds and the place of my people,' announces Sil simply as he gestures all around you to the usually invisible mounds. Then King Sil passes one of his hands over both of your eyelids. He does this so closely that you feel the suede of his gloves brush your eyelids. You do as requested and close your eyes, for now is the time to journey if you would like to take a few moments to follow your own meditative pathway in peacefulness.

* * * *

Once you have returned from your journeying, you find that King Sil has vanished and you are back where you began your pathworking at the secret entrance to Silbury Hill. The night seems ordinary once again; you hear the soft rumble of cars in the distance, the hoot of an owl in a nearby tree. It is time to depart this elfin place.

When you are ready, open your eyes, close your chakras and perform a grounding exercise. Eat and drink something to feel earthed once more and leave a small token of your appreciation to King Sil on your faerie altar.

QUEEN NIAMH OF THE GOLDEN HAIR

'Me seemed, by my side a royall Mayd
Her daintee limbes full softly down did lay:
So faire a creature yet saw never sunny day
… But whether dreames delude, or true it were
And her parting said, She Queene of Fairies hight …'
EDMUND SPENSER, *THE FAERIE QUEENE*

A Golden Enchantress

Niamh (pronounced Nee-uv) comes to us with a vivid story to tell and within this narrative the true nature of faerie is revealed. Let us find the real Niamh.

Heavenly Queen

Above all qualities we are told that Niamh is a great beauty, so beautiful in fact that she shines. In Ireland she is known as Niamh Chinn Oir, which means 'Niamh of the Golden Hair' – and indeed several meanings are attached to her name: brightness, heavenly, lustre and radiance are among them. She is so delightful that she carries her beauty as part of her name, as an innate aspect to her being. This physical beauty, which radiates an Otherworldly quality, is all part of her power. All depictions of Niamh are united in the fact that her beauty is described in vivid detail. Kisma K. Stepanich-Reidling in *Faery With Teeth* says that, 'Her golden hair hung in ringlets down to her waist. Her eyes were as blue as robin's eggs.' In Marie Heaney's *Names Upon the Harp* she is depicted '… as beautiful as a vision. Her eyes were as clear and blue as the May sky.' All sources describe her hair in varying shades from russet gold to an angelic golden hue. Some accounts describe her hair with every ringlet being tied with a bead or tiny silver bell. Descriptions of her beauty all appear to be metaphors for aspects of nature. We believe Niamh to be a metaphor for nature herself; a faerie being mirroring the most beautiful of everything in our natural world. In her we see the splendour and fullness of a summer's day.

Niamh also rides a stunning white faerie steed, a horse of its calibre like no other. It was said to wear a golden bridle with one hundred tiny, tinkling bells plaited to its shining mane. Even its hooves were shod with golden shoes and this equine was a resplendent sight. Horses are one of the sacred animals to the faerie people, and it is no surprise that Niamh's own horse should be adorned with such honour and attention.

Niamh is also associated with the symbol of the apple, which in turn often causes her to be linked with Morgan Le Fey, the Queen of Avalon and the Place of Apples and all the characteristics these portray. Apples are regarded as representing passage to the Otherworlds, everlasting youth and rebirth, indeed all traits corresponding to Niamh's story. The celebrated artist Iain Lowe says that '... she carries the apple of eternal youth that always remains whole when eaten ...'

Niamh is also connected with The Lady of the Lake, Nimue (see Chapter 14) and the goddess Badb. She is an Irish raven goddess and can be seen washing the armour of those soldiers who will die in battle. Badb is an omen of death and Niamh may be an aspect of her, as she is known to help heroes at their moment of death on the battlefield. Thus Niamh carries on her theme of transition to the Otherworlds in many guises.

As well as a faerie queen, Niamh is also hailed as a maiden goddess and some stories also describe her as a faerie princess. Some sources cite two queens with the name Niamh, both sharing very similar traits; other sources list these as one and the same. She is the daughter of Manannan Mac Lir, the Celtic god of the ocean (see page 103 for his story). She dwells in the faerie kingdom of Tir na n-og, the Land of Eternal Youth where no one ever grows old or suffers from ill health. This is the original land of milk and honey where the race of the faerie people, the Tuatha De Danann, sought refuge from the invaders to Ireland. This Otherworld is a realm of Faerie Land where there is an everlasting springtime. However, the fey that stray from Tir na n-og, especially to find love, sometimes have a price to pay for their Paradise, as Niamh's story illustrates.

The Story of Niamh and Oisin

Oisin (pronounced Ush-een) was the son of Finn, the leader of the Fianna in Ireland. Oisin was known to be extremely handsome and good-natured, and stories of his virility had even reached the ears of Faerie Land. It happened that early one May morning Finn was out hunting with his sons and the survivors of the Battle of Gowra when a comely young woman was seen approaching the band of men on a beautiful white horse. They all stopped to stare at this magnificent sight and when she and her steed halted and she spoke to Finn, they were even more in awe of her beauty. She told them all that her name was Niamh of the Golden Hair and her father was the king of Tir na n-og. She declared that she had travelled far in search of Oisin to take him back to the Land of Youth and make him her husband. Oisin, overcome with her beauty, did not hesitate to reply and said that he would gladly marry her and live in Tir na n-og. With this reply Niamh took him up upon her horse.

As they rode off together, Finn let out three mournful shouts at the loss of his son. With this Oisin returned and embraced his father and tearfully said his farewells to his brothers and comrades.

Niamh and Oisin then began their journey to Tir na n-og where the sea magically parted for them to be allowed passage to the Land of Youth. Tir na n-og delivered all that was promised to Oisin and he married Niamh, who bore him two sons, Fionn and Osgar, and a daughter, Plur na mBan, who became a goddess.

Three hundred years passed by happily, but to Oisin it had seemed as if only three years had gone by. He began to miss his father and the Fianna, and asked Niamh if he could visit Finn. Niamh gave her consent but knew that she and her children would never see Oisin again. She gave him an ominous warning which she repeated to him three times. She warned him not to dismount his horse and touch his feet upon the land of Ireland, otherwise he would never return to her again. On the third warning she broke down in tears, kissing him and pleading with him not to leave, telling him that this would be her last kiss and that things would not be the same when he returned to Ireland. Oisin felt deeply saddened, but still pined for his home and the father he had left behind.

He returned to Ireland, finding unfamiliar sights as his home at the fort was derelict and overgrown with weeds. His father and comrades were nowhere to be found and, deeply saddened, he left on horseback to the Valley of the Thrushes where he found a large crowd of people around a glen. Oisin noticed that the people appeared to be smaller than those he had left behind in Ireland. Noticing his appearance of strength and greater size, they urged him to come forward and help them shift a flagstone that was crushing several men underneath.

Oisin went to their aid and, remembering Niamh's words of warning, he did not dismount but leaned over in the saddle to lift the flagstone. However, the stone was so heavy that it caused the saddle to slip and the girth to snap. Oisin immediately fell out of the saddle and his horse bolted and fled. Oisin, a tall and handsome young man, towered above the crowd, who watched in awe. His body began to lose strength and Oisin felt himself sinking, until he lay on the grass. The crowd looked on at a blind, withered and weak old man and he later died.

Niamh's Message

Niamh conveys to us that we should always heed the warnings of the fey if they are ever given to us. This story also reinforces the knowledge that faerie glamour is only magical in Faerie Land and that, once we return to our world, faerie gifts cannot be transferred from one realm to another.

Despite her sad story, Niamh has many messages for us. Oisin was literally her chosen one and she chose a mortal husband over a fey one, indicating that she is willing to interact with us if she sees fit. As with most faerie queens, Niamh is a female siren, being sexually confident and exuding female power. She is really the Queen of Transition, guiding those who are dying to the afterlife. She is also a faerie queen who will guide you to Faerie Land in your meditations and spiritual journeying. She is known to assist people in all types of transitions in their lives, and you can call upon her for help for easy passage at these times. She can be especially called upon at baby-naming ceremonies, marriages and funerals or passing rites. She will also assist with magic and wishes with love matters.

Niamh is a caring queen and works on the love vibration of the heart. An alliance with Niamh of the Golden Hair is one that can help you in many areas of your life, as long as you listen to what she has to say.

Below is an opportunity to work with Niamh and connect with her through a simple ceremony.

A JOURNEY WITH NIAMH TO TIR NA N-OG

In this journeying ritual you are going to be Niamh. If you are male, you are going to be Oisin and you will experience Niamh from this perspective. The preparation for this journey is very simple and really just requires you to focus your mind on this faerie queen.

Prepare your faerie altar: fill a beautiful glass or goblet with either cider or apple juice to mark Niamh's associations with apples. Your offering can be an apple pie, apple cake or even slices of apple if you prefer.

You need to find one thing to place on your altar which makes you think of Niamh. This may be anything you associate with her, for example something as simple as a gold-coloured ribbon to represent her golden hair, a tiny bell or a picture of a white horse or a horseshoe on your altar. This is your focus and your signal to Niamh that your ceremony is all about nurturing a relationship with her. Of course, if Niamh is your chosen faerie queen above all others and you wish to work with her regularly, then your altar can reflect this. You can really go to town and perhaps have a golden altar cloth, attach tiny bells to your faerie besom (broom) and burn applewood incense. The list could go on; your imagination should be let loose here to create a sparkling faerie altar in honour of Queen Niamh of the Golden Hair.

To prepare yourself for the rite should also be simple and only requires a little extra thought. If you are female you need to wear one item which reminds you of Niamh. As with your faerie altar, again this is entirely your choice and can be something as simple as a ribbon of little bells attached to your hair or a sash of gold-coloured material tied around your waist.

If you are male, you are going to wear one item which reminds you of Oisin. This could be a Celtic brooch, a green sash around your waist to symbolize Ireland and the fey, or anything that would associate you with his warrior persona.

First sit before your faerie altar and invite the faerie monarchs you are going to work with.

An Invitation Blessing to Niamh and Oisin

'Blessed Be my queen so fair;
Hail, Niamh of the Golden Hair.
Your consort Oisin, to us bring,
Hand-in-hand to my faerie ring.
On this journey I will see through the eyes of
Niamh (or Oisin).
Blessed Be.'

Either sit or lie down and then close your eyes. If you are Niamh, then now begin to see yourself as her; imagine your luxuriously golden long hair and the dress that you are wearing. If you are Oisin, imagine yourself in his green cloak with Celtic knotwork design on the edging, warm clothes and a spear in your hand.

'Of Tir na n-og I wish to see,
The land of milk and honey bee.
Her hand she waved to close my eyes,
To see with my mind I realize,
Tir na n-og is just a breath away,
A wish, a kiss, but not to stay.'

Now your journey really begins. Visualize a beautiful land all around you, where the countryside is in the throes of spring. There is heavy blossom hanging from the boughs of the trees, the grass you are sitting on is lush and a deep green, punctuated with daisies and buttercups. There are birds singing and sticky buds poised to flower on the shrubs and trees. It is a gloriously sunny evening and it is almost dusk. The day is drawing close to faerie time and you as Niamh or Oisin sit beneath an apple tree in stillness. The white faerie horse grazes contentedly beneath the tree, the setting sun catching the glint in his golden shoes.

At dusk you will place upon your head a faerie crown, which sits beside you now on a green velvet cushion. It sparkles and glimmers against the last rays of the setting sun. The crown symbolizes your sovereignty, vision and enchantment. At the moment that dusk begins to descend, you will place your faerie crown upon your head and ask for a message from Tir na n-og.

Watch carefully now the orb of the golden sun almost disappearing over the verdant green horizon. When you see the last rays of the sun disappear from view, then pick up the glittering faerie crown. The stones in the fey crown are emeralds and amethysts; both gems are associated with divination and meditation. Place the faerie crown upon your head and ask the land of Tir na n-og for a message especially for you.

> '…Cast my visions, a message to see,
> The shape of magic brings tidings to me.'

This is your time in the journey to discover the magic. Remember Niamh's own message, that if a faerie tells you something it does well to listen carefully and heed their advice. A message may be given to you in many ways, including symbolically, so do not discount anything that you are given.

* * * *

Once you have received your message, take the fey crown from your head and place it on the green velvet cushion beside you. Bid the land of Tir na n-og farewell and open your eyes.

Now go to your faerie altar and it is time to bless your apple cake/juice or whatever you have.

> 'Now I seek to honour thee
> With Elphame food that blessed be.
> With this apple cake
> Of faerie food I partake.
> Two worlds are one in this rite,
> On this most enchanted night.
> Blessed be.'

Now take a sip from your chalice and eat your cake. When you have done this, it is time to bid farewell to your faerie king and queen.

Farewell to Niamh and Oisin

> 'Blessed be our queen so fair,
> Farewell Niamh of the Golden Hair.
> With your consort, now you go,
> Hand-in-hand to your faerie knowe.
> 'Til we meet again.
> Niamh (or Oisin) in this guise no more
> This faerie seeker is back for sure.
> Blessed be.'

Now take off your token that you are wearing that reminded you of Niamh or Oisin. Remember to leave out an offering of your cider and apple cake for Niamh and Oisin and their faerie court.

Below are listed several kings and queens of faerie with brief introductions, which will hopefully inspire you to contact one or more of them and learn more.

KING ARAWN

If you would like to contact Faerie King Arawn, his watchwords are strength and transition.

This king is sometimes said to be the Welsh King of the Faeries and he is also known as an ancient Welsh God of the Underworld. As a Faerie King he reigns over Annwn where he has a gigantic and magnificent castle with hundreds of rooms.

The most famous story concerning Arawn is in the Welsh *Mabinogion*. This tells the tale of Pwyll the Lord of Dyfed. Lord Pwyll met King Arawn one day while out hunting on his land. Arawn offered Pwyll a quest to exchange places with him for a year, while being magically disguised as Arawn. At the end of the year Pwyll would have to fight Hafgan, Arawn's enemy, and kill him with just one blow.

Lord Pwyll kept his part of the bargain and this cemented a firm friendship between King Arawn of the faerie realms and Lord Pwyll of the mortal world. This story is also thought to be a symbolic dual, highlighting the transition of one season to another.

- If you would like to visualize the Faerie King Arawn, here is a brief description of him to start you off. King Arawn is a large man of considerable power. He rides upon a hefty grey dappled horse and he wears clothes of many colours, which are much more vivid colours than appear in our world.

- Call on King Arawn to create new relationships and renew old friendships.

KING ARTHUR

The Faerie King Arthur's watchwords are renewal and rebirth.

It is not generally known that Arthur of the Round Table is inextricably linked to the Land of Faerie and is even considered to be a Faerie King himself. His life and death and even the question of his very existence are steeped in myth, legend and conspiracy theories. None of us may know the true King Arthur; however we present him here according to ancient faerie lore.

King Arthur is thought to be a Faerie King and god incarnate in a human body. His life was meant to be a message from the Otherworlds to save the spiritual aspect of humanity. During his lifetime he had many faerie connections. He was educated by Merlin, who was thought to be the son of a nun and an angel. Arthur was also given his magical sword, Excalibur, by the bewitchingly beautiful faerie woman known as The Lady of the Lake. She goes by the names of either Nimue or Vivienne. Excalibur was imbued with the magic of the faeries to protect the one who wielded it.

However, King Arthur's death is the part of his legend most shrouded in mystery and fey magic. It is said that upon his death, four faerie queens of Avalon, amongst them Morgan Le Fay, carried him by boat to the Isle of Avalon. Legend tells us that he now rests beneath a faerie mound until Britain needs him again – although which faerie mound is contestable! Many historians link him to Silbury Hill in Avebury, Wiltshire, England. This in turn also links him to the God Bran, the Faerie King Sil, the Fisher King and Faerie King Arawn.

No one knows the real resting place in death for this elusive king. Because his tomb has never been found many sources declare that one day he will return again to spiritually rule over Britain. As Cervantes's Don Quixote (1605) says '… this king did not die … (but) was transformed into a raven and that in due course he will return to reign … for which reason it cannot be proved that from that time to this any Englishman ever killed a raven.' The raven is his sacred animal and the winter solstice is his special time.

- King Arthur's name is legendary for his leadership qualities. Call on Arthur's help with assistance in the workplace and group projects (team work).

WAYLAND THE SMITH, KING OF THE ELVES

His magical watchwords are secrets revealed.

Wayland the Smith is an English Elf King who is thought to dwell in Wayland's Smithy. This is an ancient Neolithic long barrow situated in Berkshire, England. However, this Elf King's history goes back even further to a time when, as with many faerie kings, he was considered to be a Saxon god called Volund.

He is of course the master smith, and, as everyone knows, if the faeries have a craft, they finish it many times finer than any human craftsman. Legend goes that if a horse is tethered on the night of a full moon at Wayland's Smithy, by morning the horse will be newly shod.

Wayland the Smith's sacred animal is the horse. His optimum time is a full moon.

• Call on Wayland the Smith's assistance with perfecting creative crafts.

KING NUADA

The faerie-warrior King Nuada's watchword is restoration.

This is an Irish faerie king who was originally an Iron Age god, now of the Tuatha De Danann. Nuada is known in legend as Nuada of the Silver Hand. A warrior king, he lost one of his hands in battle and was made a silver one. (Some say this was a silver arm.) However, because his body was no longer whole and deities cannot rule if they are artificial in any way, he had to step down from his fey kingly role. The incompetent and mean Bres took over his throne.

Nuada had his silver hand/arm magically restored to flesh once again and he overthrew Bres and ruled as king. He was one of the bearers of one of the Danann's four great treasures – the sword of Nuada.

• Call on King Nuada for confidence and leadership skills.

KING MANANNAN MAC LIR

His watchwords are compassion and mirth.

This faerie king is truly an all-rounder! He is first and foremost the Celtic god of the ocean and this extends to his governing watery conditions such as fog, lakes, rivers and storms. So influential is he that he is also Manx faerie king of the Isle of Man and additionally an Irish deity of the Tuatha De Danann. He is considered to be an exceptionally caring and benevolent deity, and for those who wish to connect with him he often comes as a fatherly and friendly figure.

He has several animals attributed to him: the crane, horses, pigs and salmon. His personal qualities are known to include humour, wit, wisdom and compassion. He is one of the faerie kings who is said to ferry the souls from this world to the afterlife.

- If you have need of assistance with psychic protection, healing, astral projection (out-of-body travel) and any faerie magic, then this is the faerie king to connect with.

QUEEN CAELIA

Faerie queen Caelia's watchwords are allurement and enchantment.

Faerie queen Caelia is of Celtic/British origin and is featured in the beautiful poetic work *The Faerie Queene* by Edmund Spenser. She is said to have enchanted the illegitimate son of King Arthur, the already betrothed Tom a' Lincoln. She bore him a son and he was named Red Rose Knight, and considered to be of faerie blood.

- Call upon her when you need help with any aspect of motherhood, faerie magic in general and kindness.

QUEEN ARGANTE

Her watchword is healing.

Argante is an Elf Queen and is one of the faerie queens of Avalon, Morgan Le Fay being the other one. However, some sources say that these two magical queens are in fact the same person. The name *Argante* means 'Silvery One' and she is supposed to have originated from the Welsh Queen Arianhrod.

Argante was thought to have attended to King Arthur's wounds in his last battle, according to Arthurian legend.

- You can call upon her for help with any elfin magic and contacting the elves.

NIMUE, QUEEN OF THE ISLES OF MAIDENS

Her watchwords are hidden knowledge.

The faerie queen Nimue had truly magical beginnings as she was the god-daughter of the Faerie queen and goddess, Diana.

She is also The Lady of the Lake who kept the magician Merlin of Arthurian legend captive in an enchanted castle, although she was already married to him! She is also thought to be one of the faerie maidens (hence her title) who lives beneath the lakes of the Black Mountains in Wales.

She is said to be exceptionally enchanting and beautiful.

• Ask for her help with love spells and relationships.

QUEEN OONAGH

Queen Oonagh's watchwords are beauty and forbearance.

Queen Oonagh is supposed to be the most beautiful woman ever to walk the Earth and is a stunning creature to behold. Ironically, despite her beauty her husband, King Finvarra, is renowned for his womanizing.

Queen Oonagh is the Irish faerie queen at the court of the Daoine Sidhe. She also has the ability to shapeshift and her favourite form is that of a silver calf.

• If you would like to visualize her, see her as a delicate figure with floor-length golden hair. Her hair is studded with sparkles and she traditionally wears a silver gossamer dress with glistening dewdrops.

• Call upon her for help to cope with an unfaithful marriage with good grace.

QUEEN MAB

Queen Mab's watchwords are dreams and faerie magic.

She is traditionally the English Queen of All Faerie and has been portrayed many times in literature. Some also say that she is the Queen of Ellyllon who are the Welsh fey. She is also said to be enchantingly beautiful.

One of her main traits is to influence our dreams and bring messages to us via our unconscious. Her sacred time is night.

- Call upon her if you need help deciphering your dreams or would like to receive a dream of particular insight.

KING OBERON

His watchwords are fecundity and allurement.

Oberon is one of the best-known of faerie kings; this hails from his portrayal in Shakespeare's *A Midsummer Night's Dream* as Queen Titania's fey lover. However, King Oberon's origins are not British; he is originally a Germanic dwarf king, known as Alberon. With his many origins he also has many guises, either as the handsome faerie king in the Shakespeare play or an Elf King of small stature.

- If you would like help with any aspect of creativity, attraction and sexuality, then Oberon is the faerie king to call upon.

THE SNOW QUEEN FAERIE

Her potent watchwords are sexual energy and magnetism.

She is the spiritual embodiment of winter and although she is essentially a Germanic deity, many cultures recognize her in slightly different form and with other names. In Germany she is known as Holda. In this guise she can appear as a stunningly beautiful young woman. She has very long, dark hair and a prominent nose. Her sacred symbol is the snowflake.

Holda is also considered to have goddess status as well as faerie. At the winter solstice she rides out with The Wild Hunt, shaking out her pillows into the skies and onto the land, creating a snowfall. The Wild Hunt reigns in the skies until Twelfth Night in January. This is her magical time of enchantment when she holds most power.

Despite the bad image that Christianity and literature have shrouded her in, The Snow Queen faerie is mostly benevolent in nature. She mirrors the season of winter in her persona, though the harshness and cruelty of winter are the only facets that have normally been focused on. This is a one-sided image which now needs to be brought into perspective.

The Snow Queen faerie traditionally is the keeper of the home and all that is sacred within it. She presides over spinning and weaving, the hearth and housework. She also rescues unbaptized souls of children and takes them to Faerie Land to live there. She is also queen of sexuality and seduction.

Her sacred animals are many and include horses, wolves, geese, bears, dogs, cats and hawks. Her sacred site in Britain is The Snow Well in Greenwich Park.

- If you want to work with the Snow Queen, call on her to assist in clearing and purifying your home.

'The fur coat and the cap were made of snow, and it was a woman, tall and slender and blinding white — she was the Snow Queen herself.'
THE SNOW QUEEN (1884) HANS CHRISTIAN ANDERSON

GWYNN AP NUDD

His watchwords are romance and mystery.

This faerie king rules over two faerie realms: an Underworld palace beneath Glastonbury Tor and the Welsh faerie kingdom of Annwn. He also leads the Welsh version of The Wild Hunt.

Gwynn ap Nudd (Nudd is pronounced 'Neath') stars in a seasonal conquest to win the hand of the lovely faerie Creiddylad (Cree-thil-aahd). This marks the turn of winter to spring.

Gwynn ap Nudd is known as a powerful and mysterious faerie ruler as the realms of death are also meant to be his domain. His sacred bird is the owl.

- If you would like to visualize this faerie king, see him upon a white horse. He is a powerful fey being of great stature. As he rides upon the crest of The Wild Hunt, he wears a cloak of fur to keep him warm and a headdress of antlers.

KING MIDAR

His watch-phrase is journey of the soul.

This is an Irish faerie king who once had the status of being a god. His kingdom is the Tuatha De Danann.

His best-known story is of how he fell in love with a mortal, Queen Etain. Midar stole her away from her husband and rightful throne. Her mortal husband, Eochaid, gained her back after many trials and much effort. Midar eventually released Etain only after many battles with Eochaid and his military.

King Midar's sacred bird is the swan.

- Call upon King Midar when dealing with difficult decisions and faerie magic.

KING FINVARRA

His watchwords are mischief, transition and enchantment.

'Loveable rogue' is probably the best description of Finvarra! He is the incurable womanizing husband of faerie queen Oonagh mentioned earlier. Finvarra is one of the kings of the Daoine Sidhe (Deena Shee) in Ireland. He is also considered to be the Irish King of the Dead and also the High King of the Irish fey.

King Finvarra has a liking for mortal women, whom he lures to his faerie realm by way of faerie glamour. By dawn these mortal lovers are invariably found back, tucked up in their beds by the next morning – none the worse for wear! Finvarra's favoured animal is a horse. His time of power is twilight.

- If you would like to visualize King Finvarra, see him upon his black faerie steed. He wears a black velvet cloak and he is darkly handsome. His presence is powerful and magical.

MORGAN LE FAY

Her watchwords are sexual power and faerie secrecy.

One of the faerie queens of Avalon, England, Morgan Le Fay is one of the most famous of faerie queens and also holds goddess status. She is also documented in Arthurian legend as King Arthur's half-sister and she learnt the magical arts from Merlin.

History portrays her as a dark queen and a sexual being who had many lovers. As with many of the faerie queens, this portrayal of wickedness is not necessarily true and we have to delve a little deeper to find her true identity. She is the keeper to the key to the gateway to the Land of Faerie beneath Glastonbury Tor.

She commands magic in the deepest, most spiritual and enlightening sense of the word. She also brings transformation from darkness to light.

- If you would like to visualize faerie queen Morgan Le Fay, see her as an enchantingly beautiful woman with long, dark hair and a knowing smile.

One last story here from Bara who comes from the Czech Republic but now lives in Orkney. She experienced Morgan Le Fay within a powerful dream visitation experience.

I've been having out-of-body experiences for almost 13 years. For many years I didn't understand what was actually happening to me until I read a book about it. I became less scared and more interested in exploring these experiences. During the following years I found out that each of my out-of-body experiences reflected what I'd been reading about and thinking about during the day or days before the actual experience. Then I met Alicen and read her book, *Faeriecraft*. While I was reading her book my mind was fully occupied with the spiritual path she wrote about. There was one being that especially caught my attention and it was the faerie queen Morgan Le Fay.

The reason why it was her, was probably that she's the one who helps you to find your way from the darkness and leads you towards the light. I thought it was what I needed at that time. I felt spiritually lost and thought it would be interesting and helpful to work (or at least meet) with her.

Then one night I *woke up* and found out that I'd left my physical body. In my astral body I was sitting on my bed and there was a woman sitting on the other side, facing me. I instantly knew that it was Morgan Le Fay. She was one of the most beautiful beings I had ever seen. She had flawless ivory skin, black raven hair and she was dressed in a lovely green velvet dress. There was an aura of sparkling white light surrounding her. She was watching me silently and I felt calm, loved and understood. Then suddenly she gave me a loving, warm smile and stretched her right arm towards me and I could see she had a glowing green light in her hand. I took the light from her and watched it as it sat on my hand. Then I closed my hand with the light in it and I could see that the green light was still shining through my hand. When I raised my eyes again, Morgan Le Fay was gone and I woke back into my physical body.

CHAPTER 7

Faerie Godmothers

"'Now for a gown," said the fairy.
Her magic wand wrapped Cinderella in a dress made of
pale silver and gold threads.'
CINDERELLA

You may be wondering why we have devoted a whole chapter to 'fictional' fairytale characters. As with most of the traditional fairytales, there is more than just a grain of truth in them, as most take their origins from ancient wisdoms. The tale of Cinderella and her benevolent Faerie Godmother is no exception.

Who Are the Faerie Godmothers?

The Faerie Godmothers belong to the realms of powerful ancient magic. They are matriarchal figures with honorary Faerie Queen status, and they should be respected as a grandmother figure would be. The Faerie Godmothers are the head of the faerie hierarchy. Although our society has loved them through fairytales, we have demoted them to the cuteness of Disney. The Faerie Godmothers are waiting to wear their crown of stars once again and for us to call upon them in their traditional role.

CINDERELLA AND HER FAERIE GODMOTHER

In order to understand the Faerie Godmothers, first we must

delve deep into their glittering history. We are all introduced to the tale of Cinderella as children and, as fairytales go, it is one of our favourites. In a survey conducted in UCI cinemas in 2005, *Cinderella* was voted No.1 in the US.

The tale of Cinderella was first written down in China around 850–60 CE, but it wasn't until relatively recently that it became the familiar tale that we have come to love. The French writer Charles Perrault produced a modern adaptation in 1697 and it is this version that has endured, mingled with interpretations from the Brothers Grimm and now Walt Disney. Whichever tale you come across, Cinderella always has a magical helper, and in modern versions she is consistently graced with the assistance of a Faerie Godmother (see Chapter 9 for more information about fairytale authors).

The Secrets of the Fairytales

If we trace the history of fairytales we find that 'once upon a time...' they were stories told by word of mouth and passed down by grandmothers and mothers. Fairytales have always been the domain of women and you don't even have to look closely to realize they are often about women rebelling against the restrictions of a society where they are expected to be submissive and virtuous. Fairytales have traditionally been bound by the wisdom of women. They were originally never meant for children, but were tales of dark, macabre cruelty, fascination and enchantment. It is only in recent history that they have been watered down and made suitable for children's ears.

Knowing how fairytales originated is important, because by peeling back the hidden layers, we meet again the ancient power of the real Faerie Godmothers.

> *'Suddenly, in a swirl of blue light, a Fairy appeared.*
> *"Don't cry, Cinderella," the Fairy said.*
> *"You shall go to the ball, no matter what anyone says.*

Now hurry to the garden and bring me a pumpkin,
six mice, and a fat rat."'
CINDERELLA

The Power of Three!

The Faerie Godmothers are thought to derive from the most powerful faeries of all time: the Fates. These are three fey which have existed from the very onset of creation and are the keepers of the threads of life that bind all human beings to their destinies.

The Fates are three sisters in faerie goddess form, also known as the Moirai. Their names are Klotho, Lachesis and Atropos. Klotho is present at our birth. She is the spinner who spins the thread of our life. Lachesis is known as the measurer and she measures the thread of life and grants us our destiny. Atropos snips the thread of life and releases us from the earthly plane, escorting us to the doorway to the Land of Faerie at the moment of death.

The Fates have different names in many cultures and most cultures share in their belief. Their power over our destinies and the belief that life is a celestial thread that they spin bring them to be known largely as the weavers of fate. Early descriptions of the Fates are not far removed from modern images of what we recognize as a Faerie Godmother today. Demetra George in *Mysteries of the Dark Moon* describes them as '…dwelling amidst celestial spheres where, clad in robes spangled with stars, and wearing crowns on their heads, they sat on thrones radiant with light.'

Honouring the Faerie Godmothers

Our ancestors before us knew all about the trinity of the Fates and honoured them at the three phases of life: birth, marriage and death. When a new baby arrived, three days after the birth the family would prepare the house for the blessing of the visiting faerie. The floor and hearth would be swept, gifts of honey, bread and three white almonds were left. The door was kept open as an invitation to the faerie and a candle left burning to light her way. It was thought that the visiting Faerie Godmother would bless the child and reveal its fate; once told, the destiny could not be altered.

These customs were echoed in the fairytale of Sleeping Beauty where the thirteenth faerie curses the princess because she has not been invited to the christening celebrations. (Faeries, especially Faerie Godmothers, are partial to parties. Always be sure to invite them to yours. If you don't, you may not come out as badly as Sleeping Beauty, but it's best to be on the safe side!) The princess later pricks herself on the spindle of a spinning wheel, yet another symbol of the Fates, and falls under the curse of the thirteenth faerie.

Brides also used to leave gifts of cakes and honey for the Faerie Godmother, who is meant to appear at marriages. The faerie appears once more at the time of death when our destiny is sealed and the thread of life cut. In a dying person's room, a window is often left open to allow the departing soul access to the heavens and the faerie who will meet them.

Who Is Your Faerie Godmother?

Everyone has a Faerie Godmother whom we are allowed to call upon if we need help, rather as in the tale of Cinderella. It is a great shame that not many of us realize that we do have a Faerie Godmother who can help us. Think of her as an added bonus who complements the work of your guardian angel – yes, she's very well connected, celestially speaking! Although she does have the power to provide protection like your guardian angel, she's more about magical assistance in a crisis. She is a reminder of the loving divine force when we need it most. Your Faerie Godmother is the keeper of transformation, allowing us to blossom into our true selves. She is the solution to a problem we never thought of; the sparkle of faerie dust in a place we never knew could shine. Faerie Godmothers possess the kiss of a beloved grandmother and the key to the place we thought was locked.

Unlock the door to the Land of Elfin where your Faerie Godmother is waiting just for you …

Unlock the Faerie Door

Faerie Godmothers are never too busy to come to your aid; that's their job, so don't be afraid to ask. If you have a problem, big or small, which you cannot find a practical solution to, that's the time when you can call on her for magical help. Always see if you can find a straightforward answer to your dilemma first, as that is one of the first rules of faerie magic and common sense, too.

Asking your Faerie Godmother for help is easy. Visualizing your Faerie Godmother is the most effective and simple method of requesting her help. With this method you imagine her presence, which can also be extremely comforting, especially at a time of crisis.

Faerie Godmother Magic

When Cinderella's Faerie Godmother came to her aid, Cinderella was actively required to take part in the making of the magical solution. She was asked to fetch a pumpkin, a rat, mice etc., which where then transformed. This tells us that magic is all around us in everyday things. Our Faerie Godmother will of course come to our rescue, but will only give us the tools to help ourselves. She does not want us to see ourselves as helpless victims, but part of the already magical world, which we have access to. She can hand us the key to transform; the rest is up to us.

Anyone who has ever been on the receiving end of Faerie Godmother magic will tell you that it is usually fairly instantaneous in manifesting. It is no-nonsense and satisfyingly dramatic; so much so that sometimes it can take your breath away. So do be specific with what you ask for, as Faerie Godmothers are astoundingly spot-on. They've had a lot of practice.

Alicen: Here's a little example of Faerie Godmother magic. Quite recently my family and I were travelling home from a conference in Glasgow. When we arrived on Orkney Mainland we only had 25 minutes to catch our connecting ferry to get home to our island. Unfortunately we came across a road closure due to a fatal accident and this meant we missed the last ferry home that night. An overnight stay on Mainland Orkney was now inevitable. We tried some friends first, but they were out for the night. At the height of the holiday season we knew that the chance of finding a hotel or B&B was remote. It was 10 p.m. and the children suddenly burst into tears as they were tired and hungry from travelling since nine a.m. that morning.

As we sat in the car I asked everyone to calm down and close our eyes and visualize our Faerie Godmothers finding us a bed for the night. A tranquil few minutes were spent visualizing and then Neil hit the town to try and find us a room. After what seemed like ages he returned and, although he had finally found us a hotel, he did not have a smile on his face. When we arrived at the hotel I asked the children to be quiet as this was a very posh hotel, and they were really excited. Tam Lin, our six-year-old son, said, 'Oh yes, that's what I asked my Faerie Godmother for. I asked her for a really posh hotel with the comfiest beds we'd ever slept on.'

Tam's Faerie Godmother really had found us one of the most expensive hotels in town! While the rest of us had simply visualized a bed for the night, Tam Lin had not skimped on his visualization and now we were literally paying for it.

A Faerie Godmother Visualization

Here's a visualization you can do anywhere. All you need to do is to close your eyes and your Faerie Godmother is just a thought away ...

Simply take a few deep breaths and close your eyes. In your mind, silently ask your Faerie Godmother to be with you. Imagine a shimmering cluster of tiny stars in a haze of bright white light. As you concentrate on the starry light, see it gradually beginning to take form until the stars have transformed into your radiant Faerie Godmother. She has a gentle face and kind sparkling eyes and she wears a glistening blue dress that is studded with stars from the night sky. Upon her head she wears a faerie crown of twinkling stars. She holds in her hands a luminescent crystal wand. Her presence is calming and loving and she exudes kindness and wisdom. She is bathed in a soft blue light and there are wee winged faeries dancing around the hem of her dress. You can just see the tips of her shoes, which are bejewelled with tiny stones of blue laced agate.

Once you feel that you have visualized her clearly, ask her politely for the help that you need, always remembering to be very specific in your request. Once you have done this, imagine your Faerie Godmother waving her wand and surrounding you in a circle of stars and lovely blue light. Rest in this part of the visualization for as long as you like, and then open your eyes. Simply feeling the presence of your Faerie Godmother may help you to feel a little better.

Once you have opened your eyes, leave a token gift of honey, bread or cake for your Faerie Godmother as a way of thanking her. If this was an emergency situation, just leave a gift for her when it is next conveniently possible.

Life is always more magical and loving for knowing that we have a Faerie Godmother.

A Faerie Godmother Letter

Writing your Faerie Godmother a letter can be a lot of fun. Really enter into the mood of the occasion and find some beautiful hand-pressed paper.

Jacky: Hobby shops now sell papers in all colours of the rainbow, and even my local bookshop has hand-pressed papers with flower petals pressed between the fibres. If you are really crafty you could make your own.

If you want to, you could create the whole thing in miniature, and use particularly small handwriting. A large magnifying glass might help you. Pull apart a normal envelope and copy the shape in miniature to accommodate your extra-small letter.

If you can, use a real ink pen. Or, if you wish, use glitter craft pens to add some shine and sparkle to your note. Decorate your envelope with silver or blue stars and a sprinkle of faerie dust (extra-fine glitter!).

Write your request to your Faerie Godmother in curly script … make your handwriting as beautiful as you can. How do you wish your Faerie Godmother to help you? Remember to add as much detail as you can … don't leave anything out. Pop a few items in your envelope to represent the things you need – in true Cinderella style.

Use your imagination: perhaps a pressed flower head to symbolize a new outfit, a teeny snail shell to be a symbol of your request for a new home, and so on. Of course, if you use large objects, then you will need that larger envelope! Alternatively, you could place your objects in a silky drawstring bag and place your letter inside with the objects.

Of course, you don't necessarily have to use white mice for horses or a pumpkin for a coach, but do try and find some natural objects with a special significance ... for you!

When you have finished your letter you can wrap it in a beautiful shiny ribbon and tie it to your favourite faerie tree. If you don't have a tree in your garden, then place it under a pot of herbs (even on a windowsill if you want to – remember, it's the symbolism that counts).

As always, leave your Faerie Godmother a small offering in exchange for her help. A small shiny crystal or pretty pebble would be particularly appropriate in this case, as this can be left permanently in place. Remember not to litter!

Leave your letter overnight at your faerie tree if you have placed it in a part of your own property. If your faerie tree is in a public place, you can literally 'sit on the problem' (place your letter under you) whilst you follow the Faerie Godmother visualization.

Remember that Faerie Godmothers like to 'help us to help ourselves', so do everything in your power to create and manifest your heart's desire into your life and your Faerie Godmother will help to make it happen for you.

'I think, at a child's birth, if a mother could ask a fairy godmother to endow it with the most useful gift, that gift would be curiosity.'
ELEANOR ROOSEVELT

CHAPTER 8

⊗

Faeries and Their Lore

'...The iron tongue of midnight hath told twelve;
Lovers to bed; 'tis almost fairy time ...'
WILLIAM SHAKESPEARE

Secrets of the 'Secret People'

People are often puzzled as to why faeries have their own lore and codes of conduct; in this chapter we hope to uncloak the mystery. The fey are bound to nature by way of their being; herein lies the key to the reasons behind their lore.

We all know that although nature is our friend and sustains us, it also has to be respected for our own safety and for us to live in harmony with our environment. For instance, we understand that to be under a tree in an electric storm is a risk, so we wouldn't do it, or to be on the beach at high tide is not a good idea. When we consider these risks we are acknowledging our connection to and respect for nature. As faeries are beings of nature, when we respect their lore we are doing exactly the same thing as when we avoid a tree for shelter when there is lightning around. We are respecting their realm, the spiritual aspect of nature, and acknowledging that although we can belong partly to their realm and it can spiritually sustain us, too, we must also respect its rules.

Because the faeries inhabit their own realm as well as our world, they have developed their own customs. All cultures have their own customs and the Land of Faerie is no exception. After all, if we visit another country we learn the ways of a different culture and respect that culture's ways while visiting. We are doing exactly the same while visiting the faeries' realm … it's only polite, after all.

Much of faerie lore is mere superstition and is derived from folklore in times when Christianity was stamping out the old pagan ways and making people fearful of them. They are from a time in history when if anything went wrong it was blamed either on the faeries or on witchcraft – or both! People were afraid of what they didn't understand and it was easy to blame the little people.

There is much of faerie lore which we can identify as falling into this dubious category hailing from a time when Christianity was force-fed to the masses and the old ways were being seen as directly linked with the devil. Instead of spiritual guardians of our land, the fey were demoted to spiteful mischief-makers who would turn your milk sour, put your hearth fire out and even spit on your last harvest of blackberries. In ancient times, the fey were regarded as a race of beings that were to be respected … and feared, and at all times appeased. It was even bad luck to refer to them directly as 'the faeries' and they thus gained such nicknames as 'the good people', 'the fair folk', 'the Lordly Ones', 'little darlings', 'the Lovers', 'Men of Peace', 'secret people' and 'the good neighbours from the Sunset Land', to name but a few.

In this chapter we aim to sift through the wealth of traditions that exist. As John Matthews commented in his book *The Secret Lives of Elves and Faeries*, '… folklore serves as a last strand connecting us with a time now lost forever'. By exploring this fascinating bond with the past we hope this will provide you with a sense of the feys' historical background and also a useful body of faerie lore that will help you if you wish to work with the faeries and visit their realm. This will help you to form a safe and positive connection with them.

If you have a love of faeries we are sure that you will enjoy reading this chapter. Even after many years of studying and working with the faeries, when delving into faerie lore the subject is so complex that new discoveries always arise. If you are drawn to the fey, unearthing faerie lore often helps to make sense of certain aspects of your life. It is often that you read something and realize, for instance, that maybe the reason you have been drawn to certain flowers/trees/herbs/times of year etc. is that they are sacred to the faeries.

Marked for Mischief! – Faerie Appearance

How faeries look is bound up with their lore, as they have an appearance that is unique to their race. Contrary to popular belief, most faeries do not have wings at all and most are even human-sized, although many are around the stature of a small child, and some only a few inches high.

Many sightings are recorded of them as being approximately three feet tall. In fact, faeries are often of a human appearance with only a slight deviation indicating their fey form. These can be such physical traits as pointy ears, large slanting eyes or beautiful and unnaturally long, luxuriant hair. Many of them appear naked – this is said to be because of their connection with a more natural and less restrained way of existing. Many faeries are also believed to be exceptionally beautiful, and even if they are not so they can appear to us this way because of their faerie glamour.

Faerie hair is a common trait and is unusual to most humans. Many fey have hairy bodies, often characterized by red hair. Long hair is also characteristic, either being unkempt and knotty or beautifully tended as that of the mermaids and water nymphs. Faeries always wear their hair unbound and uncovered – this is a mark of their freedom and magical potency. Long hair has long been seen as an extension of the life force of a being, thus portraying the enchanting qualities of the faerie race.

'Queen Mab was there, her shimmering hair...'
THE DISCOVERY, PAUL LAURENCE DUNBAR

Other traits are normal bodies, though faeries may also feature parts of animals such as the beak of a bird instead of a nose, cloven, webbed or clawed feet, bird wings in place of arms and the famous fish tails of the mermaids in place of legs and feet.

In historical folklore it was thought that if you had a deformity and it looked elfin (such as pointed ears or slanting eyes) you were known to be 'elvish marked' and were said to belong to the faeries. There is a saying that you were marked for mischief as one of the fey yourself – this was not a desirable nickname to have earned!

Many faeries are also depicted as having brown- or green-tinged skin, another feature of their affinity with nature. Folklore also describes their blood as being milky-white in appearance. However, we do not know this to be true, and it is ancient folklore that any milky-white substance found in nature was instantly attributed to be spilt faerie blood.

Of the fey that do wear clothes, as in human society this is usually governed by their class in fey society. Faeries in their appearance usually echo the habitat and element that they belong to; there are particular colours that the fey wear predominantly. These colours are known to be 'faerie colours' and in folklore they are considered to be property of the fey. Faeries usually dress in red, green and white. Brown and purple are also popular colours. Green and red are especially thought to be owned by the fey, and green is still thought to be unlucky because of its connection with the faeries. The link with red is thought to arise from the faeries' association with the fly agaric mushroom, which is red with white spots and synonymous with the historical depiction of faeries.

The fabric of which faerie clothes are made is legendary. Many are clothed in the habitat of the place they dwell, for instance leaves, moss, grasses and shells of all descriptions. Faeries also have gossamer, which is peculiar to the faerie race: a fabric so fine that it could not have been made by human hands. Gossamer is supposed to be akin to the fineness of spider's thread and is the softest fabric in existence.

Faeries are also very particular about receiving clothes from humans. If a human gives a faerie new clothes as a gift in return for work that they have done, they are said to be extremely offended and will never return again ... so only pass your faerie helpers gifts of clothes if you want them to leave!

There is much lore attached to faeries and their clothes, and also to human clothes in connection with the faeries. Many fey wear pointy hats or caps and even pointy shoes. A pointy hat in folklore is seen to represent the wearer as being symbolic of intuitive magical ability and of possessing 'the sight' (clairvoyance). A pointy hat directs the wearer's psychic power to the heavens, both fey and human.

The wearing of hoods is also a faerie trait. This is thought to be because they can conceal their identity to appear in our world by wearing a hood, usually of red or green. Hoods are also associated with their rituals and may have a sacred purpose too. Faerie aristocracy are said to wear clothes made from the finest fabrics and there is every attention to beauty and luxury, as the fey are so inclined!

Faerie lore also extends to the clothes that humans wear and in folklore they are said to be useful to repel the attentions of malevolent faeries. We have never tried the following particular faerie lore tips, so we will have to relegate them to quaint historical interest, rather than the useful section! If you try them out and they work – let us know!

- If you are troubled by mischievous faeries at night, it is thought that placing your shoes with the toes pointing outwards and your dirty socks thrown under the bed will fend them off ... if

the dirty socks in our house are anything to go by, I imagine
this would work well!

- If you are pixie-led (also known as Mab-led), meaning to have
  got lost on a journey (generally through woodland), you might
  try turning your clothes inside-out. This is thought to confuse
  the fey so you can make your escape.

- It is thought that a glove thrown into a faerie ring will free any
  mortal who is captured in the faeries' realm.

When in Faerie Land ...

When you are visiting the Land of Faerie no luggage is required,
no passport or travel insurance needed. Check-in time is nil and
arrival time is ... just a wish away. But are the natives friendly?
If folklore is to be believed, then the faeries are to be feared and
you would not venture there unless you were marked by them.
However, many of these old customs associated with the fey we
can now recognize as part of a scarily superstitious age. Here are
some faerie ways, some of which hold a grain of truth, some of
which definitely do not!

All faeries are known to love dancing, and their favourite
haunts are under the full moon, in woodland, fields and meadows.
They are thought to leave behind them as a mark of their dancing
faerie rings of mushrooms or dark green rings of grass. If ever
invited to dance with the faeries it's a real no-go area and one of
the first fundamental rules of faerie lore still to be respected. It is
said that if you dance with the faeries you may die of exhaustion
or you may never be the same again.

This rule also applies to faerie music, which is said to be the
most beautiful music ever heard and, if caught by human ears,
will charm the listener to their realms. There are also a few warnings
concerning faerie music. It is thought extremely dangerous for a
young girl to sing alone by natural water such as lakes. The faeries

could sing along and lure her to their underwater palaces to become one of them and she would never be seen again in the human world. Many Irish folk tunes are also thought to have been given us as a gift by the fey. For this reason people are warned never to sing or play any of these tunes near a faerie mound, as it will offend the faeries to hear one of their melodies being played by a mortal.

WHEN TIME STANDS STILL

A particular facet of faerie lore which holds some truth is the perception of time in their realm. When in the Land of Faerie time is meant to slow down – if you have ever completed a meditation to Faerie Land, you will know what we mean! Actually visiting Faerie Land means that minutes can pass in their realm which are equivalent to whole years in our human world. The popular analogy is that if you're captured in Faerie Land you will return seven years later, but your perception of time spent in their realm will be only a matter of minutes.

The Rev Robert Kirk, who famously spent a lot of time in Faerie Land and also recorded his findings in his book *The Secret Commonwealth*, reported that time felt not to have a hold on Faerie Land, and that when he returned to our world, however long he felt he had spent in their realm, he always came back at the same time that he had gone.

THE BORROWERS

Borrowing and stealing are a huge part of faerie lore. By this they mean borrowing from humans; however, they are always said to return what they have taken with a faerie gift of some kind. Although if we borrow something from the faeries' realm the rules are thought to be slightly different for us, as if we borrow we must only give back what we took with no extras or this will cause grave offence to the fey!

Some faeries are also known to be thieves – and they won't just steal your lipstick from your dressing table: faerie lore is famous for fey who kidnap human adults and children. They are thought to be attracted only to the young and pretty among us, holding the kidnapped for the customary seven years in Faerie Land. This also accounts for the faerie 'changeling' stories. For the faeries in times way back were often believed to steal babies and put in their place a sickly or deformed child of faerie stock, or even a stick of wood left in their place. The changeling did not behave like a human child and would fade away and eventually die. We can see, now, how these stories were obviously a case of the faeries being blamed for the high infant mortality rate and any illnesses that may have been going around.

The faerie 'borrowing' theme still prevails in modern society, as they are still known to move objects around the house and 'accidentally-on-purpose' mislay items for you which invariably turn up days or even weeks later in the strangest of places. However, the modern interpretation of this is that by borrowing and mislaying objects the faeries are trying to catch your attention. They want you to notice them, and usually have some significant role to play in your life. This is often one of the first signs of faerie activity in a person's life. This leads us nicely on to …

MISCHIEF-MAKERS

The faeries have been accused of much mischief-making in the past, and some particular ailments were commonly blamed on them. According to folklore, cramps are thought to be an affliction for avoiding the attentions of the faeries. A stroke is a faerie penalty and even takes its name from the fey: elf stroke. Other illnesses such as tuberculosis, rheumatism, impetigo, lice and infant death are also fey-attributed, as are nightmares. Some faerie types even specialize in all different sorts of nightmares! Bruising was thought to be a penance for troubling the faeries. It is also a chilling thought that mischievous fey are meant to be able to steal a person's shadow.

This belief is still held in some modern societies. If your shadow is stolen you will fade away and die, supposedly because if you don't possess a shadow you cannot exist anyway ... not in a physical body, at any rate.

FAERIE MAGIC

All faeries are meant to be magical beings and possess the ability for magic-making. They hold particular types of magic to be their own, and these encompass their lore. These are most commonly 'glamour', which is the ability to appear as something they are not (mostly in a more beautiful and alluring guise), invisibility, prophecy and shapeshifting ... of course, our more modern 'glamour' is called make-up or cosmetics!

In folklore there is thought to be something called a co-walker, or doppelgänger as it is otherwise known, which is a faerie double of a person (sometimes thought of as an astral version of your physical body). This is a faerie appearing, with the aid of glamour, as a human individual. If a co-walker is seen by yourself or even if someone else sees your co-walker, this is sometimes considered to be an omen of death, and usually an unlucky sign, although there are a few instances where a doppelgänger has been seen next to the living. In these cases they served only to frighten the humans around them at the time!

According to folklore the only way humans may see through the disguise of faerie glamour is to have their eyes touched by faerie water, faerie ointment or a four-leafed clover. Faerie ointment is said to make faeries visible to human eyes and contains secret ingredients. There are speculation and stories that it may contain thyme, mushrooms and four-leafed clover among other plants.

THREE WISHES ...

The magic of the faeries is also in numbers that are said to be sacred to them and considered to be their own. The numbers three, seven and nine are all magical numbers with significance in mystical lore. The number three is seen as the magical number of completion, with many fundamental aspects of our lives having three as an accomplished component. There are three phases of the moon, the Holy Trinity and also trinities of many ancient gods and goddesses. Three is the magical number included often in faerie tales which have their roots in real faerie lore and spells.

The number seven is sacred to the faeries and is the faerie number which grants the faerie-seeker entrance to the Land of Faerie. There is a special symbol, the seven-pointed star, which is known in occult circles as the seven-pointed elven or faerie star and is worn by those of the Faeriecraft tradition. According to folklore, every seven years the faerie race has to pay a tiend (tithe, payment) to hell. However, this myth has only come about since the rise of Christianity when hell was seen as an evil place; before then, hell was merely another underworld realm and did not contain those connotations.

Seven's magical significance for the faeries arises from its associations with the natural cycles of life: for example, the seven colours of the rainbow. Rainbows were considered to be entrances to the Land of Faerie by the bridge of seven colours. There are also 28 days to a moon cycle, which is of course a multiple of seven, and the moon plays a very important part in faerie lore and magic.

Finally, nine is of course the number of months a baby gestates in a mother's womb and is also a multiple of the faerie number three. It has a mystical association with gods and goddesses and, again, faerie tales.

Faerie Lovers

Love in the Land of Faerie has a different concept to that in the human world. Although faeries marry, they are rarely monogamous. Free love is their way of life. The reason for their freer associations with love and sex is that the fey are bound to nature. Nature is continually reproducing itself, and therefore the faeries express this fecund facet. As they have been known to meld with our world and sometimes have relationships with humans, this has the effect of bringing a new dimension to a human relationship. The fey are known for their powers of seduction and their alluring beauty, and to be passionate lovers.

> '… She seemed a fairy or a child, Till deep within her eyes.
> I saw the homeward-leading star of womanhood arise …'
> HENRY VAN DYKE

A FAERIE KISS …

A kiss from a faerie is known to have unique and special powers and it is akin to a magical spell. This kiss, when placed upon human lips, has the power to transport you to their realm or enchant you. Although, sometimes being kissed by a faerie being, especially if the kiss is bestowed by a Faerie King or Queen, can be a faerie initiation upon one of their favourites. A faerie kiss is always significant and will contain hidden meaning to be unravelled. If you have ever experienced a faerie kiss it will dwell in your memory forever and can never be eclipsed by a kiss from a human. To be kissed by a faerie is to be kissed by a celestial being, a fragment of the divine.

> '… Those faery lids how sleek!
> Those lips how moist! – They speak …'
> JOHN KEATS

The fey that are known most for their powers of seduction are any of the water faeries, particularly the females, but not exclusively. The mermaids, selkies, nixies and sirens are all known to lure their chosen human males into the depths of the water, never to be seen again. This echoes the dangers of water; the fey are mimicking this with their actions.

There are numerous tales in folklore of humans being wed to a fey bride. This always involves one of the partnership having to leave their realm and live in either the human world or Faerie Land. This almost always ends in broken hearts, and faerie marriages are without exception bound by strict conditions and restrictions.

Historically, many faerie lovers are known to be dangerous. There is a type of fey, represented in both the male and female form, known as incubus (male) and succubus (female) which exist to prey on human lovers. They are known to visit their victim in their sleep, render them paralysed and have sexual intercourse with them. They can visit night after night and colour their victim's dreams with erotic images. Science suggests that this phenomenon is caused by the body becoming paralysed during dream sleep and the mind wakening accidentally during this cycle. If you've ever woken whilst your body is in this state of paralysis, then you will understand the moment of terror that this induces ... the mind makes up (or dreams) its own explanation.

However, the demonic status of the incubus and succubus was only introduced after the coming of Christianity. Before that, the concept of faerie lovers was not seen to be dangerous, but spiritual, resulting in the birth of offspring who were considered to be demi-gods. In faerie lore, to ward off the attentions of an incubus a peony flower should be kept in the bedroom. Similarly, a succubus can be kept away by a bluebell in the bedroom.

In folklore, human brides are also said to be an attraction to the faeries. In times gone by, brides were fearful of being kidnapped on their wedding day by the fey. The tradition of bridesmaids came about to confuse the fey (or the devil). Originally, the bridesmaids (or flower girls/attendants) would all be wearing the same or similar outfits to the bride herself. It is also said that if a human bride should die on her wedding night, she will pass on to become a faerie.

The Faerie Orb
The moon holds a special and significant place in faerie lore.

Throughout history the faeries have been associated with the moon, and especially the full moon, the time when lunar power is at its most potent. Lunar power affects the tides of the sea, women's menstrual cycles and the growth of nature. The phases of the moon are also meant to affect the faeries' magical powers. All these aspects reinforce the faeries' connection with the moon; as beings of nature it is logical that the moon should feature strongly in their lore. They are supposed to celebrate the full moon by dancing, revelling and feasting in woodland glades. In ancient faerie lore the moon itself is often regarded as such a mystical place that it is referred to as Faerie Land. The crystal 'moonstone', a milky stone with luminance, makes a wonderful talisman or protective piece of jewellery for women, and is said to be particularly powerful at the full moon.

Protection Against Faeries

This is a huge area of faerie lore which holds little significance today, but was almost a part of everyday life in more superstitious times. The faeries of course were blamed for more than their fair share of mischief, and much lore was created to cope with their supposed foul play. We have put together a selection of medieval tips which kept the populace safe from the meddling attentions of the fey.

Home

- It was thought that evil faeries could be scared away by the sound of ringing bells, particularly church bells. Therefore folk would hang bells outside their front door to this effect.

- The hearth is a powerful faerie portal to enter the home. This belief still exists today. It was thought that mischievous fey would fly down the chimney and steal whatever was baking, especially cakes and bread, to which they are partial. To ward against this, housewives would leave small offerings at the base of the hearth to appease them and discourage their stealing of the family baking.

- The lore of the home hearth was a powerful one and faeries are thought to be repelled by fire. For this reason fires were always kept raked and banked to keep them alight throughout the night, to prevent the entrance of evil faeries. To the same effect a broom could also be placed next to the fireplace to stop bad fey coming down the chimney after dark.

- Salt has always been a powerful repellent against the bad faerie and it was used in many ways to protect the home and those within it. If a parent was fearful that the fey would steal their small child, they would sew a tiny packet of salt into the hem of the child's dress.

- 'Witch bottles' were made up by ordinary householders to protect the family against evil faeries. These were glass bottles containing as many unpleasant ingredients as the maker could find, and generally included any combination or all of iron nails, broken glass, stale urine, blood, pins, needles, ashes, salt, rowan, oak and ash wood, and poisonous herbs and flowers. These were traditionally empowered and then buried at midnight on the night of a waning (decreasing) moon. They were commonly buried by the main entrance to a property, or in a pot of soil by the door.

- Faeries (except mermaids) are said to despise mirrors, although they adore looking at their reflections in natural pools of water. Householders would place mirrors at the entrances to their homes to ward off evil faeries.

- A protective bundle of herbs tied with red thread and hung above a doorway is said to prevent evil faeries entering.

These were usually rowan, fashioned in a cross and tied with the red thread. However, it could also be a combination of twigs and herbs tied together, such as mistletoe, clove, bay leaves, blackberry stalks, garlic, rosemary, sandalwood, witch hazel, white hawthorn and mint. Herbs were also put into home-made pouches and carried to give faerie protection. A legendary protection is to tie a trinity of oak, ash and thorn twigs together, traditionally bound with threads of red, white and black.

- Placing a sprig of pearlwort above the front door is said to prevent faeries from stealing any member of the household away.

- Incidentally, if your biggest problem is not being able to see the faeries in the first place, try drinking some elderberry wine, which is called 'faerie wine'. Drinking it is said to enable you to see the faeries.

Horses

- Horses are said to be, without exception, the faeries' most favoured animal. It is for this reason that many people were afraid that they might be stolen. If you happened to find your horse sweaty and muddy in his stable in the morning, this was an indicator that the faeries had stolen him during the night. Also, if horses' manes were tangled, this was again blamed on the faeries, and these knotty manes were called elf locks. The term 'faerie-ridden' was used when this occurred. To prevent this happening, a number of protective measures were taken, and much lore surrounds horsemanship.

- Placing an upright horseshoe over a stable door would prevent your steed being elf-ridden in the night.

- Because of their association with horses and also their work with fire and iron, blacksmiths were considered allies with the faeries. They were seen to be possessed of the faeries' secrets of magic and horsemanship. They were so faerie-favoured that it is not considered bad luck for them to hang a horseshoe upside down. Instead they are the only mortals who can get away with doing this, as the good luck of the horseshoes is meant to pour down on the forge.

- The faeries are thought to have their own race of faerie horses which are never shod in iron, but with gold and silver horseshoes instead.

Jacky: I always suspected the faeries stole away a gold ring from my bedroom!

Faeries are known to adorn their horses' manes with small jingling bells. It is only evil fey who are afraid of bells; the good faeries are attracted by the sound.

After Dark …

- Most fear about evil faeries was at night-time when we are most vulnerable and the uncertainty and mystery of darkness sometimes remove rational thought. Faeries were often blamed for nightmares and people being stolen in the night.

- Any stone with a hole in it was thought to contain magical and protective powers. One theory is that these stones were said to belong to the goddess. For this reason, if a holed stone was placed under the sleeper's pillow at night, it was said to prevent nightmares. You can also thread your holed stone on a leather thong and hang it around your neck during the daytime.

- To prevent faeries entering the bedroom at all, scattering flax on the floor would be a preventative measure, or a trail of salt across your doorstep.

- Keeping a piece of iron under the pillow or under your bed would stop a sleeper from being troubled by the faeries. Faeries hate iron.

- The herb St John's wort is said to prevent a person being stolen by the faeries in their sleep.

- Placing the herb purslane under the pillow will prevent the faeries from entering the sleeper's dreams uninvited.

Faerie Favourites

Some humans are traditionally marked out as being favourites of the faerie race. These people are generally described as being 'faerie-blessed'. They will all have certain qualities favoured by the fey. It is said that the faeries favour those born on a full moon. They especially favour those who are beautiful, graceful, simple in lifestyle, unpretentious and sincere, and who love animals. Those whom they favour may be exempt from their lores and are often treated as honorary faeries. In return the fey may bestow on them magical powers including the sight (clairvoyance), youth, luck and a comfortable life. Other traits might include a faerie-like appearance, complete with their luxuriant hair. Healing is a particular gift they like to bestow on their favourites. It is most likely to be the water fey who grant this faerie offering, and they are known to favour witches.

The fey are ill-favoured towards those who are greedy and boastful, nosy and mean-hearted. They are also thought to steal from those they are not inclined towards, but will only take what they believe the humans do not deserve.

A Modern Guide to Faerie Lore

From reading this chapter we can gain a sense that our ancestors were very afraid of the faeries and they were only respected because people feared them. We now live in a more educated and informed world, where superstition, although it still exists, does not rule our lives. We can look upon our history with a sense of perspective and realize that these lores stem from what was an oppressive society, living under the fear of God and all the pagan and heathen traditions turned evil by the Church.

It is living proof that the book you are holding now means that we still have a belief in our modern societies of magical beings such as the faeries. The fey as a race were once revered and given god-like status as our connection to the spiritual aspect of our living world. It is for this reason that the faeries are still with us today and because of a heightened sense of growing spirituality in our world, the faeries wish us to reclaim their relationship with humans. We can now take a fresh look at faerie lore and take the elements which help us to connect with the fey and form a positive and safe relationship with them. We have compiled the following guide to help you connect with the faeries, using ancient faerie lore as our inspiration.

USING THE FAERIES' LORE

We now leave the faeries gifts, not to appease them for fear of them harming our loved ones or entering our homes, but to thank them for their presence in our lives and to befriend them. As part of their lore, faeries do not like to be thanked, but prefer an exchange of energy by giving gifts. Their favourites are small amounts of honey, bread, cream, milk and cake left in biodegradable or natural containers in a special place in the home such as by a vase of flowers or a quiet place in the garden.

If you would like to attract the faeries into your home, do not have large amounts of iron present, as this repels and offends them. By the same token, if you wish to ward troubling faeries off, use iron for protection. Metals which the fey can tolerate are gold, silver and copper.

The old faerie lore guidelines of never dancing, eating or drinking in Faerie Land still hold true, unless of course you are a faerie favourite. However, I would not advise putting this to the test. If you visit the Land of Faerie while in a meditation, ceremony or dream, it is wise to remember these guidelines.

Always be respectful to all living creatures and to nature, and the faeries will look upon you kindly. Try to be aware of your impact upon the environment and live as green a lifestyle as possible. Look after the environment in your community and if you see litter near your home, pick it up and bin it properly. If there are any community schemes to clean up your home town, such as a pond-clearing day, beach clear-up or tree-planting programme, then get involved. These practical steps, as well as spiritual ones, will strengthen your relationship with the faeries. These things are often fun, too!

Always work with the intention of attracting loving and benevolent faerie beings. If you do this they will enrich your life and help you in your spiritual development. As with all things, there are light and dark, so when working with the faeries always ask for protection from the Faerie King or Queen, your Faerie Godmother or guardian angel or any other benevolent being you usually work with. The faeries are non-dogmatic, so they can cross over to any belief system you may already be comfortable with.

The faeries today are reaching out to empower us and enhance our lives, not to disempower us as was the case in times gone by. Working with them should be as easy as taking a lovely relaxing walk in the woods and noticing all the beautiful aspects of nature around you. If you respect nature, then working with the faeries will come naturally ...

Please note: The subject of faerie lore is almost inexhaustible and far too extensive to be put into one single chapter. To prevent repeating material too much, we have placed other aspects of faerie lore such as the lore of trees, animals and flowers in other sections of the book. To simplify, we have only included the main aspects of the way of faeries in this chapter.

CHAPTER 9

Faeries in Culture

Of course you do not hear it, child. It takes a fairy ear ... '
VACHEL LINDSAY (1879–1931)

Famous Faeries

Throughout time, faeries have been written about in poems, plays and stories and made guest appearances in films and television programmes. Who are these famous faeries? Some of course are 'fictional' faeries who in time almost take on a life of their own ... in the other realms, at least. Others are 'real' – at least as real as we can tell by tracing back through traditional tales, and legions from countries around the world ... sometimes, I'll admit, it gets difficult to tell where fiction ends and begins! Here's a quick look.

Faerie Who's Who

Famous faerie	Background information
Ariel	Ariel is a sprite from Shakespeare's *The Tempest*. In the play Ariel has the ability to create illusions. It is not known if Ariel was a male or female character. 'Coincidentally', Ariel is also the name of an Archangel and the name of the principal character in Disney's *The Little Mermaid*.
Blue Faerie, The	The Blue Faerie appears in *Pinocchio* by Carlo Collodi. The Blue Faerie gives Pinocchio (the wooden boy) a gift.

Famous faerie	Background information
Cottingley faeries	The famous 'Cottingley fairies' were photographed in 1917 by Elsie Wright and Frances Griffiths, two young cousins aged 16 and 10 who lived near Bradford in England. The faeries and even a gnome were photographed by the girls after they had reported seeing them on several occasions. Several well-respected people, including Sir Arthur Conan Doyle (author of the Sherlock Holmes books), supported the girls' stories, believing the photographs to be genuine. Doyle even went so far as to write a book about the faeries and the girls' experiences. It was not until the end of their lives that they admitted the photographs were fakes. Whether the photographs were real or not might not be relevant. Elsie says that the two cousins did really see the faeries and only faked the photographs under pressure. The fifth photograph was real, and she maintained this right up until her death.
Faerie Godmother	One of our most well-known faeries and always seen with a magical wand, the source of her power. She is found in both Roman and Greek mythology and is known as 'the Fates'. Some references suggest there are three Faerie Godmothers altogether, and many more appear in our common faerie tales. The Faerie Godmother is often shown as a kindly creature with guardianship over children. Beware, though: not all Faerie Godmothers are good-natured.
Green Faerie, The	The Green Faerie (La Fée Verte) is another name for absinthe, the green-coloured alcoholic drink. In the film *Moulin Rouge!* (2001), the Green Faerie is played by singer Kylie Minogue.
Oberon	King of the faeries in folklore and married to Titania; featured in the Shakespeare play *A Midsummer Night's Dream*.

Famous faerie	Background information
Peter Pan	The character Peter Pan is from the story of the same name written by J M Barrie. Peter Pan has been made into animations and films including one by Disney. Peter works closely with his friend Tinkerbell, the faerie.
Puck	The imp of English folklore made famous by Shakespeare's *A Midsummer Night's Dream*.
Sugar Plum Fairy	The Sugar Plum Fairy became famous when composer Tchaikovsky included her in his *Nutcracker Suite*. In the ballet, the Sugar Plum Fairy and her attendants welcome Clara at her court in the Kingdom of Sweets.
Tinkerbell	Tinkerbell is a character from the book *Peter Pan and Wendy* by J M Barrie. Tinkerbell gained greater fame from the Disney film version of the same name. Tinkerbell is sometimes called 'a pixie' and she leaves a trail of 'faerie dust' wherever she goes.
Titania	Another character from Shakespeare, this time from *A Midsummer Night's Dream*. Titania is the Queen of the Faeries and married to Oberon. Shakespeare borrowed the name Titania from Ovid's *Metamorphoses*, where Titania is a name given to the daughters of the Titans.
Tooth Fairy	The Tooth Fairy is popular in Western culture, although didn't make her or his appearance until the early 1900s. Young children leave their milk teeth or 'baby teeth' under their pillow (after they fall out naturally, of course) and in the morning the 'Tooth Fairy' (usually Mum or Dad) leaves some small change – or occasionally a gift – in exchange for the tooth. In Italy, the Tooth Fairy (*fatina*) is thought to be a mouse!
Willo the wisp	'Willo the wisp' was the name of a British cartoon series in the 1980s. Willo the wisp was narrated by the actor Kenneth Williams. The character of Willo was a blue 'ghost-like' faerie with a long pointed nose!

Fairy Tales

Ancient fairy tales didn't necessarily contain tales of the same faeries we know from stories … not obviously at least. Often these stories of 'myth and magic' contained creatures of other descriptions – and faeries, but often in disguise. As mentioned, many faeries have the ability to 'shapeshift' and take on other forms (discussed in more detail in other chapters), at least temporarily, and these were the ones more likely to appear as butterflies, birds, mice and even rats, as in the fairy tale *Cinderella*.

Traditional fairy tales have lived on for generations and have been passed on by word of mouth to adults and children of all ages. Strictly speaking, many of these stories – which contained such delights as poisonings, killings and even characters wanting to eat each other – are hardly appropriate for children (using today's standards anyway). No one could say that these tales were not exciting! Most stories were written for adults.

Many of the more well-known stories have several variations (appearing in different countries as folktales) and are passed through different families, often with men's versions being more humorous and women's versions, by and large, more mystical!

FAMOUS FAIRYTALE WRITERS

Here are a few of the more famous fairy tale authors.

Hans Christian Andersen

Hans Christian Andersen was born in Denmark, in a place called Odense (named after the pagan god Odin). He was born in 1805, the son of a shoemaker. He was an only child and by his own admission he was spoiled, even though his family were poor. His father read to him often and took him for walks daily in the local woods. His life was one of magic and even though he didn't have professional schooling as his father wished, Hans learned a lot at his father's knee.

Hans actually wrote his own life story in the work *The True Story of My Life: A Sketch by Hans Christian Andersen* (1847). Famous stories include his books *The Snow Queen* and *Thumbelina*.

'Every man's life is a fairy-tale written by God's fingers.'
Hans Christian Andersen (1805–1875)

Brothers Grimm

The German Grimm brothers collected old folktales the way that other people might collect stamps or coins. Jacob Ludwig Carl Grimm (1785–1863) and Wilhelm Carl Grimm (1786–1859) were born in Hanau, Germany. They had nine other siblings. They both studied law and began collecting traditional folktales in 1806. Their first book *Kinder- und Hausmärchen* (Children's and Household Tales) was published in 1812 (see Faerie Films, page 147).

Asbjornsen and Moe

Peter Christen Asbjornsen (1812–1885) and Jorgen Moe (1813–1882) wrote many tales together … classic Norwegian 'Folktales'. Stories include the scary *The Three Billy Goats Gruff.*

Peter was born in Oslo (or Christiania as it was known then). He heard many *eventyr* (or tales) in his father's glazier workshop. Peter met Jorgen in 1826 at the Norderhov School they both attended. Jorgen was born on a farm in Hole, Ringerike.

Both were interested in writing from an early age and longed to be poets! They wrote up their first collection of Norwegian folktales in 1845, which was much influenced by the Grimms' *Kinder- und Hausmärchen*.

Marie-Catherine d'Aulnoy

Marie-Catherine Baronne d'Aulnoy (1650–1705) was one of the earlier fairytale writers whose works included *The Yellow Dwarf* and *The Blue Bird*.

She was born into a noble family and later married Baron d'Aulnoy, who was 30 years her senior. The two, along with their children, travelled widely around Europe and this created much of the inspiration for Marie-Catherine's stories. She published many books including two fairytale collections which were very popular (although not aimed at children).

Giambattista Basile

The Italian Giambattista Basile wrote his book of European fairytales almost 200 years before the Brothers Grimm put pen to paper. *Il Pentamerone* was published in 1634 (translated into English in 1847). This work contains stories which are very similar to those which are now well-known to us, including *Cinderella*, *Sleeping Beauty*, *Rapunzel* and *Snow White*.

Thomas Crane

Born Thomas Frederick Crane (1844–1927), he wrote *Italian Popular Tales* in 1885, which included the magical stories, *The Fairy Orlanda* and *Puss in Boots*.

Joseph Jacobs

Joseph Jacobs (1854–1916) wrote several fairytale collections including *English Fairy Tales* (1890; includes the stories *Fairy Ointment* and *Jack and the Beanstalk*), *Celtic Fairy Tales* (1892) and *European Folk and Fairy Tales* (1916; includes *Beauty and the Beast* and *Snow White*).

Charles Perrault

Charles Perrault was born in Paris in 1628; he died in 1703. The author was well-schooled and went on to become a lawyer in 1651. His fairytales were very popular and he wrote up famous versions of stories such as *Puss in Boots*, *Cinderella* and *Little Thumb*.

FAERIE POETRY

So many poets have included faeries in their work that it is hard to go any way towards doing it justice here. Faeries have been the inspiration behind many great works, particularly during the Victorian era.

> *'... There sleeps Titania sometime of the night,*
> *Lull'd in these flowers with dances and delight ...'*
> A MIDSUMMER NIGHT'S DREAM

The great playwright William Shakespeare (1564–1616) included faeries in several of his plays, including Oberon and Titania in *A Midsummer Night's Dream*. The mischievous Puck is one of the literary world's most famous characters. Shakespeare makes full use of magic and humour in his writing.

There is no doubt that Shakespeare influenced many later poets, especially William Browne (1591–1674) and Harritt Prescott Spofford (1835–1921).

> *'...Merchantmen poise upon Horizons, dip and vanish with fairy sails.'*
> EMILY DICKINSON (1830–1886)

Faerie Films

Faeries make great film subjects. Here are a few of them.

- *Fairy Tale; A True Story* (1997) – starring Harvey Keitel, Jason Salkey and Peter O'Toole. This film is based on the story of the Cottingley faeries, the faerie photographs taken by two children in 1917.

- *Photographing Fairies* (1997) – starring Toby Stephens, Emily Woolf and Ben Kingsley. Photographer Charles Castle (played by Toby Stephens) is a photographer who goes to war following the tragic death of his wife. The story follows

Charles's search for the existence of faeries after he is given some photographs which are said to be of the little folk.

- *Snow Queen* (2002) – starring Bridget Fonda. The innkeeper's daughter travels across the winter lands to save her beloved from the clutches of the Snow Queen.

- *Peter Pan* (2003) – This version of J M Barrie's tale of the boy who never grew up stars Jeremy Sumpter as Peter, Richard Briers as Smee and Lynn Redgrave as Aunt Millicent. Peter Pan himself was a faerie and Tinkerbell, the 'pixie', also plays a prominent part. The teeny Tinkerbell sprinkles faerie dust wherever she goes.

- *Peter Pan* (1953) – The original Disney version is an animation and still considered one of the best Disney films ever.

- *The Brothers Grimm* (2005) – A fantasy version of the life of the famous faerie-tale authors. In the film, Will and Jake Grimm are travelling con-artists who have to face a real fairy-tale curse. Stars Matt Damon and Heath Ledger.

Disney Fairy Names

Disney included a fair few fairies in his films. Here is a quick list.
- Beck
- Bess
- Fawn
- Fira
- Iris
- Iridessa
- Lily
- Luna
- Mother Dove

- Peter Pan
- Prilla
- Rani
- Rosetta
- Silvermist
- Terence
- Tinkerbell
- Vidia
- Violet.

Faeries in Songs and Music

William Shakespeare actually wrote a poem called *The Fairy Song* and Louisa May Alcott wrote a poem entitled *Fairy Song*. Both were based on the idea that the faeries themselves sing … usually when they think that humans aren't listening, of course.

> '… *And though unseen on earth we dwell, Sweet voices whisper low* …'
> LOUISA MAY ALCOTT

Modern-day musicians have been inspired by the sound of the faeries. *Journey to the Faeries* and *FaerieLore – Journey to the Faerie Ring*, both by bestselling composer and musician Llewellyn, and *The Fairy Ring* by Mike Rowland are beautiful examples. Using natural sounds to take you on a magical journey, the atmosphere created on these recordings makes them the perfect backdrop for your faerie meditations. Check out your local New Age store or search the Internet for more examples to help you on your own faerie journeys.

Don't forget *The Sugar Plum Fairy*, composed by Tchaikovsky for the ballet, *The Nutcracker*. My children used to love dancing to this when they were younger and I remember the English comedy duo Morecambe and Wise once did a famous sketch to the tune.

I'm sure you will think of many more examples of your own.

CHAPTER 10

Faeries in Religion

'In the past when Christianity was at its most fanatical,
faeries were said to be fallen angels or demons sent by the devil.'
FAERIE MAGICK, MARIE BRUCE

Faeries, Faeries Everywhere …

Faeries, in some form or another, have a presence in every culture
in the world. It is no surprise that they have also filtered into
many of the world's religions and become an intrinsic part of
those belief systems.

The popular belief is that faeries existed before any religion
was established in the human race, as they are part of our 'pagan'
past. This seems to be an aspect that we have been reluctant to
lose. Whether this is sentimentality, superstition or still an
overwhelming belief, the faeries have indeed stood the test of
time, millennium after millennium finding a presence in every
culture and most world religions. They may only be represented
by fairy stories, a watered-down echo of the faeries' true power,
but this is still a reminder that there are truly faeries everywhere.
Even the most evangelical and purist religions include fairy
stories in their teachings. In this chapter we explore the presence
of the fey and their fundamental influence on human belief.

Christianity

On the surface of it this may seem a very odd section to have in the book, as we are sure that many of you are thinking, 'Have they gone mad? What on earth has Christianity got to do with faeries?' Well, 'Ah ha', we say! Much more than you may ever have imagined. Indeed, the way faeries are beginning to be perceived in our modern world may even be a significant link to the general spiritual resurgence. Surely the belief that the faeries are actually spiritual beings, God's earthly messengers and workers, must come from somewhere? History is a wheel, ever repeating itself, and if we look deeper, we will find out ...

SEEK AND YOU SHALL FIND ...

There are three main ways in which faeries and Christianity have intertwined. Probably the best place to start is with the man himself ... Jesus? We pose this with a question mark because the information we have researched is largely down to interpretation and may actually introduce more questions than it answers. However, there is certainly a debate here, and this is what we wish to highlight and propose.

> ***Alicen:*** About 18 years ago when I was just beginning my spiritual pathway and still a teenager, I belonged to a Psychic Developing Circle. During a session with the Circle, while in a very deep meditation I unexpectedly received a vision of a figure whom I knew to be Jesus. This experience I have shared with very few people, for fear of being ridiculed, but now is the time. He was standing with a Bible in his hands and then he very deliberately threw the Bible over his shoulder. He looked at me and said, 'Follow me, not my book.' Those were his exact words and he said nothing else, then he was gone. I was stunned by his appearance and also his action, as it seemed a shocking and contradictory gesture for him to be discarding the Bible. I had never seen him before and I have

never seen him since. However, his message rang clear and often played on my mind over the years that followed.

For a long time I have had a gut feeling that Jesus is connected with the faeries in some way. Of course, it is not enough to just have a feeling about these things, so I set about trying to find some evidence. Since the meditation experience with Jesus, my personal belief has been that what was left *out* of the Bible has as much to teach us as what was left in.

Our first exploration into such information was with the Dead Sea Scrolls and the Nag Hammadi Library. The Dead Sea Scrolls were discovered between 1947 and 1956. They were largely found to be written in one of the two dialects of Hebrew, Aramaic and some in Koine Greek. Our research focuses specifically on those documents thought to have been written and secreted away by a spiritual community of people called the Essenes. The main body of our research in this chapter has been taken from *The Essene Gospel of Peace Book Two* which was, in this version, translated by Edmond Bordeaux Szekely. By the author's own admission his translation was a creative interpretation of the text and not a literal one, so as to make the text more digestible to a modern readership. The relevance of this will become clear as this chapter unfolds.

THE ESSENES

Some theorize that the Essenes wrote much of the material found in the Dead Sea Scrolls, among others. They were thought to have lived in the vicinity of the Qumran area, where the Dead Sea Scrolls were eventually discovered. They were a community who felt that they were part of a divine spiritual mission. According to the Essenes, Jesus belonged to their community and at some time lived among them. Many other notable figures in the Bible belonged to the Essene community and shared their mission. The most striking and controversial aspect of the Essenes was that they communicated directly with angelic beings and practised spiritual healing.

The Spiritual Dimension of Nature

In the texts written by the Essenes, the faerie connection to Jesus and the traditional view of God is not only hinted at specifically, but also alluded to through an emphasis on the significance of nature. In *The Vision of Enoch, The Most Ancient Revelation, God Speaks to Man*, there is an unmistakable framework of natural references implying that God communicates to us through nature and that this is where God exists to be sought.

'I speak to you
Through the grass of the meadows
Be still
Know
I am
God.
I speak to you
Through the trees of the forests …'

One of the very first things we learn when working with the faeries is that their realm is that of nature. By becoming close to nature we may commune with the nature spirits and, by doing that, become more connected with the divine, with God. This is our first correlation.

Mother Nature

In the Essene book of *Moses, The Ten Commandments*, we are told that communion with the four elements (earth, air, fire and water) is prescribed as a holy way of living. 'The Earthly Mother' is also to be honoured equally with 'the Heavenly Father'. Some sources interpret 'the Earthly Mother' to mean Mother Nature and/or the goddess. In ancient times the faerie kings and queens were once considered to be of this pantheon. You can see where we are going with this, can't you?!

'Angel of Sun,
Holy messenger of the Earthly Mother,
Enter the holy temple within me
And give me the fire of Life!'

In these communions we are told of the high significance of the angels of the four elements, among others. Some sources interpret these 'elemental angels' to mean our modern understanding of the elemental spirits or faeries. And faeries are commonly referred to as 'angels of the Earth', being God's spiritual messengers and workers of the earthly spheres. When looking into Angel Lore, these elemental angels are not mentioned by name in any of the traditional spheres of angels. We wonder why the translators of the Essene Bible chose the word 'angel'? Was this a literal translation or a creative one?

To try and make sense of the interpretation of the use of the word 'angel' in this context we have looked in the Nag Hammadi (13 papyrus documents of Gnostic writings discovered in 1945, considered to be heretical), where we are told that '... the angels, are in the form of beasts and the gods ...'. Maybe this is saying that angels are not always as they traditionally seem?

Also significant is the number seven, which is considered to be the sacred number of faerie and the mystical number of spiritual completeness. The most critical link between Jesus and the faeries may perhaps be found in *The Communions* when Jesus says, 'And the Angels of the Earthly Mother Number Seven ...'. Without much effort we could easily interpret this to mean that the goddess has seven prominent angelic/fey beings.

'Angel of Water,
Holy messenger of the Earthly Mother ...
Angel of Air,
Holy messenger of the Earthly Mother,
Enter deep within me,

… That I may know the secrets of the wind
And the music of the stars.
The Lord sent the Angel of the Earth,
Holy messenger of the Earthly Mother …'

These words of Jesus in *The Communions* read more like the invocations of a pagan ritual than passages from a religious text like the Bible. This may give us a clue as to why these references were never included in the definitive text: they may have been considered too dangerous or heretical. In particular, the references to 'the Earthly Mother' would have given power to the feminine aspect in society. This could have been another political reason why these 'Communions', which have dominant female, lunar and nature references, have been omitted from the Bible we are all more familiar with.

Again within the words of *The Communions,* Jesus gives great relevance to nature:

'And hear, O earth,
The words of my mouth.
My doctrine shall drop as the rain,
My speech shall distil as the dew …'

By deciphering Jesus's words from millennia ago we can tie them in with current spiritual thinking about what faeries are and how they connect with the divine aspect of ourselves and the Earth.

The above is, of course, theory and, who knows, maybe the beginnings of a debate … we hope so! The validity of the Dead Sea Scrolls as an actual record of the words of Jesus, and maybe some of the lost books of the Bible, has inevitably surrounded them in doubt and conspiracy theories. We say to you, take this information where your heart leads you and make of it what you will.

CELTIC CHRISTIANITY

References to 'the Earthly Mother' and 'the Heavenly Father' lead us nicely to the second thread the faeries have woven for us with Christianity.

Celtic Christianity was a form of worship practised by much of what we now call the British Isles from approximately the 4th to the 9th centuries. Characteristically, Celtic Christianity recognized a 'Mother Goddess' as well as 'God the Father'. At a time when the Christian Church was melding with people who had always practised pagan beliefs, the Celtic Church became dualistic in nature. Celtic Christianity, at the time when it was widespread, and even now, embraces the divinity of nature and the female aspect in God. This often includes teachings on the faerie realms. Maureen Duffy in her *The Erotic World of Faery* comments that '… the Celtic Church … was extremely important for the preservation and development of the faeries'.

Many people practising Faeriecraft (the melding of the faerie faith and witchcraft) today also link this with the practices of Celtic Christianity. Often those who are interested in faeries admit to 'having a Jesus thing going on'. However, this is always said in whispers, as it is not seen as 'cool', in pagan company, to be talking of Jesus!

THE DEMONIZING AND DEMOTING OF THE FAERIES

Once the Church had become more established in the British Isles, faeries – and indeed anything else linked to magic and nature – became demonized and demoted. Faeries were blamed for stealing your milk or your wife, or seducing your daughters, and they were thought to be on a par with demons. Simple folk looked for a source of blame for anything they couldn't understand.

Christianity spread the belief that the faeries were unholy and actually fallen angels. They were depicted as being connected to the devil and, according to Celtic folklore belief, they were cast out of heaven for their pride and vanity. When they fell to the Earth, the devil took command of them.

Also, anything that the faeries enjoyed, such as dancing, for instance, was seen as unholy. The Reverend John Brand, a minister in Orkney, wrote in 1701 that the faeries were evil spirits, no less, who could be seen feasting and dancing in wild places.

Many Christian symbols were said to be protection or means of banishing the faeries. A Bible is said to break the magic of a faerie spell. Men of the Church also did very odd things with Bibles to rid people or beasts of faerie enchantment. One method was to tear pages out of the Bible, roll them up into pellets and feed them to anyone or any animal who had been struck by 'Elf Bolts' (faerie arrows believed to be shot at livestock or people to cause harm). A cross or crucifix was also a deterrent against the magic of faeries (not just to frighten off vampires, then).

All faeries were deemed to be 'mischievous spirits' who were not to be consorted with. Not only were they considered to be fallen angels, but some believed that they were the damned souls of dead humans. Other folklore, however, held that faeries did not have souls at all, damned or otherwise.

In medieval times, faeries were just not popular and even seen as dangerous to the point of being life-threatening. All sorts of strange superstitions surrounded them. At the end of the day, however, this is just what they were: superstitions.

Many of the great faerie kings and queens, once considered to be gods and goddesses, were demoted in significance. This is thought to be one reason why faeries are now considered to be small in stature, as Christianity has diminished them in importance and size.

In the Victorian era the faeries lost their demonic guise as they began to be depicted by artists such as Cicely Mary Barker as cute and whimsical creatures. This image prevails today and most people still perceive faeries in this manner, as innocent, childlike and fictional beings.

Now in the so-called New Age this may be changing and coming full circle. The faeries are beginning to enjoy a renaissance where once again they are being considered to be spiritual beings who are part of the divine.

Paganism

The link between faeries and paganism is an unquestionable reality. As W Y Evans-Wentz comments in his book, *The Fairy-Faith in Celtic Countries*, '… the evidence of paganism … concerning the Fairy-Faith is so vast that we cannot do more than point to portions of it …'. This is because faeries belong to the fabric of the pagan world; they are part of the pagan religion.

The pagan faith has eight major festivals known as sabbats (Sabbaths). These are also celebrated by the faeries, when they are known to feast, dance and cross the veil into our world with ease.

Faerie sightings and communication are also most favourable at these festival times.

Faerie Festivals

Samhain	31st October and the Celtic New Year (Halloween)
Midwinter solstice/Yule	21st December
Imbolc	2nd February
Spring equinox	21st March
Beltaine/May Eve	30th April
Midsummer solstice	21st June
Lughnasadh	31st July
Autumn equinox	21st September

Other significant times for pagans and also for faeries are the phases of the moon – most notably the full moon, when lunar energy is at its most powerful. Pagans also honour the gods and goddesses, worship through ritual, and respect the spiritual dimension in nature. Recognizing the four elements is also an intrinsic aspect of the pagan path. As faeries belong to these four elements, they naturally fall into a pagan belief system. Making a differentiation between faeries and paganism is just not possible; they are one and the same!

Shinto

This is the native Japanese religion and, indeed, was considered to be the state religion before the Second World War. However, this is an important religion to highlight because it still forms the basis of religious behaviour in Japanese culture today. Shinto is also widely thought to have had Buddhist influences from very early on; and Buddhism has a definite nature theme which we will explore shortly. Shinto also has, to some extent, a complicated and political past which it is not so significant to discuss here; rather, we will focus on its spiritual practices and core beliefs.

Although Shinto is no longer considered to be the state religion in Japan, it has definite influences on the country's culture and has endured as more of a folk religion. This means that although many people in Japan today don't consider themselves religious, they still practise many aspects of the Shinto ways, such as having a shrine in their home and wearing an amulet (*o-mamori*).

THE ESSENCE OF FAERIE

The most dominant feature of the Shinto faith is a belief that nature and all of life are sacred. This leads on to the belief in *kami*, which means 'spiritual essence'. The Japanese largely believe, as a result of Shinto influences, that everything upon this Earth contains a *kami* and, because of this, must be respected. This is where the faeries come in: although not actually called 'faeries' in Japanese culture, this is what the *kami* are. Western pagan and faerie tradition believe that all life is sacred also and that everything in the natural world has within it a god consciousness. The nature spirit is alive and well in Japanese Shinto and still prevails in the culture of Japan today, expressed in their customs of general respect. Shinto's main doctrine is to live 'a simple and harmonious life with nature and people'.

Shinto has a close harmony with all the natural elements and places much importance upon revering them. The faith, similar to Western pagan beliefs, includes venerating the gods, and Shinto in particular reveres its sun goddess Amaterasu. Many shrines are dedicated to her. Thus, Japan has its faerie equivalents in the *kami* and in the universal perception that these spirits should be respected and honoured among men.

The *kami* have a similar domain to Faerie Land and are acknowledged to dwell in another world, parallel to our own. This distinction is made in Japanese shrines by the *torii*, which is a gate which separates the world in which we live from the shrine of the *kami*, where they dwell in their other world. These shrines are similar to the faerie altar in faerie traditions.

Natural magic is also a Shinto belief that cannot be disunited from faerie presence, for faeries (or *kami* in this case) are the magic within nature.

Japanese culture also has its own fairy stories, passed down over centuries, demonstrating that the spirit of faerie exists in their society and integral beliefs. Fairy stories are in any culture a throwback of belief in magic and how humans have used these natural forces to learn lessons and find transformation.

MAKE A SHINTO SHRINE

Bring the simplicity of the Japanese fey to your home by creating a Shinto shrine of your own. Many Japanese have a small corner or even just a shelf in their home devoted to the *kami*. The *kami* are believed to inhabit all living and non-living things such as stones and shells. The Japanese also write names and messages to the *kami* on pieces of paper and attach them to their shrines.

If the serene Japanese *kami* appeal to you, then bring them into your life by creating a special place for them. This can be decorated with finds from nature and may help in a special connection with the fey. The *kami* are petitioned by the Japanese to help them in everyday life as well as special times; they can help with something as simple as leading a happier life to a significant event and time such as the birth of a baby.

You do not have to be of the Shinto faith to create a shrine for the *kami*, as everyone is considered in Japanese culture to be divine regardless of their belief.

Buddhism

Many of us may already be familiar with the Buddhist version of faeries, who are known simply as the *devas*. This is because the *devas* have seeped into our own spirituality, made famous by such spiritual movements as the Findhorn Foundation in northern Scotland, which became known for its phenomena with *devas* or 'nature spirits' as they are sometimes known. (The people at the Findhorn Foundation worked closely with the plant *devas* to grow extraordinarily large and healthy plant and vegetable specimens on poor soil.)

This is where the Japanese Shinto is very similar to Buddhism and, for this reason: Shinto and Buddhism are practised together by the Japanese, with no distinctions between them. The *devas* also resemble the Western Elemental Faeries, with their Elemental Kings and Queens. However, the Buddhist *devas* seem to have a far more complex and sophisticated hierarchy than their Western counterparts.

The *devas* share many traits with the Western Elementals: they are mostly invisible, have no need to drink or eat, have the power of glamour and magic, many can fly, they are related to the gods and are long-lived, and they also dwell in a different sphere from humans. They are ranked in different classes, too, as are the Western fey. The *devas* are described as being 'blissful' and, as well as dwelling within natural things such as mountains, for example, they are also believed to have their own realms and spheres, which are described as the three *dhatus*.

The *devas* are an important part of the Buddhist spiritual path and are used to explain why everything should be respected as having a 'spiritual consciousness'. Buddhists also believe that some of the *devas* can be contacted by way of meditation.

Among devic belief, it is said that human beings were once akin to the *devas*, in that humans could at one time fly, had magical powers and had a luminary light shining from their being. Over time, we evolved to become solid and live in more Earthly ways and we have now forgotten how to be devic. This coincides with the current thought in Western culture among the faerie tradition that we need to bring ourselves closer to the fey once again to remember how to be the Shining Ones once more.

Hinduism

The *devas* are also embraced by Hinduism, with a slightly different emphasis of definition. Hinduism defines them more as gods or even angels, with some lower *devas* being akin to the faerie beings as we know them. They are divine beings who are close to god and take on myriad different forms within Hinduism. Many of the Indian *devas* represent the forces of nature such as earth, air, fire and water and also such creations as trees, the sea, rain, storms etc. They also have higher beings of these elements which are named, such as Agni and Soma, who represent fire. The devic beings are worshipped and honoured. However, not all *devas* are nature *devas*. Some go into the realms of the gods.

One example of a Hindu nature spirit is called a Yaksha or Yaksi (feminine). The Yaksha is shared by the Buddhists, too, and is described in a similar way in that religion. The Yaksha has a fierce dual personality and is associated with forests and mountainous areas. Sometimes it is depicted as being harmless, while on other occasions it is an ogre, phantom or demonic creature which will lie in wait for travellers and eat them!

A FAIRY PRINCESS

In Indian culture there is a tradition of fairy stories, one example of which is the tale of The Ivory City and its Fairy Princess. One of the characters sees '… a fairy. She is the fairy of fairies.' This tale follows the traditions of fairy stories from other cultures: a fairy has supernatural powers and is revered above humans. It is also a tale of intrigue and morals, and shows us that evil ways never pay the rewards that they can sometimes promise.

Hinduism is considered to be one of the oldest religious traditions in the world, and the faeries have been included in this long journey.

Islam

The Middle Eastern cultures have one of the most exciting and most widely portrayed fey types in the world in the shape of the Jinn/Djinn or Genie. The *Jinn* appears in the Qur'an, where the prophet Sulayman (Solomon) is given dominion over all beings including the supernatural *Jinn*. In one account Solomon is offended by the Queen of Sheba's gifts to him, so he quickly sends a *Jinn* to bring him the Queen's throne before she arrives at his court. The *Jinn* is said to have done this 'within a twinkling of an eye'. This is typical of the kind of magic that *Jinn* are said to have performed.

Jinn are thought to be controlled by binding them to a physical object. This peculiarity is portrayed in the story of Aladdin, where the *Jinn*, or Genie, is bound to the lamp (or, in some versins of the story, to a ring). The *Jinn* also appear in literatures of the Middle-East such as *The Thousand and One Nights*.

NEITHER GOOD NOR EVIL

Jinn seem to behave much in the way of Western fey traditions. They are thought to live in societies that mirror that of the human culture they derive from (much as is suggested above). They are also invisible to humans, although they will sometimes make themselves visible to humans at will.

Muslims believe in the *Jinn* wholeheartedly and consider them to be real entities. Unlike most Western fey, they are thought to be formed by God from fire which derives no smoke from it. They are also beings which, like humans, have the ability to be either good or evil. They do have free will, unless they have been bound by a human. *Jinn* also have the ability to shapeshift and appear as other humans and animals, their favourite being a snake.

The Qur'an states that the Devil was not an angel, as in Christian thought, but a *Jinn*. This is because a *Jinn* has the ability to choose whether to follow a good or evil path, while angels do not: angels have to follow the good will of god.

Evil *Jinn* have the ability to possess human beings, much like Christian demonic possession. Muslims have sayings to protect themselves against evil *Jinn*, which are called *Ifrit*.

I GRANT YOU THREE WISHES

The presence of *Jinn*, as a Middle Eastern cultural icon, is thousands of years old and continues to live on in our popular culture. *Jinn* have captured the imagination of movie-makers, writers and artists alike. Many people do not realize that the tame Genie from the story *Aladdin* has such a significant part to play in one of the world's religions.

Incidentally, more recently in Western society, the 'Genie' is thought to be the power of our own thought processes. Films such as *The Secret* suggest that our thoughts create our reality, just as the Genie says, 'Your wish is my command,' meaning, 'Your will be done' or 'Whatever your thoughts can imagine, you can create.' This means that, although the original Genie of popular films cast just three wishes, our wishes are now limitless. The Genie (our own limitless power) can create anything we wish. Many books and films now teach that we all have the power of 'the Genie', or the gift of manifestation.

Hassan's fascinating account is an example of a Middle Eastern fey encounter. He gave his permission for Neil Geddes-Ward to relate his story here:

On the flight from London to our family holiday in Spain in 2006, I was seated with my son Tam Lin who was next to the window, and on my left was another passenger whom I did not know. We got chatting and he said that he was from Iran. We asked what each other did, and I told him that I was an artist and my wife and I also ran 'Orkney Faerie Museum and Gallery', which told of the legends and stories of Faeries of Orkney and Scotland. He said that he thought there was a lot more to this world than what we can normally see and know. This prompted the man, whom we shall call 'Hassan', to relate to me his story.

When he was much younger and lived back in Iran, he was enlisted in the army. One night he was on patrol with a fellow soldier in a village and a storm blew up. So they sought shelter in a nearby mosque. They both agreed to stay there all night or until the storm had at least passed, but would take it in turn to sleep whilst one kept watch. So Hassan's friend went to sleep first. Hassan kept watch but, because he was sitting on the floor with his back to the wall, he soon also drifted off to sleep. Some time later Hassan awoke and saw a young attractive lady crouching near him and staring at his feet, along with a young female child looking at his friend's feet. At first he thought he was dreaming but then soon became fully alert. The two strange visitors were still there, right by the soldiers' feet, staring intently at them. Hassan thought that they might have walked into the mosque and possibly pose some threat. He tried to wake his sleeping friend by pressing his arm heavily onto his companion's chest in an effort to rouse him. No matter how hard he tried, he could not wake his friend. Hassan said the lady then looked directly up into his eyes and stared straight at him. He knew then, somehow, that this strange lady and the child with her were 'not of this world'. He thought his best bet was to then escape. So, as he had his machine gun upon him, he started to wrap the gun strap tightly around his arms so it would not swing about as he ran away. As he was doing this, very quietly and carefully, the strange lady got up along with the young girl and turned to walk away. They walked towards a wall, and Hassan noticed that both the strange visitors' feet were not human at all, but were hoofed, like those of a cow or goat! They then proceeded to walk right through the wall and disappeared.

Judaism

The Jewish faith is no stranger to the faeries and has a strong tradition of fairy stories associated with both the secular and sacred Jewish culture. Although fairy stories do not always mention actual fairy characters in their plots, they always have magical and transformative elements to them: traits which are known to belong to the fey of all cultures. It is in the guise of the fairy story that the faeries are most prominent within the Jewish faith. They also have the other ingredient which is common to fairy tales: a moral. Most often in Jewish versions the reader is shown examples of where faith in God repels evil desires.

A really beautiful story among Jewish fairy tales is *The Fairy Frog*. It tells of how a young man, Hanina, does not question the words of his dying parents and follows their last wishes to the letter. Although this causes him much hardship, poverty and suffering, he carries on with his parents' last wishes. Through doing this he acquires a larger-than-life frog, which turns out to be a talking frog. The frog imparts much spiritual knowledge to Hanina and brings him every living thing and plant, which is a gift to Hanina. The frog says, 'All these belong to you,' pointing to the jewels. 'Of equal worth are the herbs and the roots with which ye can cure all diseases.' The frog then reveals himself to be the '… fairy son of Adam, gifted with the power of assuming any form'. He then returns to the size of an ordinary frog and leaps into the forest, indistinguishable from any of the other creatures.

Again we see the magic of the faeries in this tale, which has an additional message, that wisdom is to be found within nature.

Faerie Tangles

It would seem that faeries are such an ancient part of human history that it is hard to disentangle them from any part of our existence. This is strangely so within religion, where we would probably assume that faeries do not have a place. We hope that we have enlightened you as to the faeries' sacred nature within many religions. They are still found in the more 'folk' aspects of many religions. The faerie hold upon us, it would appear, is so strong that even religion can't shake it off. Faeries weave their way invisibly through our doctrines and continue to transform and bring magic to us in their own special way.

Chapter 11

Faeries in Our Lives

'Of all the minor creatures of mythology, fairies are the most beautiful,
the most numerous, the most memorable.'
Andrew Lang

Do You Believe in Faeries?

First, a word on faerie experiences. Once you begin to acknowledge the faeries and become a believer, then you really are opening your personal doorway to the Land of Faerie. Our thoughts are very powerful things and no one knows that more than the faeries, for in their realm, thoughts are things and desires are indeed readily manifested.

Alicen: Over the years my own relationship with the faeries has deepened and with this bond and increasing belief, my experiences of the faeries' realm become more frequent.

My own faerie experiences have become so common, in fact, that not a week goes by without encountering a faerie-happening in some shape or form. However, just a little word of caution here: the fey are known to be extremely private and secretive people and they like to guard their ways and whereabouts most closely.

Faeries do not take kindly to their magical moments with you being divulged or boasted about. It is perfectly acceptable to tell of a faerie experience if you genuinely feel that it will benefit others or it will help someone who is open to such things to know the faeries more intimately, by inclusion in a book or a work of art, for instance. However, the vast majority of my encounters with the faeries are kept between the fey and me and will never, ever be told to a third party. Always think twice before telling a faerie secret, for if shared unwisely, it could be your last one. Treat them with respect and love and you will have a lifetime of wonderful faerie encounters – such as this next story, which was kindly emailed to us for inclusion in this book.

Faerie in the Kitchen

'I was cleaning out my kitchen once and I saw a small, male-looking faerie (about four inches high), wearing overalls and a red shirt. He just peeked at me from behind a pan on the stove. I only saw him briefly and thought nothing of it except … *what a funny place for a faerie to hang out!* This made me stop and look again, but he was gone, of course. I laughed out loud and called my husband to tell him about it. That was the first time I ever actually SAW a faerie!'

A Faerie Renaissance?

The author of *Peter Pan and Wendy*, J M Barrie, famously wrote: '…every time a child says, "I don't believe in fairies," there is a fairy somewhere that falls down dead.' Now, maybe that was a little dramatic of J M Barrie, but there is actually a grain of truth in what his character, Peter Pan, said.

Belief in faeries and the possibility of magic denotes whether or not the fey are present to any degree in our world. It is no accident that once the Industrial Revolution was underway, the faeries departed further into their hidden realms. It is only now, in the New Age where magic has undergone a revival, that we are beginning to ride the wave of a Faerie Renaissance. Now that we are coming to believe that perhaps material pleasures and science leave us spiritually malnourished, the belief in faeries is once again growing and the fey are again emerging.

When we set about writing a book like this, we automatically assumed that readers would already believe in faeries. If perchance you happen to be dipping into this book and you *don't* believe in faeries – hold that thought. Faeries have been lumped together with Father Christmas, the Easter Bunny etc. in our culture and, quite naturally, once we find out that we have no evidence for their existence we leave them behind in childhood. This is rational, grown-up behaviour; a belief in faeries is quite clearly – NOT. Or is it?

If you had the knowledge that faeries aren't really fluttery pretty things that take your milk teeth from under your pillow but are actually the lost gods and goddesses hailing back to pagan times, might things begin to look a little different?

Some people say that they don't believe in faeries because they can't see them. We cannot see x-rays, radio waves or even God, but most of us accept that these exist. Faeries are not always what they are cracked up to be if you believe their popular depiction. They have certainly been given a misrepresentative and bad press for the last millennia. We challenge you to suspend your disbelief for just a while and entertain the idea that they might exist. After all, what have you got to lose?

As humans we do tend to base our belief system on what we can see, hear and feel, but as we know, this makes no logical sense. Science brings us new tools to see, hear and feel all the time. The 'sensitives' amongst humankind don't need this new-fangled equipment and have been telling us for years that there is 'a whole other world out there'.

Think back, it is not so long ago that humans thought the world was flat. Of course it never was and we laugh at that now … bear that thought in mind as you read on.

FAERIES IN MY LIFE

Jacky: When Alicen and I first decided to create this book, I knew that I had to make a shift in consciousness. Faeries are all around us. Their world is interwoven between, in, under and around ours and I wanted to be a part of that. How could I dip into this mystical realm of enchantment?

Meditation has always worked well for me. It has taken me on 'out-of-body' journeys both above our immediate stream of consciousness and to a magical world in the heavenly realms. Would I be able to see faeries by using this technique? Anyone who meditates regularly will tell you that there can come a time when the 'spiritual' body begins to vibrate. It seems like your heart will beat right out of your chest, but it doesn't. This usually occurs when the body is in a very deep state of relaxation, so it can also happen as you drift off to sleep and occasionally at other unexpected times as well.

Here is one of my experiences that occurred one night whilst I was drifting off to sleep.

An Out-of-body Journey

I could hear myself snoring. Was I asleep? Yes, I was asleep but yet, as I had planned, my mind was wide awake and very aware of what was going on around me. I was still lying in bed with my husband fast asleep beside me and I could hear him snoring too. The light in my room changed. I had my eyes closed but I could still see the room around me. I was seeing with my newly-acquired clairvoyant vision. The room had taken on a greenish-yellow glow and I could see my chest of drawers in front of me where it always was.

Suddenly I snored loudly but my physical body remained asleep. I felt my spiritual body go through a strange vibrational shift and the room around me seemed to melt away and a new vision popped up in front of my eyes. I was floating above a scene of rolling hills with beautiful old oak trees laid out before me, but I was flying and floating as if I had the wing power of a bird.

This was no dream. I was well aware that my body was asleep on the bed but my soul was soaring above the ground, free and with the normal vision that you would expect if you were doing this for real ... heck, it *was* real, but a different type of reality than I had experienced before.

Confident now, I decided to swoop down closer to the ground. With my arms outstretched I drifted to the ground. I could even feel the breeze rush past my spirit body as I soared up and down, moving a little closer to the treetops. I remember thinking at the time, ... *This must be what it's like for a bird. What an amazing sense of freedom.* In time my consciousness faded out of this realm and I drifted back into normal sleep. The experience had been more real than real, and nothing like any dream I'd ever had in my life ... I knew it wasn't a dream.

In a dream we just follow along as if from an observer's point of view. Even if we take part in the action we don't have any conscious control of our actions, but in this scenario I had. I had decided exactly where and how I moved. The land below me was lit as if in daylight.

Of course, I realized much later that this had been an out-of-body experience or, as some people call it, 'astral projection' (often used to describe trips to other realms when out of the body). This shift in consciousness ... could I use this same technique to visit the faerie realms?

Many years later, my family and I were lucky enough to take a very short trip in a helicopter. We were at an air show and for the price of £25 each (quite a lot of money when there are four of you) we joined the very long queue to take our very short ride over the local countryside. No sooner did we fly over the treetops in the adjoining field than this out-of-body memory came flooding back to me. This was exactly what I had experienced many years before! It could almost have been in the same place, except this time I was sharing my flying journey with the three people closest to me.

To create faerie vision, I knew I had to find a way of recreating this shift of consciousness. Many times I had read that anyone could 'see' faeries if they took their vision away from the 'normal' world around us. Can we 'tune out' of one dimension and 'tune in' to another? I believe we can, and although sometimes this happens as if by 'accident' we can try and create these experiences on purpose.

Dandelion Seeds

When I was a little girl we used to pick the wild dandelions which grew in the grass in our gardens and in the fields near to our home. When the yellow flowers had turned to seed we would take great delight in blowing the fluffy light seeds high up into the air and watch them float on the breeze. Of course, we were always asked not to blow them in the garden ... my mother was not keen to have more weeds in the garden and our childish games would distribute the seeds everywhere.

Whenever we saw the random seeds blowing in the air my mother would say, 'Look, there's a faerie ...' We always called these seeds with their wispy fronds 'faeries' and now, whenever I see them I think the faeries must be close by. It's amazing how many I have seen in the last few weeks. Perhaps someone is trying to tell me something!

BUTTERFLIES

Many people believe that where butterflies thrive, faeries do too. In faerie picture books their wings are often shown to be similar. Butterflies, too, seem to appear on a regular basis as we write this book.

Jacky: At this time it is November here in England. November is a cold month, late autumn, and leaves are turning all shades of brown and red and falling to the ground. November is not a typical month, then, for butterflies, but as I was standing in my bedroom yesterday, talking about the next chapter of this book, I heard a loud knock. As I looked up, I was just in time to see a beautiful butterfly flying away from the window. The butterfly must have struck the window, although how it had done so and made such a loud noise is beyond me! Sometimes you just have to accept that there are magical things at work.

Gill has written to us about learning the art of meditation to its fullest effect. She uses her meditation skill to take her to many fantastic realms ... both in this life and apparently others! She told me, 'I had a great meditation yesterday, where I went to my planet of origin. It has three moons, and is so lush! Fluttering around the river were dozens of multi-coloured fairies, accompanied by many butterflies. It was an absolute picture ...'

From another reader, Laura, we hear that '...I've been using Faeriecraft every time I'm in a garden or out and about. Butterflies have begun to follow me everywhere and it wasn't till I checked up the meaning of butterflies that I realized they are connected to the faeries. Next time you see a butterfly go by, remember to say hi, it could be a faerie in disguise.'

Faerie Stories

Whether you believe in faeries or not, there are literally thousands of people around the world who have encountered faeries in one way or another. In some instances the experiences are subtle and in others more dramatic.

In the traditional sense, a 'fairy story' would appear to be something made up, a tale to entertain children. Have you ever considered where these tales would have come from in the first place, their origins? Certainly there is enough material to suggest that faerie stories come from legends based on real sightings.

THE FAERIE MUSEUM

Jacky: Although my interest in faeries is something which has grown as I have researched and written this book with Alicen, she lives very much with faeries as part of her everyday life.

Alicen: When we first moved to Orkney, we knew that one of the reasons for moving there was to set up Orkney Faerie Museum and Gallery. However, when we arrived at our new home on the Orcadian island of Westray, we had no idea where we were going to house our museum. We live in a rented house with outbuildings, which at the time were not rented by us but were full of furniture in storage by our landlords.

Within a week of moving into the house, one morning very early I opened the front door and noticed that a perfect faerie ring of mushrooms had sprung up overnight right in front of one of the outbuildings. I quickly went to tell our two children, who were very excited. We all felt that the faeries were welcoming us into our new house. We decided to leave a little bowl of honey as a thank-you in the faerie ring. For the next few days the circle of mushrooms kept popping up and then more faerie rings appeared around the garden that surrounds the outbuildings. These were of a different variety of faerie ring, which is a circle of darker grass. Every day another faerie ring would appear, either in mushrooms, grass or both, until there were ten or more at one point. Then one day they all disappeared.

By now we were searching for a building to house our museum and we seriously investigated two properties on the island, but nothing seemed quite right. We then discovered by reading a book of local folk stories and by talking to a neighbour that the house we lived in was opposite an ancient Pictish dwelling known as a faerie mound, with lots of faerie legends connected to it. This all felt very exciting, as we felt that the faeries had helped us to choose this house, since before we had moved there I had not seen the house or even been to the island!

Soon after we found this out our landlord was visiting one day and said that he would like to show me the inside of the outbuildings. As soon as I walked in the door it felt magical and I knew that, if possible, this was where our faerie museum should be housed. We approached our landlords and asked if they could move the stored furniture so we could use the buildings. They agreed, and then we didn't know why we hadn't thought of it in the first place. After all, the faeries had been trying very hard to tell us with their many faerie rings circling the outbuildings!

Quite a while after we had opened the museum a local man popped by to tell us of a tale of the outbuildings, which are now Orkney Faerie Museum and Gallery. He said that as it used to be an old croft house a man used to live there and he kept a cow there too. The floor was also earth and not concrete then, as it is now. However, what the man could not understand was that, although his cow never went to a bull, it had a calf every year. The man would sometimes see tiny footprints next to the cow's hoof prints and he deduced that the faeries were the ones who were taking the cow to the bull!

Sensing Faeries

Can a faerie experience be something you sense? We believe it can. The awareness of the fey energy can be something that we pick up using many senses, not just sight or hearing.

This charming story is from Nicole, who wrote to Jacky after visiting the faeries pages at Jacky's website (www.jackynewcomb. com).

Faerie Beads

My parents live in a beautiful hamlet on the west coast of Scotland, among hills and countryside. I took my daughter Amy, then five years old, up there for the summer holidays, and we explored the woods and countryside.

One day we went into a hilly field that had a large area covered by gorse bushes. In one particular set of bushes there was a small hollowed-out part of the bush, and on the ground a small groove in the soil that looked like a little pathway. On either side of this tiny entrance were beautiful yellow flowers and I told Amy that in the bush was a home for the faeries. I explained to her that the groove was the pathway into their home and that the flowers either side were their lanterns and lights to show them where home was.

She was so fascinated that the look of belief and wonder on her face was magical in its own right. Whilst bending down and peering into the hollow, hoping to see the faeries, Amy snapped her red popper bead necklace, causing the beads to fall to the ground. They lay near to the hollow and, although she was upset, she said she would leave them for the faeries.

The following day she wanted to go back to the 'faerie den' as she called it, so off we went. When we got to the hollow, the beads had moved and were now in the hollow under the bush. She was in awe, and so pleased that the faeries had taken them into their home.

I've always wondered, how did the beads get into the hollow? Was it the wind? Was it the sheep in the fields that had nudged them in? Or was it the faeries? I like to think it was.

FAERIES IN DREAMS

Jacky: From the moment I first sat down to write I felt that I was being influenced, guided in some way. Each night as my head hit the pillow I had a spirit source begin dictation. Chapter after chapter they wrote to me, and I would dream myself writing down their words of faerie wisdom.

This was important. I know that whatever knowledge they were sending me in my dreams was information they wanted me to share. But of course there was a problem, as there always is. The moment I awoke, the dream information trickled away from my mind like sand through fingertips … where had this information gone that they sent me night after night?

I knew that the information had to be filtered through my own mind, and to be interpreted in my own way. Although they had given me dictation, this wasn't to be a channelled vision but should arrive as inspirational thought. Then I realized we can all ask for information in this way. We just kind of 'plug ourselves in' when we drift off to sleep!

Remember to ask for the guidance and inspiration from the spirits of the Earth, but don't expect it to arrive as a list of answers in the way that I had. We have to filter the information through the human brain. We are the voice which alights the thought, and each person will translate that knowledge in their own way, using their own personality.

FAERIE DREAM VISITATIONS

Faeries like to visit us in dreams. Their powerful messages can be more easily absorbed during the dream state. Here are two amazing and true faerie dream experiences.

Faerie-dusted

I once had a faerie encounter in my dreams. I was sleeping soundly when I was approached by a beautiful faerie with strawberry-blonde long hair. The faerie kissed me and then started to throw fairy dust in my mouth! I could actually feel the faerie dust coming into my soul as if something strong and potent was entering my soul and spirit!

The experience was so intense! I believe I was actually faerie-dusted in my dreams by the fae whom I deeply love.

This next story is from Jamaica. Dylan works a lot with her dreams anyway, so faerie dream encounters are not such a large leap, although Dylan tells us that she wasn't particularly interested in faeries before her encounter …

Faerie with a Headscarf

Even as a child I have always felt a deep connection to the natural world around me, both seen and unseen. Without knowing how to explain it I knew that I was not alone and that there were always others around me.

As I grew older I think I became separated from that part of myself because of difficult and painful experiences in my life. I was sad for a very long time. As I tried to bring myself out of my sadness I began to yearn for that connection I'd once had with the natural world around me. I began to truly explore my spirituality.

I do a lot of dream work and my dreams are very important to me. One night I had a dream. In the dream I was alone in my apartment and I was feeling quite upset because I had new neighbours and they weren't very nice. Then this woman appeared. I don't remember meeting her specifically, she just appeared. In the dream I felt confused because although she was not human I was not quite sure what she was! She was smaller than me with a very round forehead and she had a distinct 'other-worldliness' about her. She wore a scarf around her head, and at the time I remember thinking that she reminded me so much of a faerie.

In the dream she became my confidante. She really empathized with me and this helped me to heal some of my pain. The dream's meaning has become even more profound to me because I have since discovered the Faerie Path. I have come to believe that this dream was the beginning of the answer to my desire to tread a spiritual pathway.

Faeries Helping

Not all faeries are naughty tricksters as people like to believe! Some faeries like to help their human neighbours and they can do this in amazing ways. Jacqueline shared this special story of healing.

Bringing Comfort

As a child I was always claiming to see fae by looking through a magic mirror that I would make from bending a twig over and gathering frosty spiders' webs in the loop. I feel sorry for poor spiders whose hard work in building their beautiful webs so often goes to waste.

As an adult I forgot about my childish faerie play until a couple of years ago when I was newly pregnant with my son. My husband and I had only got back together six months previously after a trial separation, so it wasn't an ideal time to get pregnant. However, I was delighted by my news, although my husband didn't react as I had hoped.

We were temporarily living in a bungalow borrowed from a friend whilst our new cottage was being renovated. I had suspicions that my husband was misbehaving and I had found some upsetting text messages on his phone whilst he was out one evening. I was lying on the sofa sobbing and I felt so lost and alone, wondering what on earth to do.

As I looked up I noticed first a little head and then the rest of a teeny body pop out of the fireplace. He was all shades of brown with an enormous hooked nose. He had a sloppy well-worn hat on his head and bare feet. His eyes were brown pools and he had such a kind, concerned face. We looked at each other for a while and then suddenly I had this feeling wash over me that everything was going to be fine. And he disappeared.

My son was born 18 months ago and my husband and I couldn't be happier. It seems that from that moment on things have gone from strength to strength.

Faerie Music

Jacky: I remember when I was writing my first book about angels. A lady wrote to tell me how when she was a small girl she would go to the local fields to play with her brother and that they often heard faerie music. It was something she grew up with and was used to.

Caitlin heard faerie music, too.

From One Musician to Another

I have also heard faerie music, which is so sweet. It was on a flute outside my window in the countryside in Pennsylvania. I also saw the biggest faerie I've ever seen outside that same window. It was about a foot tall and it was glowing yellow. I could see the outline of its head and shoulders.

I am a musician myself, and I used to like to go into the woods and sing to the faeries before I moved to the city. When singing at night in certain forests, I would always see faeries. Later I moved to the city so that I could learn to sing to people, and learn how to relate more with people than with nature. The faeries have given me so much love and inspiration and helped me through many hard times, when I didn't have anyone else.

Ona is from America and currently living in Argentina. She is a musician as well as a singer. Ona told us that she has believed in faeries her whole life:

Faerie Carousel

One day I was in desperate need of help. I was feeling lost and totally alone in the world when suddenly, in the silence of my home, I heard music. It was the most beautiful music I had ever heard and it seemed to be coming from some other dimension … but from behind a mirror in my room. It reminded me of carousel music, like you hear in children's music boxes.

It sounded as if the magical notes were trying to get my attention back home and to remind me of my heritage. The music played for just a few seconds, but as soft and subtle at it was, I felt it was also very intense. It seriously changed my life forever! I felt that I had been touched by the fae!

Faerie Lights

Jacky: When I first started looking for faeries I had a preconceived idea of what I might see. I know that I was looking for a flower-faerie type of faerie. Where is the little being with wings and clothes made of leaves and seed heads?

I remember when my niece came to stay and we decided to go for a walk around our country village in England. As we strolled through local woodland I peeked under boughs of overhanging trees, and squatted down to look at the base of bushes and shrubs. At the end of the walk I couldn't help but be disappointed at seeing nothing at all.

It was time to walk home and we strolled through the modern estate-type houses. We were chattering away about nothing in particular when I suddenly spotted a flash of red light at my feet. I actually jumped back in surprise because the light looked like the flare from a match. Where did this red light come from? I have no idea but was annoyed that neither of my human companions had seen it! Was this a faerie? Research suggests that this bright red flare was probably a salamander, a fire faerie.

Others, too, have seen the faerie lights. Caitlin is American but is of Scottish, Irish, French and German descent. She is 23 years old.

Open to Faerie

I first saw faeries when I was 15 and on a three-week outdoor trip in Maine, under an organization called Outward Bound. We canoed for 10 days and then hiked for 60 miles, which took us another 10 days.

Like many teens, I had been sent on the trip by my parents to have an attitude adjustment! Although other kids sometimes go on this program voluntarily, seven out of the ten people in my group had also been sent by their parents.

On this particular day we had been canoeing in a lake when lightning and thunder flashed and rumbled overhead. We quickly paddled to a nearby island and sat on our sleeping pads to wait out the storm. I was chatting away with my friend when I noticed a red light flashing behind her. I was so stunned I literally stopped speaking mid-conversation and she knew I had seen something unusual.

I knew immediately that it was a faerie, and although I'd assumed that faeries no longer existed any more I had always believed in the existence of angels. I told everyone that I had just seen a faerie and you know that they thought I was crazy.

Over the entire trip I saw many faeries, particularly green and blue faeries and one green faerie which appeared to be dancing. Red and yellow faeries were common in this area, too.

The faeries made me laugh a lot, but there was one night in particular when I saw a group of about six white faeries and I knew it was something special. I was on 'solo', which was part of the trip where all the campers spread out and have to stay in a small area for two days without much food. The idea was that we were not to contact each other throughout this time. I was lying down in my sleeping bag at night and I saw tiny white lights everywhere, near the ground. I wondered if these were little plant faeries that help the plants grow, as I hadn't seen such tiny faeries before.

Then I saw about five or six white faeries flying near me. They were much larger than the tiny ones near the plants on the forest floor and they were also much larger than any I had seen previously on the trip. I assumed that the one who was leading must have been the queen and I could see an outline of her head and shoulders.

I told one of my leaders about the night when I saw the white faeries. Several nights later he came to my tent and asked me to show him the faeries, so I did. We just walked over to some plants and I showed him the green and blue faeries and we both started laughing.

Since this trip I have been lucky enough to see angels, too, and I've even heard faerie music too, which was sweet.

Here is another of Alicen's magical experiences.

Faerie Lights

Many years ago, before we had children or were even married, Neil and I went with a small group of like-minded friends to Glastonbury in Somerset for a day trip. When we arrived we discovered from a poster that we were there on a full moon. At that time we were all very new to magic and spirituality and had not yet got into the habit of following the natural tides. After attending an organized full-moon meditation in Glastonbury town centre we headed excitedly for the Tor. When we reached the foot of the Tor it was dusk. All the guys decided to walk to the top of the Tor and have an impromptu jam with a guitar and drums that they had brought along. This left me and my two girlfriends in the meadow at the base of the Tor. For a while we just sat on the grass and chatted until something stunned us into complete silence.

What we saw was the full moon rising over Glastonbury Tor, and it was as if this spectacle had been arranged for us! We had never seen the moon appear so large and imposing; it seemed to fill the whole sky. It appeared to be so illuminated as it rose above the Tor, as if it was a message for us. For a while we just sat in silent awe at the sight of the rising moon and by this time we felt that we should be whispering! Then I noticed in the long tufty grass lots of orbs of light bouncing as if they were bubbles across the meadow. I whispered to my two friends to look where I had seen them and they saw them too! Indeed, once my friends sighted them too, the illuminated orbs seemed to increase in number.

These orbs were in many different colours and they are known as 'faerie lights' or sometimes they are called 'Will o' the wisp'. We all watched the faerie lights bobbing and dancing in the meadow for what seemed like a very long time, and my friends were very excited that they were seeing faerie forms. I will always remember the night of the rising full moon over Glastonbury Tor and the faerie lights. The experience made a huge impression upon me at the time and I remember feeling on a natural bubbly high, which took about a week to come down from.

The Hidden Fey

As we have mentioned before, faeries are sometimes known as the 'hidden folk' or the 'secret people' etc. This is because it is rare to see a faerie, as they dwell in their own realm. However, this does not mean that we cannot sense them and they cannot touch us in other ways throughout our lives. Most people in Western society today view faeries as fictional fantasy creatures enjoyed by children. It is not generally realized that faeries underpin our core beliefs, and although we think we have left them behind in childhood, faeries make their presence felt by weaving their way, silently and subtly, throughout our lives. As can be seen by the research that we have presented in this book, faeries are indeed everywhere in our adult lives, from religion to literature, movies and advertising, to the environment. They are like the silent watchers who are waiting for us to awaken and realize that, although they are supposedly hidden, they are making their voices heard loud and clear, if only we know how to listen and find the right places to look.

From the readers' true faerie experiences that have been kindly donated throughout the book, you can also see the many different ways in which faeries communicate with and make themselves known to us. This is evidence, too, that the faeries want us to know that although like the wind in your hair you cannot see them, you can definitely know they are there. Just because you can't see faeries (most often anyway) it doesn't mean that they don't exist!

Here is a good example, as Laura discovered.

Cheeky Altar Faerie

My experiences with faeries have been that they can be a bit cheeky … not in a bad way, though.

After I had arranged my faerie altar at home (which took a great deal of thought and planning to do, including lots of sewing), it wasn't long before I started noticing that the little faerie figurine which I have on my altar kept moving. Now, by moving I don't mean it jumped down and ran off, I mean it moves about 180 degrees at a time.

I have asked my family if they have moved the figurine; they've all said no. It still moves to this day and I check it every morning and night to see if there has been any movement, but it always happens when you are not expecting it, of course.

Sensing Faeries

This is probably the most common way in which we experience the faeries, by our intuition and by simply having a feeling about something. If you have a set of faerie oracle cards, you will know that the faeries guide you with your intuition.

Have you ever gone for a walk in the depths of winter in woodland? If you are sensitive, you will be able to feel the fey in the atmosphere, for a woodland is one of the easiest places to try this out. This is because natural life is in close proximity all around you. Each tree has its own fey guardian, not to mention all the ferns, bracken, wild flowers, mosses and fungi that populate the wood. Woodlands are positively heaving with faeries!

Here is a visualization for you to try. As faeries also come to us very strongly through our imagination, so a visualization or meditation is a great way to sense the faeries.

We have chosen a woodland in winter because during this dormant season, although the trees and vegetation are resting, and indeed many animals are hibernating, the fey are certainly not! They are active throughout the year. In a wood in winter you will not have the distractions of the growth energy of spring and summer. All life is resting and listening, waiting and pausing. It is the secret time of repose, when faerie magic is visible to the naked eye. It can be seen in the lacing of frost on cobwebs, the crisp crunch of frost on leaves underfoot, the separate spikes of a snowflake as it comes to settle on a leaf. The woodland waits magically and secretly, and to sense the faeries in this suspended city of trees is an experience well worth delving into …

The Watching Woodland Visualization

Choose a time when you will not be disturbed, and find a room where you are comfortable and warm.

Sitting down, close your eyes and breathe deeply. Once you are feeling relaxed and ready, imagine that you are in a wood. This can be one that you already visit near your home, perhaps, or one that is from your imagination. You are alone at dusk in the woods and wrapped up in warm clothing, quite, quite safe. 'Sensing' is the watchword here and you need to be open to new sensations and ideas.

Begin to follow a footpath that takes you deeper into the woods. Do not rush along the path, but walk slowly and mindfully, taking in all your surroundings as you walk. If there is anything that catches your eye along the way, make sure that you stop for a moment to take a closer look. This visualization is meant to be a sensory experience and now we are going to explore that concept.

The time is December and the air is damp and a swathing mist has moved in. This mist lies near the ground and anything above knee level is clear of it. You feel the mist draping around the base of the trees and threading itself throughout the bare bracken. You can feel the dampness in the air and the cold beginning to pinch your cheeks as the sun's warmth begins to fade. The dampness clings to the trees' bark.

The most startling observation is the silence all around you. It is a magical silence which seems to hang in the air, just like the mist. Do not be afraid of the silence; it is really magic hanging in the air, waiting for you to touch it and enter it.

Although the woodland is damp, cold and silent, be assured that you are truly welcomed and you may share in the magic that is just a thought away. As you walk along the pathway, stop at the next tree that you feel most attracted to. Put your hand out and touch the damp bark; can you feel any lichen or moss? Is the surface slippery or rough? Run your hands up and down the bark for a few moments and feel that you are being welcomed by the tree. Now send a thought out to the tree's faerie guardian, that you would like to be a part of the woodland's magic.

Take a step back from the tree and look all around you. Look at all your surroundings and begin to feel comfortable in the silence. The movie-makers do not go far wrong when they depict magic as showers of tiny stars. If we could see it, this is how magic in nature would really look. Therefore, you are now going to 'sense' this magic. Imagine all around, in between the trees and hanging in the air, magic everywhere; the air is thick with it. However, although this magic is there, you can't quite see it. You know it is there, so you will have to 'sense' it first with your imagination. After a while of imagining it is there, you may actually be able to see or feel it in the air. The quiet of the trees, the dusky atmosphere and the draping mists all lend themselves to sensing more readily this natural magical faerie dust.

Really enter the silent world of the woodland for a few moments and imagine that you are surrounded by invisible tiny stars. Concentrate on these images and feelings for as long as you can, and when you are ready you may open your eyes.

This is a visualization which you can do regularly. Not only is it very relaxing and peaceful, but your experiential results of sensing magic should improve and strengthen each time that you practise it.

Some people also feel that they are being watched while doing this visualization. This is a very common experience and it is really the guardians of the trees and the faeries who are watching you, so there is no need to feel uneasy about this sensation.

Another way that we may sense faeries is by receiving the powerful energy that they bring with them. If you have had the good fortune to feel that you are bathed in God's love or the presence of an angel, you will know exactly what we mean. As the king of faerie artists, Brian Froud, also recognizes in his book *Good Faeries/Bad Faeries*, 'Faeries are not seen by the eyes but through the heart.' Most often you will be looking in the wrong place if you are trying to see a faerie, as Brian comments, 'Keep your eyes and your heart wide open. Only thus is faerie revealed.'

Whenever many people encounter a faerie experience it is accompanied with spiritual feelings and is often a life-changing experience. These experiences come to people in many ways, visualization and meditation often among them. Do not think that just because you have never seen a faerie that you have not experienced them, for we have so many ways of sensing them around us. The more we are open and receptive to these potential experiences, the easier it is for faeries to communicate with us.

Hearing Faeries
Was it a rat or a mouse ... or a real-life faerie? Can we always tell? Usually yes. An encounter with magical energy leaves a

magical trace behind, that certain feeling of excitement which can't be explained in any other way! You just know that something special has occurred.

One of the most magical and possibly quite haunting ways in which faeries communicate with us is by music. This can manifest in two different ways. First, musicians and composers receive inspiration from the faeries and this filters through into their compositions. Second, it is possible actually to hear faerie music and, as in sensing faeries, it may be all part of a spiritual experience. Like the stories which have gone before, it's amazing how many musicians pick up on the sounds of faerie music – maybe they are already naturally tuned in!

Alicen: In the year 2000 on a summer's night, I remember that I had flopped into bed so tired that I didn't bother to pull the curtains properly. There was a big gap in the middle, which I didn't really notice as I went to bed.

Sometime in the dead of night I awoke, as I felt that I had almost been pulled awake. That is the only way in which I can describe it. The first thing that struck me was that I could hear enchantingly beautiful music, except that this was different because I knew that although I was definitely hearing it with my ears, I was hearing the music in another, deeper way too; however, I could not tell you what instruments created it. The only way in which I can describe it is that it was ethereal music which penetrated everything. There seemed to be nothing that it did not touch.

I remember sitting bolt upright, as I knew that something weird was up! As I did so, I was exactly opposite the gap in the curtains, where in the black starry sky I saw, at that precise moment, the full moon glide perfectly into the gap of my window.

Unfortunately, words do not do justice to the immensity of this experience. The music was the most captivating and enchanting that I had ever heard, and I just knew that I was hearing faerie music, with its unearthly beauty. The moon appeared on that night as if it were there at that particular moment for me to see and experience. The music was all-consuming and I simply sat in bed enraptured and mesmerized by the whole experience. Also, time had done that weird faerie thing and it felt as if it didn't exist any more.

I do feel changed by that lovely experience, as if I had been woken up to witness that special happening. Otherwise I have no idea why I had awoken.

A good friend of mine told me quite recently that after coming home from a night out in the early hours of the morning, she parked her car in the driveway and, as she got out she heard lovely music coming from her back garden. She had no doubt that it was faerie music and although she wanted to investigate, she didn't quite dare and she ran into the house as quickly as she could!

Faerie laughter is also a common way to hear faeries. The fey are known for their sense of fun and mischief, so if you hear giggling one day and you turn around and no one is there, then maybe it could be a faerie.

This story is from Christina:

Midsummer Faeries

One Midsummer's Eve while a group of us sat around a bonfire after a ritual, I heard the sound of children laughing in the dark woods (another friend also heard the children). We both stared and looked back at each other and knew it was the fae celebrating Midsummer. That was quite uplifting. Our group had no children in it and we were the only group of people for miles.

Seeing Faeries

It is also possible to see faeries with your own eyes. There are many ancient tips and tricks for ways of helping you to be able to break through to the faerie realms, even momentarily.

For the lucky few, if all circumstances come together at the right time in the right place, the little people can be seen ... usually for just a moment or two. This experience is life-changing and many spend the rest of their lives trying to recreate the magic once again.

This is a tricky one, as you'll discover. There seem to be three ways that people most commonly see faeries. The first is with their physical eyes, as you would expect. The faerie being is sighted as you would see any other ordinary person.

The second is seeing them psychically, usually described by someone who has the sight (clairvoyance), the natural ability to see supernatural occurrences. This would probably take the form that the only person able to see the faeries would be the person with the sight. They are known to see such things through their third eye, which is the psychic centre in the middle of the forehead, between the physical eyes.

The third way would be a combination of the two. The person sees the faerie as a physical form with their actual eyes, but also simultaneously receives information psychically through their other senses and third eye. This one is a little difficult to understand unless you have actually experienced it. This is usually encountered by people who are multi-gifted in the psychic department (not a technical term, we know, but an easier way to explain it!). However, it can be likened to being in a cinema with surround-sound and a larger-than-life screen ... in full 'Technicolor™'. In other words, it is a multi-experiential sighting.

It is sometimes theorized that faeries do not really have form, and especially not wings. It is really our own collective perceptions of and expectations for these beings that determine their form. Also the fact that we need to personify everything that we can't explain. We will leave this out there as a theory and let you decide what you think of it.

Faeries in the Guise of Men and Women

Jacky: Like angels, faeries can come in the guise of humankind. My sister and I sometimes 'people watch' when drinking coffee in public places. Is that person a faerie in disguise? Could that person have been a gnome in a previous life? Look at the way people dress, the way they hold themselves, even the way they communicate … the clues are there!

Science Fact?

Faeries have long been thought to be able to live among us in the guise of men and women. This may sound like a programme on the Sci-Fi Channel to those who have never heard of the concept before, but really, we're being perfectly serious. Let us explain …

Although faeries are generally known to stick to their own camp – Faerie Land – they are part of our world, too. They also need to interact with humans, as we are a branch of the natural world, so it is part of their mission to connect us with nature. Because of this function they sometimes find it necessary to live among us in human form. They do this to achieve work that they would find difficult in their fey form, which is not naturally a physical state.

These faeries are born into human beings, but are considered to be humans with a faerie soul. Throughout history they have been known as faerie temptresses or enchantresses, or in their male form faerie tempters/enchanters. Now in the 21st century they have sometimes been given the more modern terms of faerie priests and priestesses. Similarly, Doreen Virtue in her book *Earth Angels* calls them 'Incarnated Elementals'.

Humans with a faerie soul are typically very sensitive individuals who are drawn to the faeries as children and carry this through into adulthood. They usually work for the faeries and feel that this is their life purpose. This can take on many guises, from working for the environment to helping sick animals, counselling and healing or pursuing a magical career. All these people usually learn about herbs and the magical arts at some time in their lives, maybe working with aromatherapy oils and so on. It is often the case that these people have known that there is something different about them all their lives. They are often searching for the reason why they feel so sensitive and drawn to the faeries all their lives. Sometimes it is not until they read about what a faerie priest or priestess is that they come to realize what they have been all along. This can be a tremendous relief to many people, to find that there are others like them.

These people do carry out the faeries' work in human form. They also communicate with the faeries for guidance on their life pathway and in the work that they do.

These fey-like people not only have faerie traits in their personalities, but also have an appearance that may remind you of a type of faerie, pixie, elf or leprechaun, for instance. By the same token these folk are often sensitive, artistic and may have a wickedly mischievous sense of humour. These are very often the faeries who walk among us. It was thought that when these fey-touched people died, they went back to the Land of Faerie and became fey beings once again.

Shapeshifting

Another way in which faeries may appear to us in the guise of men and women is a more temporary state than as faerie tempter or temptress. Many faeries need to appear to us to fulfil a particular function for our benefit, but only for a short time. This is usually to deliver an important message or to give us a sign.

One such example is that of Faerie Godmothers. They are said to appear, sometimes momentarily, as old women, to give help in a particular situation. If your Faerie Godmother appears to you as a human being, this is historically thought to be in the form of an old woman you would never have met before. She would come to you at a time of crisis, to give you advice on your troubles.

Faeries in the Guise of Animals

Jacky: There is a tradition that suggests that hedgehogs are faeries in disguise. My sister recently found a young hedgehog wandering around in front of her house in broad daylight. Hedgehogs are creatures of the night and we discovered that they usually only come out in the daytime if they are cold, hungry or ill. This applies even more so to baby hedgehogs, who can easily die if their mothers get run over or killed by wild animals.

The hedgehog responded readily to a lunch of slugs and quickly snuggled down to sleep in my sister's back garden. Later in the day that poor baby was again found wandering around in the road in the middle of the day, meaning its chances of survival were lessening by the hour.

Everyone set to work. According to several specialist hedgehog websites, baby hedgehogs need to be kept warm, or even brought into the house. My husband was persuaded to create a wooden 'faerie house' for the hedgehog with felt roofing to keep out the rain, and straw in the bottom for warmth. The house had a small door and we even joked about creating flower boxes, decking and maybe windows. I was stunned to discover that many petshops in the UK actually sell boxes of hedgehog food, so 'Grandma' bought some ... we're a little soppy over animals in our family!

Several weeks later I am pleased to announce that 'Arnold' is doing very well! Will his presence encourage faeries into the garden? Perhaps if we sneak out at night we'll discover him in his true pixie body ... maybe it was a test of human kindness after all. Who knows?!

Other Disguises

Faeries use animals as their messengers to us. They do have favourite animals in which they like to appear. Birds are the most favoured of these. This may be because it is easiest to deliver a message if you can alight anywhere! Other animals favoured by the faeries are hares, horses, toads, frogs, deer, black dogs, cows and cats. According to Anna Franklin in *The Illustrated Encyclopaedia of Fairies,* '... shapeshifting is a power possessed by most fairies'.

Sometimes the animal who is the faerie in shapeshifted form can appear slightly different to an earthly animal, instantly giving us the clue to take notice.

Alicen: A friend of mine once recounted an experience to me that had a profound effect upon her. One night she was awoken by a loud tapping on her window. She immediately got up to see what it was and drew the curtains back. As she did so, behind the window was a raven which she said was formed entirely of what seemed to be moonlight. She instantly knew that this was a spiritual messenger and of course not a real raven. She was also going through a very tough personal struggle at the time and she found this experience very comforting.

Ravens are said to be closely associated with the faeries, and among other things are thought to be symbols of prophecy. Because of this they are considered to be a sacred bird and are shrouded in mystery.

Faeries are often thought to blend in with trees, plants, flowers and things like mosses and toadstools. Be careful where you tread!

In this next story the cheeky faeries stole their own 'offering' from Kathy. I'm sure there is a lesson for us all here.

Goblin Wood?

Last year my husband and I visited a small forest called Fairy Glen in a place called Appley Bridge near Wigan in Lancashire. It was a very dark wood and you could feel a strange atmosphere straight away. My husband really didn't like it and said he'd felt something tap his shoulder a couple of times!

I was quite pleased as I found a lovely fallen branch on the ground, which I asked the forest for permission to take. As we came out of the other side of the trees, my husband looked at me and asked what had happened to my hair ... I'd had my hair in two pigtails, and somehow my glittery elastic bands had completely vanished and my hair was unravelled!

I had no idea how this happened, since we were just strolling along, but I suddenly wondered if it was because I hadn't left a thank-you offering in return for the branch.

I went back weeks later and left some rose quartz crystals in the little stream. It was where I saw real red-spotted 'faerie' toadstools for the first time! Funnily enough, a friend of mine took her two children there and one of them got quite frightened and said he'd just seen a 'creature like a goblin'!

Faeries in Dreams

Our dream state is one of the most significant ways in which the faeries may communicate with us. This is because in our dreams we are already half way to the Land of Faerie, so to speak. Hence the saying 'away with the faeries' when we are sleeping (we have one foot in the other dimension). We are also open and receptive, without our rational and questioning mind and more able to accept messages and encounters from the fey.

When we sleep we enter a state very similar to that of Faerie Land, where time does not exist and we do not need a physical form. Faeries can reach out to us more easily and when we awaken it is easier then to decipher any messages or symbols that would seem to be faerie-given.

There is one Faerie Queen who is very linked to our dream states and this is thought to be her favourite way to communicate. This is Morgan Le Fay, who is the queen of the subconscious, delivering her messages under the cover of darkness to the most fertile aperture of our minds: the sleep state.

An Exercise in Faerie Dreaming

Here is an exercise to help you to make sense of your dreams from a faerie perspective. In fey mythology dreams are considered to be messages from your soul, guiding you through life.

Find a special notebook, one that reminds you of the faeries, to write down your dreams in. Place this book together with a pen by your bedside. On the first page in your Faerie Dreaming Book, write a short letter to Queen Morgan Le Fay. Ask her politely if she will kindly illuminate your dreams to reveal more clearly the messages she brings from your soul and the faeries.

Over the course of the next month, as soon as you wake up in the morning, jot down what you can remember of your dreams. Don't leave it until any later in the day, as dreams have a habit of fading.

After a month has elapsed, read back all your dreams. You should see a pattern emerging and you will soon learn that certain things jump out at you as symbols and messages. Any recurrent themes are also things to watch out for and are significant. Faeries usually send messages to you in code or symbolic form; don't expect everything to be straightforward! Deciphering the messages is all part of the faerie journey – as you will discover.

Honouring Faeries

Faeries deserve our respect. We might not understand their ways or ideas but that doesn't mean that we must disrespect them. Goodness, you don't even have to believe in them if you don't want to, but imagine if the fey didn't believe in us?

Of course, sometimes we disregard them by accident. Linda was especially attuned to faerie energies when she was a child, and had these sad experiences.

The Toadstool Garden

When I was four or five we had just moved to a new house. I went alone to explore the garden and remember it was somewhat unkempt. I found myself walking round a circular flower bed. It was overgrown and quiet and I had the feeling that there was a faerie presence there. It was quite beautiful and I guess I seemed open to the fragile energy of the garden. In time the new garden was landscaped by my parents and I remember feeling sad that the faerie place had been taken away.

A number of years later I actually saw a gold- and cream-coloured fairy when I was looking for strawberries amongst the strawberry plants. There was a glow to it and I remember looking for it everywhere afterwards.

A few years later a large toadstool grew from the bark of a tree. It was an interesting cup shape and I had that same feeling about faeries then. One day I saw small shapes looking out from the cup but unfortunately my brothers got wind of my interest in the toadstool, and threw stones at it until it came down. I do remember feeling as if something special had been desecrated.

We do too, Linda. Remember to teach your children respect for all living creatures, especially faeries!

WORKING WITH RESPECT BRINGS RESULTS

We were particularly keen to include the experiences of Cath, who is lucky enough to connect very closely with the little people! Cath specifically asked that we leave in her full details.

Faeries of the British Isles

I am Cath Vause-Hooley and have been blessed with many encounters with the Faerie peoples since I arrived in the

British Isles almost five years ago from New Zealand. These are not the little sparkly-winged 'fairies' flitting and fluttering around the foxgloves in the flower garden (although I have spoken to and worked with these). They are the Sidhe, the Tuathans and the Fianna. The Fey folk. The tall god and goddess beings of the old religion. Deep as the Earth, powerful and beautiful, mysterious, dangerous, dark or shining. Warrior-smiths, healers, makers of miracles. They are the ones that our ancestors accepted as neighbours who inhabited the numinous borders of our own lands.

For me, it began three days after touching down in London. I headed for Glastonbury, to finally see the enigmatic Tor that had drawn me like a magnet right across the globe. On that Samhain Eve (31st October 2001, the night when the veil between our worlds is thinnest) it was also to be a Taurus full moon. It is said that when this occurs (the full moon falling exactly on Samhain night) that Gwynn Ap Nudd, King of the Faeries, who lives within the hollow hill of Glastonbury Tor, will ride forth through the skies with his Faerie host and the hounds of Annwn (luminous white dogs with spectral red eyes and ears to match) to gather up the souls of the dead and then return with them to his realm. It is the Faery Rade.

It certainly looked set to be an atmospheric night. I stood atop the huge Faerie hill beside the Tower, facing west, and watched as the sun set on one horizon, while directly behind me the moon rose up over the other. I stood between them, held in their balance. As darkness grew, people emerged from the shadows to begin the celebrations. All sorts of people. My friend from London was with me and a fellow called David that we had met in the George and Pilgrim Inn where we were staying. Amid the drummers and didgeridoos, dreadlocks and druids. It was wonderful.

At midnight, with the huge golden moon high in the sky above, the three of us spontaneously began chanting the name of the god, and dancing and jumping around in a circle while holding hands. We were spinning faster and faster, calling louder and louder, 'Gwynn!, Gwynn!, Gwynn!' on and on. Raising the power.

Everything went suddenly silent but for our chanting and then came the eerie howling of dogs. There was a feel of chaos with the rising energy. It clearly unnerved some of the people up on the Tor, who started shouting, 'Stop it! Stop it!' but I think it was too late by then. We had called him up. He who would become one of my helpers and allies as I traversed the 'watery mirror realms' and quagmires of emotions that unravelled when I moved permanently to Glastonbury a few months later. Even though the monks of the old Abbey had drained the water from the surrounding lands, it remains on the etheric planes, and water, being akin to the emotions, can certainly magnify and distort!

During that turbulent first year and a half in Avalon I would seek refuge out of doors and often find myself in the evenings walking the dark lanes up to the Tor. On rainy windswept nights, under the light of the moon or under blue-black skies with starlight only to light the way, I would reach the summit and find myself alone of human company, not another living soul up there. The rainy nights were the best, everyone else stayed inside in front of the TV and the streets were empty. I began to take offerings with me of herbs and honey, silver and copper to the Faerie King and I would place them carefully at the foot of the Tower (which I had secretly always believed to be part of Gwynn's Faery castle).

I would speak to the Faery King during my challenges and also my successes. I petitioned his help regarding finding a new home to rent (when all the letting possibilities in town seemed to have vanished and it looked like there were no options open. My then partner and I moved four times in those first two years: landlord returning from Spain and needing her cottage back, landlord going through a divorce and selling up to divide assets etc). I would climb the path with wish lists, read them aloud and then let them blow shredded to the four winds. I knew he could hear me and I was certainly not 'alone', I could feel many eyes watching me. I'd see shapes flitting past in the shadows.

Remarkably things would begin to take a new shape effortlessly and stuck situations would often free up in the time it took me to descend the steep pathway down. I would be engulfed in a feeling of peace that everything was being taken care of in the right time and order if I could just 'trust' and let go, take a leap of faith into the void. Sometimes there would even be a phone call before I got back into town. I found help to find the right work, with inspiration for creative projects and also to let go of my relationship that had become unhealthy and intolerable. It was a powerful magic and one I learned not to take for granted.

It is said that Glastonbury Tor is haunted. I say it is one of the Hollow Hills, home to the Fey folk. There are many stories locally about a tunnel going into the hill from an entranceway at the back of the White Spring Café building. It is apparently blocked off with stones and I have heard from several sources about a guardian that protects this closed gateway. Then there are tales of the people who have journeyed in, some returning in a state of madness, some never returning at all.

I've had several wonderful Faerie encounters in Ireland during the summer of 2004. It was Midsummer Day when I made a pilgrimage to the heart of County Meath, to visit Tara, Fourknocks burial chamber and Newgrange on the banks of the River Boyne. All these places were 'alive' with the ancestral spirits or Faerie. I saw a tall warrior at Fourknocks. He was waiting at the entranceway, a tiny door cut into the side of the high domed grass mound, and then he stepped past me and disappeared from sight.

I went on to Tara, 'Rath Grainne', seat of the High Kings of Ireland in times gone by. I had purchased a beautiful ring with a very dark purple amethyst set in it while back in Dublin, as a way to commemorate the feeling of closure and healing I had arrived at, having now spent many months on my own after the end of the disastrous relationship the year before (the one with all the house moves round Glastonbury).

I felt it was time to honour myself, put Self first, in fact, time to draw together the masculine and feminine aspects (the animus and anima) within my own psyche. If I could call for a harmonious balance within myself, then I would attract another balanced healthy individual at some point in the future, or at the very least increase the chances of that happening. I wanted to perform an 'inner sacred marriage' ritual of sorts.

I walked across the green splendour of the Tara hills under a glorious midday sun, past the Lia Fail (the Stone of Destiny) and over to the hawthorn tree that was well known locally as 'The Faery Tree of Tara'. I paused to see that the gifts I was bringing would be accepted and called on Danu, the Great Mother of the Tuatha De Danann. I placed the bread and honey and silver coins around the tree and walked three times sun-wise around the trunk. A luminous being appeared and I had a lengthy conversation about my intention for being there and I offered her the amethyst ring and also a silver claddagh ring (known as an Irish wedding ring). She hung them in the branches of the tree while chanting blessing words over them.

She placed them in the palm of my hand and when I looked up she was gone. I put the rings on my finger, thanked her quietly and departed. I was not alone for long, however. I was being followed by a curious American tourist with a huge camera round his neck, who was desperate to know what I had been doing by the tree!

Six months later, back in Glastonbury at a druid gathering, I did meet the man of my dreams. His name is Dan. Ten months after that I was preparing to move away from colourful Glastonbury (my soul home) to be with him in Llangollen, North Wales. Dan and I climbed up the Tor one evening just before it was time for me to go, to ask for a blessing on my journey north and also to see how, if possible, I could be of service to his kind.

It was near the end of our visit and I was voicing my thanks for deeds past and expressing thoughts for the future, when Dan and I both saw a massive shape move across the stones of the tower on the Tor. A HUGE man, like a shadowy giant rose up and stood beside the doorway. I let out a gasp. Incredible. I thought maybe I was the only one who could see him, but to my surprise Dan could also. Sensible, grounded Dan (who has a psychology degree and has studied forensic behavioural sciences) could also see the King of the Faery castle of Avalon. It was incredible.

Ironically I was moving up to the tiny town of Llangollen which had a direct connection to Gwynn. Old tales spoke of St Collen, a pious monk who lived in a hermit's cell at the foot of the Tor, who had been invited several times to visit the Faery castle up on the summit to feast with Gwynn Ap Nudd and his court. Finally he accepted and entered the castle. But not only did he refuse the faerie food and drink he was offered, but spoke insults and threw holy water he had taken care to bring with him all over his host and assembled party, who promptly vanished along with all trace of the castle. It is said that St Collen drove Gwynn and the Faerie peoples out from the Tor and some stories say that they fled north into Wales, where St Collen continued his chase. Llangollen means 'Church of Collen'.

On the festival of Lugh (August 1st) Dan and I got engaged and we chose bands of the stone circle 'Ring of

Brodgar' from the Orkney Islands. On the night before they arrived (they were being sent down from Aurora Orkney in Scotland, and we had a card saying that they were awaiting us to sign for them at the post office) the dark purple amethyst 'faeries' ring' blessed at Tara, vanished. I can't explain where it went. It simply disappeared from my finger! A new chapter was obviously beginning.

There have been other mysterious occurrences too. In the woods at the foot of Camelot Castle Hillfort, seated in a 'fairy ring' of daisies on the lawn at the ruined abbey at Lindisfarne, rites of passage, celebrations and druidic initiations all taken on the tree covered Faery Hill up behind the cottage where we live in Llangollen. And of course the profound and scary night spent atop the Long Barrow burial chamber of Wayland's Smithy (as recorded in the article on the sweat lodge on our website: www. druidshaman.com).

CHAPTER 12

Faeries and Children

'Every child can remember laying his head in the grass, staring into the infinitesimal forest and seeing it grow populous with fairy armies ... '
ROBERT LOUIS STEVENSON

Faeries are Freedom

Children have always been open to the magical realms of the faerie. In whatever form, they belong to the fabric of childhood from Peter Pan to Cinderella, and 'imaginary' friends in between. In however small a way, each of us is touched by the magic of the faeries as children. Do you remember making faerie houses? Writing letters to the faeries or seeing the faeries in your own garden? Even if only in your imagination, many children feel the joy of faeries in these early years.

Children are also credited with having far more fey experiences and closeness to the faeries than adults. The reason is simple: faeries inhabit an untouchable place similar to the realms we all came from before we were born and came into our physical bodies. Children are closer to the Land of Faerie because, it is theorized, they are still loosely connected to that previous existence.

The Austrian philosopher Rudolf Steiner, who founded the worldwide Waldorf Schools movement, put forward the idea that children from birth to seven years old were still 'settling in' to their physical bodies. Therefore, fairy tales were suitable forms of education, as this was an art form which retained elements from the Otherworlds. Also, according to Hamilton Wright Mabie writing in 1905, '… the fairy tale records the free and joyful play of the imagination'. Similarly, Rudolf Steiner also believed that older children from the ages of seven to 14 were in the realm of 'imagination and fantasy', exactly the most effective standpoint to communicate with the faeries.

It would therefore seem that all children are naturally predisposed to closeness to the faeries' realm. For, according to Hamilton Wright Mabie, '… children not only possess the faculty of imagination, but are largely occupied by it during the most sensitive and formative years'. All of us as children move and live in the realms of our imaginations, a place indeed on the cusp of the Land of Faerie.

Faeries and the Realm of the Imagination

According to the Concise Oxford English Dictionary, imagination is 'the faculty or action of forming ideas or mental images, the ability of the mind to be creative or resourceful'. Indeed, the dictionary seems to struggle a little to pin down adequately in words exactly what the imagination is, so …

Delving further, other sources provide more accurate descriptions of what it feels like to imagine. For such an innocent and straightforward mental function, most sources completely get their 'knickers in a twist' over exactly how to define imagination.

It seems fitting, then, to draw upon other people's perceptions of the imagination to illustrate the connection to faerie. Peter tells us:

> … First about me, I was never mystically inclined, had no interest in such things, neither had my parents. I was a small boy of five who was more interested in cars, guns and World War Two than fairies.
>
> The occurrence happened sometime in 1964 in a terraced house in Abercairn Road in Streatham, South

London, of an evening. I was not, nor had been, ill, and was attending primary school. My stepfather didn't like me so I was always sent up to my bedroom where I would be left on my own until my grandfather, who shared the same room, went to bed.

I hadn't been asleep yet when my grandfather retired. My bed was next to the window and I could see the dusk sky between the curtains and the wall. In the far distance I could see against the otherwise cloudless dusk sky the occasional small white cloud heading towards my window. As one cloud got closer I could see it was ridden (as a horse is ridden) by a small man who had a round pointed helmet, a round shield and carried a trident. The man wore chain mail and had a black bushy beard; he would have been about 12 to 14 inches tall.

I was stunned. He bumped his cloud against my window as if trying to get in, while others were approaching in procession. I was somewhat concerned though not frightened by this event, so asked my grandfather if I could get into bed with him. The light was still on, I got into the side of his bed that was on the opposite side of the window and next to a single wardrobe.

The next thing that does read as slightly odd is that what I took to be the carpet of the room was now wrapped around the wardrobe, a few inches higher at the top, and a few of these men from the clouds were arranged around the top of the wardrobe like soldiers guarding a castle, their lower bodies hidden behind the top edge of the carpet.

The carpet moved as the door of the wardrobe opened and inside was a female fairy. She looked older than me but was still a girl; she had long black hair and would have been maybe three foot in height. Her clothing was white and looked as if it could have been made out of light, for it radiated pure white light. I cannot remember if she had wings or a wand now, as it was so long ago, but she was the classic representation of a child's fairy.

She was looking at me without expression or word, but I would say she had a look of wise concern. Whilst this occurred and after the door closed and everything returned to normal, there was what I have always described as a glowing cobweb of energy stationary and hovering in the corner of the room.

This cobweb of energy was permanently stationed there for about a further two weeks.

I would come home from school, have some tea and then my mother would take me up to bed, still in the light afternoon where I would see this thing. She can still remember me pointing up at it and asking her, 'What's that?' though she could never see it and told me I was having an hallucination. These things were as real to me as anything I've ever seen, though.

Later that year my parents put me in a children's home for a few years.

I have never seen such a thing again since. It was only in my late 20s that I became a Christian and pursued a spiritual train of thought. But I have always wondered about the fairy and why such would come to visit me?

The cobweb of energy I have come to believe may be what people describe as orbs. It would have been around two to three feet diameter. I don't recall it being a sphere, though, but a two-dimensional circle.

Childish imagination, or a young child with the ability to see through to the other realms? It certainly sounds real enough to us!

Brian Froud in *Good Faeries/Bad Faeries* really does hit the nail on the head when he says that 'Faery is a land of paradox, being both outside and within us.' This is precisely what we refer to when we say that the imagination is the most effective way to enter Faerie Land. The imagination is generally perceived to be a mental state in which images are formed at will, but, according to an online dictionary, '... is neither perceived as real nor present to the senses'. We would like to challenge this premise and suggest that, perhaps, in the case of the imagination, where all things are considered possible, we should have an open mind to exactly what is real within the imagination. This is the fertile ground in which reality is sown.

As Dr Robert Anthony says, 'Act as if you have already achieved your goal and it is yours.' There are many books that now show us how the 'imagination' forms the basis for our reality. Each and every thing which humankind creates starts at first as a figment of the imagination. What the mind can create, can become reality. Do we create these things in our imagination or are they already there waiting for us to tap into them? Do we somehow draw down these images from a realm which already exists outside ourselves?

When does it stop being your imagining and become part of reality, and where is the bridge from the imagined to the actual? Your imagination may be as real a place and state, as real as you are sitting, reading, breathing and holding this book now. Your imagination is just a different kind of real – potential reality and a bridge to other parallel worlds such as Faerie Land.

Most novelists will tell you that when they are writing about a storyline or characters, these 'imagined' people in the novel come to have a life and voices of their own. One writer once said that she *had* to sit down and write every day about her characters and describe their narrative. If she didn't write every day she feared that she would miss out on what her characters were up to and the story would have developed further, much like missing an episode of a television drama, and she would not know what was going on! Many writers say that they just listen to what their characters say and then record it. The characters become real. Wallace Stevens sums this up when he says that 'In the world of words, the imagination is one of the forces of nature.' Who's to say what is 'real' and what is not?

This is the kind of imagination that the faeries belong to. Almost a real place that our minds can tap into. It is not a reality that we can touch, but one that we can enter fleetingly and with beneficial results.

So we have discovered that to contact the faeries our imaginations are an essential tool, and because children inhabit the realm of the imagination they are naturally inclined to experience their wonderment. Although there is no reason why as adults we should have to wave the faeries goodbye if we don't want to ... we just have to use our 'imagination'!

Twenty-nine-year-old Susan sent us her story.

Faerie Rings

When I was around four years old I awoke early one summer morning. It was about 6 a.m. and I remember getting out of bed and looking out of my bedroom window. It was a lovely sunny morning with no hint of rain.

Outside the house was a green area, and I sat watching as light, about the size of a golf ball, appeared moving around on the grass below. It was creamy-white with just a hint of yellow, and looked as though it was purposely creating frosted rings (each about one foot wide) on the grass. There were already a couple of well-defined rings, and it appeared to be making another. It definitely moved with a purpose, as though there was intelligence behind it.

I remember thinking at the time that I was watching a fairy, and that it was creating rings of fog or mist. At that age I thought nothing peculiar of it. It moved slowly and hovered at each point for a couple of seconds, then moved slightly before hovering again and forming another white ring.

It's only as I've got older that I now wonder what it was that I really saw, and can only assume that if it wasn't a fairy, and if I wasn't hallucinating, it must have been ball lightning.

At the time it seemed quite normal, so I never mentioned it to anyone, although I never forgot it. The memory still sits with me quite vividly, so I am absolutely sure it was real, whatever it was.

If you would like to make your own faerie ring, see Chapter 18 for some fun ideas.

Fairy Tales – Fact or Fiction?

Well, a bit of both, actually! In Chapter 7 we explored the origins of the fairy tale, discovering that they are ancient magical and historical knowledge all wrapped up in a morality story that has been watered down over the centuries.

Many stories are called fairy tales, yet they contain no reference to actual faeries whatsoever. This is because the term 'fairy' is used broadly here and may mean that they put the reader in touch with qualities akin to faeries and their realms. Hamilton Wright Mabie in *Fairies Every Child Should Know* suggests that 'In the fairy story, men are not set entirely free from their limitations, but by the aid of the fairies, genii, giants and demons ...' (incidentally all considered to belong to the realm of faerie) '... they are put in command of unusual powers.' For example, in *Rapunzel* the beautiful princess locked in the tower possessed the distinctly fey quality of peculiarly long and luxuriant hair, which eventually gave her the means to escape her prison.

Marie Bruce in *Faerie Magick* points out that fairy tales are rich in 'magickal symbols' linking them to the faeries. She observes that 'midnight ... the number three ... [and] magick mirrors', to name but a few, are elements which reveal themselves and you don't have to look far to unveil the hidden faerie magic.

Each fairy tale is a link to the faeries and perhaps our first experience as children of their realm. As Marie Bruce again rightly comments, 'Faerie Tales hold a key place in faerie magick, as they are the vehicle that first introduces us to the realm of the elementals.' They allow us to passively learn about magic and wonderment without being encumbered. If we draw back to any given fairy tale that we experienced in childhood and unpack the story to reveal the symbolism within, each one is a lesson in magical living in itself.

Let's take one fairy tale as an example. *Sleeping Beauty* has many magical ingredients of ancient symbolism, irrefutably connected with faerie. The core element is the spinning wheel of the thirteenth faerie. Spinning is a faerie attribute and also wielded by Klotho, one of the three Fates who measures out the thread of our lives. Strangely, this tale is also about a life which involves missing time and a life that is very long. In Sleeping Beauty's slumber of 100 years, did she visit the Land of Faerie? The elements for such are all there in the story. For Beauty, along with her whole royal court, falls into an enchanted sleep where, although the rest of the world outside carries on as normal, Beauty and her castle begin an inner journey of dreams. It is said that if you visit the Land of Faerie, when you return time will have moved on, whereas you will return the same age as when you left, although you will have no perception of passing time. A kiss is the only thing that will awaken Beauty's enchanted state. Yet another faerie symbol of power and sexual initiation.

Sleeping Beauty tells us about the power of faerie magic in respect to transformation. Before you come to know the faeries and magic you could be sleeping through life in respect to spiritual awareness. Magic and wonderment can awaken you to a new destiny. There are many interpretations that we can place upon the symbolism within *Sleeping Beauty*. Maybe it has awakened a personal meaning for you? Take any of the fairy tales – everyone has a favourite – and see if you can unpack the spiritual and magical meaning. For as children we read fairy tales in the dreamy state of childhood, and as adults we may awaken to their true meaning and magical wisdom.

(For information about fairy tale authors, see Chapter 9.)

Magic in Everyday Life ... Start Young

Most of us will have performed our first piece of magic by the time we are one year old. The tradition of blowing out the candles on our birthday cake and making a wish is a ritual performed in many places throughout the world. Many rituals and rhymes become part of our everyday life and are so natural that we are not even aware that we perform them.

When we spill salt, a natural cleanser (and used in purification and clearing), many would throw the salt over their shoulder to prevent bad luck. In some parts of the world it is bad luck if a black cat crosses your path, but in other parts of the world it is considered good luck. Different traditions, different places. Humans are very powerful beings with the ability to manifest on many levels. Magic is 'thought made good'.

We can choose to include magic in our lives or not; it's our choice. Begin introducing the most powerful magic of all to children from the earliest age by letting them know that they have the ability to manifest goodness in their lives. Manifestation comes about as confidence, the confidence to succeed in their chosen path. Most people realize that they can do pretty much anything they set their mind to once they try.

Jacky: Most millionaires the world over succeed because they always 'knew' that they would. Failure is another step on the journey to success. When I first heard about this magical ability, I was told, 'If you think you can't ...you're right, but if you think you can, you're right too.' Teach this magic to your children and always back up their goals ... you'll be teaching them a wonderful tool for life.

Creative Ways for Children to Connect with the Faeries

Children of both sexes delight in making things for and with the faeries. All these activities use their imaginations and inspire them creatively. If you have children, grandchildren, nieces or nephews or even work with children, all these tried-and-tested faerie projects will bring wonderment and joy.

FAERIE WALK

Make faeries the theme of your nature walks with children and the whole thing becomes a more magical journey. Take along your camera to photograph in hidden glades, or just search at the base of trees for natural 'faerie doors'. Help children to weave stories around their experiences. (See Chapter 18 for more details about photographing faeries.)

Share with them the secrets of the faeries' favourite trees and plants (check the lists in this book), and show them how to make magical daisy chains to hang around their necks. Watch out for pretty mushrooms and toadstools (remind them not to pick them, as so many can be poisonous), and search out faerie rings and natural-looking 'faerie' paths through the shrubbery!

Learn the names of butterflies and birds as part of your nature walks – all things in nature connect back to the faeries! Or create a list of things to tick off when you find them – maybe drawing pictures as you go. You could take a book with you so that you can identify species of plants and wildlife on your travels.

When you get home, your children can make a faerie 'map' of your local woodland, drawing in the most likely places for faerie homes, or draw some potential sightings – who knows? Children can be very perceptive and they may already have spotted the wee folk with their 'inner eye'.

FAERIE DOLLS

Old dolls can be recycled into faerie dolls. You can use old scraps of flower-strewn fabrics or fine pieces of netting to create skirts and faerie dresses. Felt is useful for shoes because it does not fray, or you can glue pieces into place if you are intending to keep your masterpiece afterwards.

Try adding silk flowers and leaves – these are especially pretty woven into faerie hats and crowns. You can also use natural dried flowers, although these would need gluing into place by an adult using a hot glue gun to keep them secure. Consider adapting seed heads, pine cones and so on to make jewellery and shoes – heaps of fun!

Make your own faerie dolls at the same time as your children … you won't be able to help yourself! If you're pleased with the result, consider framing them in a wooden box frame.

Faerie Dollhouses

If you have a creative woodworker in your home you might be able to persuade them to create a faerie dollhouse. Adapt an old log by cutting out dollhouse windows and doors, or transform an existing dollhouse. If not, you can glue bark to the side of an old wooden box and then the creative fun really begins. Even a strong cardboard box has potential.

Decorate the outside of your faerie house with flower pots (green tube lids or bottle lids filled with dried or silk flowers). Create a faerie house name using cardboard, or mould one out of dry set modelling clay (ask your local craft shop for this clay, which comes in a wide range of colours). Maybe even add faerie lights to the outside and weave in and out greenery that you glue to the frame of your faerie home. 'Grow' dried flowers outside your faerie house.

Inside, look for 'rustic'-style dollhouse furniture or make your own. Paint or decorate in natural colours. Imagine a magical mirror (a compact mirror decorated with leaves and seeds, perhaps), a faerie bed (a cardboard box with layers of gauze and netting in greens and golds decorated with fabric flowers), a faerie kitchen (mini jars of honey, bread and bottles of faerie milk or cream made with clay, plastic tubing and pieces of cork as bottle tops) … and all the faeries' favourite foods. You can make fairy cakes – using your clay.

Make your own faerie pictures to hang on the wall. Raid your local dollhouse shop for catalogues of images, or look online for inspiration. Let your imagination run wild … you know you want to! Just remember that many adults collect dollhouses so it's a perfectly legitimate activity for adults too … as if you needed an excuse!

DRESSING UP

Many toy shops and fancy-dress shops sell children's dressing-up clothes and faerie wands and crowns, or you can have some fun and make your own with tin foil and glitter! If Grandma or Aunty is good with the sewing machine, then get them stitching up some gorgeous Faerie Queen gowns. If you prefer the pixie look, then consider green waistcoats, brown trousers and a green felt hat decorated with feathers – very Robin Hood. You can even buy faerie wings and pixie ears (made of latex) from specialist shops on the Internet, so that you can really get in the mood.

FAERIE TEA PARTY

Have a faerie tea party in the garden. Remember to lay a pretty cloth, and use your children's china tea set (many toy shops sell these). You could have a picnic cloth or take outside your children-sized tables and chairs. Don't forget to dress for the occasion.

Make your own necklaces by threading seed heads onto elastic. Perfect for wearing in your very own faerie house …

MAKING A FAERIE HOUSE

This is a little different from the faerie dollhouse described above, as this is a creation which is entirely made from natural materials. This is perhaps an addition to your faerie altar and somewhere that the faeries may come to visit when you are not around! It is a place to leave your faerie gifts and to decorate seasonally as you feel inspired. Here's how:

Decide on the size of your faerie house and how much room you have to accommodate it. Some faerie houses can even be outside structures, so if you prefer this, you can think even bigger!

First, find a wooden base. This can be a natural piece of flat wood that you have found in the woods, or it can be the base of a wooden pallet, for example. It really doesn't matter, as this part is going to be covered up later.

Once you have found your base, you need to decide what your design will be. For younger children it may be easier to make a 'wigwam' type of structure, as all you do is find three sticks of the same length and put them together at the tips. Tie them together with wool, ribbon or string. Then place this frame onto your wooden base. All that's left to do is to find some suitable fabric to cover your frame. Finding a faerie colour such as green, purple, black, red or silver is appropriate. Cover your base with moss or the same material as your frame. Now it's time to decorate! Use finds from nature to adorn your faerie home, such as feathers, shells, stones and crystals. Make it so beautiful and inviting that any faerie would be delighted to visit.

If you are a little more ambitious, then a faerie house with four sides can be constructed with more adult involvement. Four holes need to be drilled at each corner of your wooden base. Each needs to be big enough to fit a stick, but not so big that your sticks wobble! Once you have your stick frame in place, then you need to put in place the walls and floor. This can be material in a faerie colour draped over the sticks and a hole cut in the front for the door. Cover the floor with moss or material and then decorate your faerie house. If you are making an outdoors faerie house, then thin fabric may not be a suitable cover and you may want to use straw, rushes or a waterproof material, for example.

And inside the house: whichever design you have made, once you have decorated the outside you can really go to town with your imagination. There is a lot of scope for making it a welcoming place for the faeries. Illuminate your faerie house at night. If it's outdoors, get an expert to fix up some pretty garden lights.

Leave little gifts for the faeries in natural containers. For example, honey, milk, cream, a tiny slice of cake or bread left out in half a walnut shell or a sea shell. Children will delight in leaving these little gifts out for the faeries at bedtime. In fact, if you are a grown-up it's great fun too!

Decorate your faerie house to reflect the season. At Christmas you can string fairy lights around the roof and use Christmas tree decorations to hang from the corners of your house. At Halloween place some ornamental gourds (or mini pumpkins) on the doorstep. In spring you can sprinkle dried flowers on the roof and place a small pot of miniature daffodils by the front door. Children absolutely love the concept of a faerie house and the idea of making a magical home for the faeries. It is a really special project which can be very consuming and provide hours of fun. Let your imagination run riot. Don't forget, even if you don't have any children to help you, this is no excuse for not having some creative fun and bringing some of that childhood magic back into your life.

Jacky: If you want to make something more permanent than this, consider adapting a garden shed. When my girls were little we had several different garden-shed houses. One of them had an upstairs level and stairs but it was always too small to be useful. The best one we ever had was a little larger than a normal children's play shed. It had a barn door (in which the top of the door opens independently if you wish) and pretty windows.

We made chintz curtains (a 'must' in any faerie house), which closed properly, of course. Our faerie home had carpet on the floor which, although not terribly authentic, meant that the shed was a comfortable and warm place to play. We added trellis up the side and grew honeysuckle and roses. Each daughter owned one of the flower pots outside the front door of the house – a trip to the local garden centre soon had them filled (although older children might enjoy growing plants from seeds, younger children want results NOW!).

Let your imagination run wild.

MAKING A FAERIE LADDER

Such a simple idea, but beautifully effective. All you need to make these are two long and straight sticks found in the woods, garden or brought from the garden centre. These make the main structure of the ladder, then you need lots of little sticks which are approximately the same thickness and length. Wool, cotton or string will effectively secure these together.

Place your two long sticks parallel to one another on a table. Then, to make the rungs of the ladder, place on top of the two sticks, evenly spaced apart, your smaller 'rung' sticks. Once you have it all arranged so that it looks like a real ladder, but in miniature, secure the rungs to the outer sticks with your thread. This needs to be wound around each rung and can be a little fiddly, so adult help may be needed to tie knots etc. This project is fun to do, as children imagine faeries climbing up the ladders as they are making them.

Once you have your faerie ladder, here's how you can use it. If you have made a faerie house or dollhouse as described above, then the ladder can be placed on the outside, or inside for the faeries to use as stairs! If you have a garden, you can place these little ladders against trees and shrubs for little faerie feet to climb! Place on a bird table, against a flower pot, next to the cat flap! Your children's imagination will find the perfect place, and if you manage to make a few of these (they can be addictive), they look so enchanting, as if you have magical visitors to your garden.

These faerie ladders really do encourage the faeries to visit your home or garden, as they work on the same principle as making a faerie altar. The faeries will be very pleased indeed to have things made in their honour. Any project such as this which uses the imagination so creatively will encourage the fey into your life.

MAKING A FAERIE DOOR

This can be made from wood, cardboard or even clay. The idea behind a faerie door is that when placed against or attached to a wall or human-sized door, this is then the faeries' own entrance to your house! As they are astral beings they are able to pass through objects; making an actual door for them is simply a symbolic way of inviting the fey to your home. Children will love the idea of this project. If you are making the cardboard version, this needs very little adult supervision.

For all versions, cut out a template for the shape of your faerie door. This is traditionally an old-fashioned arch-shaped door, the sort you would find in a secret garden, for example. However, this is your faerie door and the choice is ultimately up to you. Whatever reminds you of faerie is just fine. Then use your paper template to create the faerie door from cardboard, wood or clay. If you are using cardboard, of course it is fun to colour or paint it to attract the faeries. Don't forget to draw a door knocker and a keyhole!

Faerie doors are now so popular that they can be ordered from and made by craftsmen. See the Resources Directory at the back of this book if you would like to buy a ready-made one.

CHAPTER 13

The Land of Faerie

'The fairy world is just like ours – there bloom again our faded flowers …'
JOHN PETER ALLAN (1825–48)

A Place of Enchantment

Never has a place been more shrouded in mystery, longing, myth and entrancing fascination. The Land of Faerie is to many people a symbol of childhood dreams, a place of hope that magic may still exist; where glamour, beauty and fairy tales are eternal. However, in Celtic times Faerie Land took on different meanings, as the place where the soul travelled on its way to the Otherworlds – and there are many more ancient beliefs where that one came from.

The Land of Faerie is all of these things and more. If you have even a snippet of wonderment within your being, then Faerie Land still has the power to delight and enthral you and bring light to the darkest of days. It's a place of transformation, healing, bewitchment, magic and love; let us explore this magical realm and un-turn the stone to the entrance of the Land of Faerie.

Where Is Faerie Land?

The faerie realm has no geographical location, for when Peter Pan said 'Second to the right and straight on till morning,' he really summed it up. There are ancient sites which have long been considered to be entrances to this land, but you can't find Faerie Land on a map because it is other-dimensional. It is on the cusp with our reality and co-exists in our world, but it also inhabits a state that is only accessible when we come loose from our physical bodies. Faerie Land is known as an astral realm, where it has been linked to such places as heaven and hell and the old Celtic Otherworlds and Underworlds. This ancient idea where souls travel after death is also true of the belief that the Otherworlds were also home to the souls who were yet to be born in our world. It is truly the place of dreaming, of imaginings, safe haven and astral travel.

Faerie Land can be very much a place of dreams and magic ... we can wish ourselves there (although traditionally it can be a dangerous place; make sure you are well protected!).

'... Ah no along the paths of song do all the tiny folk belong ...'
Paul Laurence Dunbar

Can We Visit?

This brings us on to our next question: if Faerie Land is a place we can't ordinarily go to in our physical bodies, how can we visit? That is the beauty of Faerie Land: we may visit in this life and the next, in our sleep and when awake. It is a multi-dimensional place and, because we are able to go there in our present life, we are able to stay connected to this spiritual dimension – to touch a part of God and remind ourselves of the real meaning to our lives.

Jacky: I've had many out-of-body experiences myself, and some of these were spontaneous. Although most of my own flights have been around my home and local neighbourhood, I've spoken to many who have travelled to other realms. Science questions whether these realms exist outside ourselves or in our own minds ... I know what I believe, but perhaps it doesn't matter after all?

When we are sleeping, we often come loose from our physical bodies and astral-travel. Some people also practise astral travel consciously, and this is an art which has to be learned (Jacky has done this herself and wrote about her experiences in her book *An Angel Saved My Life, and other true stories of the afterlife* (published by HarperElement).

Visiting the Land of Faerie is also possible through our imaginations and dreams, meditations and visualization. All these states of mind do not belong to the everyday realm of consciousness and intersect with Faerie Land if we wish to go there. This is also something which can be practised and learned; later on in this chapter we have included a visualization especially for those who would like to begin working regularly on journeys to the faeries' realm.

The more often the visualization is practised, the more effective your journeying will be and the more vivid your experience … practice certainly makes perfect in this case! It can seem as if nothing happens for such a very long time and then, miraculously, we break through to an alternative existence – where the magic begins to happen. We both believe that astral travel can be an amazing psychic tool. You can travel as far as your confidence will allow. Fear will certainly hold you back. Make sure you read up on other people's journeys and experiences first of all. If you are armed with knowledge, then it will help your confidence no end. Feeling (and being) safe is important, so do read all the tips on working with and visiting faeries before you start.

Oh, and if you prefer a more hands-on method of reaching the faerie realms, it is said that if you touch a fairy rock with a posy of primroses, as long as it contains the right number of blossoms (try five) you can open the way to Faerie Land and faerie gifts. Take care, though: if you use the wrong number of flowers, it is said to bring about certain doom! Here is another of Alicen's experiences.

Faerie Land in a Bubble

I had been writing about Faerie Land a lot in the few days leading up to this experience, so it had definitely been on my mind. It was a Sunday morning and I was in the lovely drifting place between sleeping and waking. This all changed in an instant as an image was plunged into my head as if a bolt of lightning had struck it there! I could see an image of our world, and within that world was a bubble which contained what looked like a splendid Faerie Castle. This bubble fitted into our world exactly, although I knew that we couldn't see it and I knew that they were showing me Faerie Land.

Then the faeries spoke, saying that this was the Land of Faerie they were showing me. They said that it was a hidden place within our world. They explained that the Land of Faerie was not a realm outside our world, but one that existed, mostly concealed, around and about us all the time. They also said that if we wanted to see and touch faeries we had to become attuned to this hidden world, because really they are only a thought away …

> '… O'er the mountain, through the wild wood,
> Where his childhood loved to play …'
> THE FAIRY BOY, SAMUEL LOVER

Doorways to the Land of Faerie

In different cultures Faerie Land is known by other names and all have their own ancient portals, considered magical places of entry to this realm. In England Faerie Land has many portals, one of the most well-known being Glastonbury Tor, which was once the Isle of Avalon. Faerie Queen Morgan Le Fay is the protectress of this particular faerie doorway together with Gwynn ap Nudd, who is the Welsh Faerie King. Glastonbury Tor is believed to lead to this faerie kingdom, Annwn/Annwfn, which is the Welsh Faerie Land.

In Scotland, Faerie Land is known as Elphame/Elfame/Elfhame, which means 'Elf Home'. Doorways to the Scottish faerie realm are many and are very often in faerie mounds. These are burial mounds, which are common in the UK and usually date back to Neolithic times. In fact, any mound, whether burial, barrow or buried ancient site, is considered to have magical faerie properties. The fey are thought to make their homes in them, and there are even stories that they glow at certain phases of the moon when the faeries are revelling. They are thought to be passages to the Otherworld from this world to the next.

In Ireland, Faerie Land is known as Tir na n-og, which means The Land of Youth, because no one ever becomes old there. It is the Otherworld nirvana of the Irish Celts.

Lakes are also sometimes considered to be entrances to the Land of Faerie, with underground faerie palaces located at the bottom of the lake. Water is a constant magical feature in faerie lore and certain rivers, streams, seas and wells are all thought to be portals to the magical realms.

Visualization to Elphame

This visualization is split into sections so that it is approached in three parts which all follow on from one another: the Pathway, Elphame, and Wish Me Home.

Find a comfortable place and a peaceful time for this exercise to the Scottish Land of Faerie: Elphame. Close your eyes and take a few deep breaths and once you feel in a relaxed state you may begin.

The Pathway

First visualize your guardian angel behind you, bringing their protective presence to you throughout this exercise. Ask in your own words that they guide and protect you. Once you are satisfied that you have vividly visualized their presence, concentrate on feeling relaxed and receptive.

See before you a pathway. There is nothing else except this to focus on and it is important that you visualize this pathway in glorious detail, for this is your pathway to Elphame.

You stand at the beginning of the path and see it stretching before you, as far as your eye can see. It is winding and wending its way to a destination that you can't yet see. The pathway is an illusion that you will build, an illusion because Elphame is reached by way of desire and a wish, not by a direct route. The pathway to Elphame is a paradox in faerie lights, and the only way to enter that realm is by building the path in your mind and not actually walking it.

Confused yet? Don't worry about how you are going to reach your destination – just visualize and sit back and enjoy the ride, for enjoying the journey is all part of the magic.

Now, in your imagination, look down at your feet. You see that the path is made from springy, velvety moss: the most luxurious and perfect moss that you have ever seen. Of course it can't be ordinary moss, but one that holds hidden secrets.

Now take one little step. As you do so, you see the moss light up with a luminous emerald-green glow. The light illuminates your shoes and bathes the mossy path in a luminescent shimmer, for just a fleeting instant.

Stand still on the pathway for a few moments and simply look down at the moss. As you look closer you will see peppered within the mossy carpet starlight and sparkles, glittering and winking at you as if you are walking upon magic itself.

Now walk a little way along the path. With each step that you take, see the emerald light surrounding you. Also with every footstep the glittering starlights bounce up and envelop you. It is as if at every step you shower yourself with a powder puff of glistening faerie dust.

The further you walk upon the path, the more encompassed you become in shimmering green light and sparkles of starlight. The light and shimmering dust have now risen so high that they dance around your head and before your eyes.

You are all at once surrounded in a brilliance of green light and stardust. You are so engulfed that you can't now see the pathway ahead. You are encircled by elfin magic. Take a few moments just to take in the experience and watch closely the dancing spectacle of light and luminosity.

Elphame

Now comes your wish. Ask for Elphame to be revealed to you and concentrate on this wish. See the light and stardust evaporate away and in their place is a green wooden doorway directly before you.

The doorway is an arch shape, as if it belongs to an old chapel or secret walled garden. Now all you have to do is gently push the door and it will open for you.

Walk through the doorway. Now you discover that you have entered a Faerie Mound. All around you are earthy walls and the floor is a continuous carpet of moss. Upon the earthy walls are fixed flaming torches to illuminate your way. You are in a short passageway that you now make your way along. Feel safe in this environment, for you are in the womb of the earth and the heart of magic.

As you reach the end of the earthy passageway it suddenly turns a tight corner. As you follow the corner around you are presented with another green wooden door, similar to the first one, only somewhat smaller. The doorway is so much smaller that you realize that you will not be able to pass through it.

As you come to the door you begin to hear strains of enchanting and melodic music that seems to enter you, not only through your ears but through the pores of your skin and every particle of your body.

Now tap gently on the wooden door three times. Now you will be granted a peek. Simply nudge the door softly and it will open wide for you. You may not enter the doorway, though, for this is not entirely your realm. However, as a visitor you are allowed to sit and respectfully watch and listen to the proceedings.

As the door opens, sit down on the mossy floor and peer through the entrance. Before you is a huge earthy cavern, so vast that it is like a natural cathedral. You are at the position which in a conventional cathedral would be level with the stained-glass windows. In this elfin cathedral are wooden doors all glowing with emerald luminous light instead. You look down upon the gathering of a hundred elves who are illuminated by many wall candles surrounding their reverent atmosphere of song.

As you watch them you realize that they are human-sized, yet quite different. Upon your visit they are all wearing white dresses and robes with hooded cloaks of white velvet. Yet they are surrounded in a shimmering silvery-white glow: as if they are immersed in a shower of moonlight. Each of them holds a candle lantern as they sing.

Every so often you catch a glimpse of one of the exquisitely beautiful faces of both male and female elves. They all have kindly elfin, slanting eyes and singing voices that whisper magic into the air, as if it is almost visible.

You are allowed to watch this elfin spectacle for a few moments. Feel calm and peaceful and simply let the elves infuse you with their restful magic in song. Their singing is enhanced by a few of the elves who play the lyre, a faerie instrument.

After you have watched and listened for a while, a female elf pulls off her white velvet hood. She reveals plaited red, long and lustrous hair and eyes as green as the moss that you sit upon. She looks up at you and looks you straight in the eye. As she blinks her heavy lids it is as if a spell is cast upon that blink and your time in Elphame must draw to a close.

The little wooden door gently falls shut of its own accord and you must now get to your feet.

Wish Me Home …

Although the earthen passageway is warm and gently inviting, with its soft torch-light, it is not your home and you are only a visitor. Now imagine the room that you began your journey from. See any furniture the room may contain, remember where the windows are and see where you are sitting.

Firmly wish yourself back home and say goodbye to the enchanted Elphame which has shared part of its magic with you. Thank your guardian angel and see them vanishing behind you. Now open your eyes. Perform one of the grounding exercises in Chapter 16, and do be polite to the elves and leave them a small gift as a token of your appreciation.

Perform this visualization any time when you feel it would be comforting to be in the company of elves. They do have a healing energy, and Elphame contains and radiates a fragment of God's love which is yours to delve into whenever you feel the need.

CHAPTER 14

Faeries and How We Can Help Them

'Fear closes the door to the magical life.'
TED ANDREWS, *THE ENCHANTMENT OF THE FAERIE REALM*

The Future Is Faerie

It has been a long time since the faerie race has been as close to us as they are now. We are living through a very special time in history, as indeed it has been hundreds of years, according to Katherine Briggs in *A Book of Fairies*, where she says, 'From the time of Chaucer onwards [14ᵗʰ century] the fairies have been said to have departed or to be in decline, but still they linger.' She sadly reports that the fairies left altogether at the beginning of the 19ᵗʰ century, when an account of two children in Aberdeenshire, Scotland was recorded. The children were reported to have seen '… a long cavalcade of small horses and riders being wild and unkempt, wearing … antique jerkins of plaid, long grey cloaks, and little red caps, from which their wild uncombed locks shot out over their cheeks and foreheads'. Fascination overcoming his curiosity, one child asked the last rider in the fey procession, 'What are ye, little mannie? And where are ye going?' The faerie man replied to him: 'Not of the race of Adam … The People of Peace shall never more be seen in Scotland.'

It is thought that the faeries were once much closer to man; however, since we have distanced ourselves from the land and believed that we could become masters of it, instead of being in harmony with it, the faeries in turn have also distanced themselves. They have completely retreated into their own realms and left humans to get on with exploiting our planet.

Wake Up, World

Not until now has the realization occurred to us. We have woken up and it is not only the green activists who are saying that we have to turn back the clock and undo the damage that we have done to our Earth. No longer is being green the domain of the few; all of us are having to think twice about the way we travel, the energy we use, the food we eat, what products we buy and even that suntan cream is now obligatory! We are all paying the price for industrialization and mass consumerism. As a consequence we all know that our lives have to change on a practical level. The faeries know that as a by-product of this eco wake-up call, our spirituality has already shifted and will continue to change for the better.

This is why the faeries are now tentatively making a re-emergence into our world and inevitably into our consciousness. Now that we have remembered that for the human race to survive, we must stop destroying the environment that we rely on, we have also remembered the faeries.

Faeries have a number of ways in which they can reach out to us and touch our thoughts. One of these is predominantly through creative people. The prolific faerie artwork of Cicely Mary Barker, Arthur Rackham and Mabel Lucie Attwell, to name but a few, began to change the way that we viewed faeries. Instead of them being the wicked and mischievous folk that would steal your baby and turn your milk sour, they were now portrayed as childlike, innocent, romantic and utterly enchanting.

This shift in how we view the fey in general set the scene for what was to follow. The faeries sacrificed their true power and grace for a while so that they could pave the way for acceptance by the human race.

They are now just beginning to remind us of who they really are and how much we have forgotten of their power. This in turn rekindles our own spiritual power, which is locked into our relationship with the Earth that we call our home. We are finally discovering and remembering the true nature of faerie, a race with an intrinsic relationship to the land and even us. They are our bridge to enjoying a spiritual relationship with our environment with its natural cycles. They need respect, because the Earth does. They are often exceptionally beautiful, because the Earth is too. They are wild and free because the grass, the trees and the sea are too. They are nature's mirror in a personified form, and the sooner we welcome them back and remember how as a race we used to live alongside them, the sooner our world will heal.

Now can you see why the future is faerie?

A Faerie Is the Earth Calling for Help

We all know that the Earth needs our help to heal and only we can make that change. This message comes to us every day through the news on TV, newspapers, magazines, the weather report and books that we read. Even advertising is sending the message that it is now cool to be green. The fact that the faeries are drawing close to us now is one message to us that they need our help to put things right and restore the balance. The faeries are nature's messengers and are seeping into our daily lives through art, literature, films, product labelling etc. to try to reach out to us and convey their message of help. If the Earth becomes sick, then the spiritual qualities of our land diminish too. A faerie is indeed the Earth's messenger calling for help.

THERE'S NO TIME TO LOSE

Most importantly, though, the faeries also know that there is hope and that we can restore the Earth to its full physical beauty. We are able to learn respect once again and regain a sense of harmony. The faeries are emerging, but they would like to be here to stay. It seems very significant that they have emerged to ask for our help, for such wise beings would not offer their hand of friendship if they didn't think that there was at least a good chance of us succeeding. The message to us is also that there is no time to lose and we must act now to make change.

THE COLLECTIVE UNCONSCIOUS AT WORK?

Many people around the world are also recognizing this shift and fey presence. They are receiving similar messages about the faeries' role in the ability for the Earth to heal. Doreen Virtue, in her beautiful book *Healing with the Fairies* recognizes this and has received messages from the fey conveying the same. The faeries impressed upon her that '... we can all put our collective hearts and minds together to reach the common goal of a cleansed and healthy Mother Earth'.

What Can We Do to Help the Faeries?

By helping the faeries we are also helping ourselves. We are taking steps to heal the environment and also re-forging our spiritual link with the realms of fey. Doreen Virtue received the faeries' message to us: 'Please tell them about the power that even one person has to impact the environment positively.' Every one of us can make a difference to our environment. So what can you do?

- Don't be a litter-bug. Litter harms wildlife and spoils our environment. If you visit a natural place to picnic or walk, leave it cleaner than when you first came. Bring along some plastic bags to clean up the mess you and others have made. Encourage children not to drop litter in the first place.

Jacky: My own daughters remember a speech I gave when they were young, which went something like 'If everyone were to leave a sweet paper on the floor, how long before the world becomes one big trash can?' It seemed to do the trick anyway. It's easy to get into the habit of saying, 'Just one piece won't matter,' but of course it does.

WHAT DO YOU DO IF YOU SEE OTHERS LITTER?

Jacky: I remember sitting in my car in our local shopping centre car park one day. The woman in front of me was enjoying a meat pasty meal and was rubbing her hands out of the window, brushing off the pastry onto the car park floor. This was quickly followed by the paper bag and the plastic which wrapped her meal! I was cross but decided to handle it gently. Getting out of the car I picked up her litter and handed it back to her, saying, 'You seem to have dropped this by mistake.'

The woman looked very embarrassed and said, 'Sorry,' whilst her friend in the car chastised her, 'I told you not to throw it out of the window!' The gentle approach can work well with others, so try this first of all.

If you see litter anywhere, always pick it up and take it home. Get into the habit of taking a plastic bag out with you and make it a rule never to walk past litter without picking it up. Imagine what a difference it would make if each person picked up just one piece of litter every day and placed it into a wastepaper basket?

If you live in a countryside or coastal area, then you can join in the local annual clean-up schemes which are often run by the council or environmental group. If there isn't one in your area, why not start one?! As well as helping your own corner of the world, these can be great fun and social events when you can get to know your community better.

Alicen: Over the past couple of years my family and I have become involved in the Orkney version of one of these clean-up schemes called 'Bag the Bruck'. (Bruck is an Orcadian term for rubbish/trash.) This means that each spring many locals join together on a special day to collect litter from the seashores and general environment. It is mostly debris which has been blown or swept ashore by the winter storms.

Our children absolutely love 'Bag the Bruck' day and set one another a challenge to see who can collect the most bags of bruck. They did so well that they wrote to the children's BBC show *Blue Peter* and earned themselves a badge! The local press also gets involved and prints articles and photos of the most industrious bruckers and often people who have found unusual things on the beach, the most recent being a real message in a bottle!

Have fun collecting and walk in groups chattering or singing as you go – wear gloves and make a litter-picker for yourself (a stick with a bent nail on the end to help gather small pieces of paper). Children can use a special 'grabber' created for the disabled or elderly.

- Create a wild patch in your garden. Do not cut the grass there and grow some wild flowers, particularly varieties that will attract butterflies and bees. You could even make it a place where you leave presents for the faeries.

  By creating a wild garden you will not only be helping insects and wild animals, but you should soon notice that the atmosphere is different from the rest of your garden. Invite the faeries in by hanging gentle-sounding wind chimes from a tree. Decorate patches of earth with crystals and unusual seashells and grow some herbs, as their energy is known to be very harmonious and healing. You may create such a peaceful setting that you can use this wild place as your sanctuary to meditate and visualize the faeries when the weather is warm. (See Chapter 2 for more details.)

- Feed the birds. This is such a simple act, which takes very little time and effort. The faeries are really impressing upon us to look after our wildlife. Everyone can do this one, even if you live in a tower block in the city. We all have access to a local park where you can take food along to feed the birds. (For more information see Chapter 2.)

- Write to your MP on any 'green' issue which you would like to see change. OK, so maybe this is not the most exciting suggestion on the list! However, just think that if everyone who reads this book wrote just one letter, what a difference it could make!

Alicen: For example, only yesterday I filled in a form on the government's website as they were asking for voters' comments and ideas on the coming year's policies, one of them being their proposed action to reverse climate change. It took only 15 minutes out of my day to propose they try to get manufacturers to reduce packaging for the consumer, thus cutting down on the landfill site legacy we are inevitably going to be leaving for our children. Who knows? I may have made a difference and I also felt much better for getting it off my chest!

- If you know of a natural place which is under threat from thoughtless people, such as litter-bugs, fly-tippers or developers, here's what you can do.

An Elven Protection of Place Spell

Use the preparation techniques for meditation outlined in Chapter 16. Once you have closed your eyes, simply visualize the place in nature which you feel requires protection and healing. Now imagine a vibrant and protective beam of light surrounding that place in a circle of luminosity. Imagine a vibrant sphere of light sparkling with tiny stars and faerie dust; make it magical. Also send loving thoughts to that place and ask your guardian angel/Faerie King/Queen etc. to help you in this task.

Then ask the faeries who dwell in that place to help you too. Sometimes they will give you an answer straight away. For example, you may see a ring of mushrooms pop up in your meditation or a troop of elves walking around the perimeter of your chosen place. You may feel the help being transmitted to you with feelings of love. You may even get a physical sign. Not everybody will receive their answer straight away.

Once you have visualized the sphere of light and asked for the help of the faeries, mentally or aloud just say, 'The spell is done.' Open your eyes and leave a small gift out for the fey, ideally in the place that you asked for protection.

Alicen: Recently my Faerie Ring and I knew of a place that needed protection. At our Faerie Circle we asked the faeries to help us protect the place and performed the spell above together. A couple of days after the spell I was walking past the place in question and saw that there was a perfect ring of red-capped mushrooms which had popped up overnight. A sure sign of faerie activity!

Jacky: I remember a few years ago that the centre of my Staffordshire village was getting scruffy and litter-strewn. Several friends and I asked for higher assistance to help with this small corner of our world. Within days people began painting their houses, placing pots of flowering plants and collecting litter … coincidence? You decide!

- Find out all you can about how you can undo global warming. See our Faerie Resources Directory at the back of the book, where we have done a lot of the hard work for you in the special 'Be a Green Faerie' section. There are stacks of ideas on how to live green on websites and in the books and magazines listed there.

- Plant a tree in your own garden or get involved with local projects to 'green up' an area. Plant more flowers – put a flowering plant pot on your desk at work, herbs on your windowsill and flowering tubs by your back door!

Jacky: We had a profusion of poppies in our front garden one year and I had great fun collecting the seeds which I spread under the trees around my local lake! Imagine the surprise for everyone when the poppies came into bloom the following year! (Do bear in mind that the birds love the poppy seeds too, so make sure some are hidden away if you want to try this yourself.)

What the Faeries Want Us to Learn

Whatever way we engage and connect with nature, we are also connecting with the faeries, whether we realize it or not. It does not matter if you are not the meditating type or you live in the city. If you make any conscious efforts to connect with nature and improve the environment, the faeries will be thankful and you will have achieved on a personal and also a collective level one more step towards bringing the Earth, and ultimately the faeries, back into harmony.

This is just the beginning of our journey as humans to remembering and deepening the relationship we have with our Earth and the spiritual dimensions. Not everyone who goes on a beach clean-up day will see a faerie or realize that they are also helping to make ripples in the Unseen realms, and not everyone will want to be a part of that aspect of it. For those who do, recognizing and working with the fey realms is a wonderfully magical bonus and something that will make your life all the sweeter.

Faerie Fans Stop Builders

Before closing this chapter we want to share one last word with this lovely story reported by a UK newspaper.

On the 21ˢᵗ November 2005, *The Times* ran the headline, 'Faeries stop developers' bulldozers in their tracks.' The newspaper went on to explain how villagers in St Fillans, Perthshire asked builders not to move a rock on a proposed building site for new houses, for fear that it would harm the local faeries.

This particular rock, which rose from the middle of a field, was surrounded by the Dundurn mountains. In the 6ᵗʰ century the Celtic missionary St Fillan visited the area with the intention of converting the Picts from the pagan darkness of superstition. Builders thought that phone calls about local faeries were nothing more than a joke, but later they even tried to work around the rock, hoping to keep the locals happy!

Local people felt that the rock (as with all 'standing stones') had special historical significance, and that this particular rock had even had kings crowned upon it. We can't say if the rock stayed or went, but local planners say that local customs and beliefs have to be taken into account before permission is given for building works to go ahead! No doubt the faeries would have had their say!

CHAPTER 15

Faerie Transformation

'The healing energy that is raised in contact with nature can be sent out into the world.'
ROSEMARY ELLEN GUILEY, *FAIRY MAGIC*

The Keepers of Transformation

There is no one faerie or group of faeries who are the guardians of transformation. ALL faeries, even the ones you wouldn't want to meet in a dark alley, hold transformation as one of their key roles. It is impossible for anyone to have any kind of faerie experience without it touching a deep part of them. Call it a necessary side effect if you like. Faeries connect with us through transformation; that is how they work. If you do not want to begin an inner journey of self-discovery, then do not seek the faeries! For this is one of their gifts to us. The dictionary definition of transformation is 'a change or alteration, esp. a radical one'. This is exactly what we mean when we talk about transformation in connection with the faeries. So hold on to your seats ...

Faeries Help Us to Heal Ourselves

Faeries are the angels of transformation, holding our hands through personal crisis. If you ask the faeries for help they will hold your hand and never let it go until you are safely out of the darkness and into the sunlight.

The way that they work with us is of course not ordinary, but magical. By magical – as Marcia Zina Mager says in her book *Believing in Faeries* – we do not mean '... casting spells or making elephants disappear. Magic is a natural state of wonderment.' The faeries want to make us aware of the magical process of life itself and of the transformation potential which arises from simply becoming aware of this. It is also wise to heed the certainty that the fey will not always instantly wave a magic wand to cure all ills and predicaments. If you ask for their help in any healing, be it something physical, emotional or a situation, the faeries will point us in the right direction. They illuminate the path of shadows so that we can find the light. This is their versatility and that is why they are able to facilitate transformation. They know and walk with us through all the spectrums of human emotion. In his book *Good Faeries/Bad Faeries*, Brian Froud sums up this self-healing process when he observes that 'on the portal to Faeryland are carved two words of magic and power: Know thyself'.

This is the key to faerie magic, and indeed any magic. The faeries will hand you the key to assist your own healing. Faeries shine a magical mirror onto ourselves, a mirror laced with shimmering, dazzling elfin lights. They let us see our soul lights and, if we have the patience to look, we will see our true potential as well as the answers we are seeking. Our answers will be waiting for us, sometimes in twilight and mysteries, of course, for faeries will rarely hand you an answer on a plate. Discovering the pathway to an answer is as valuable as the answer itself.

If you have ever read Doreen Virtue's book *Healing with the Fairies* you will see a classic example of a faerie transformation in Doreen's own journey at a challenging time in her life. Doreen's experience is a wonderful example of how working and listening to the faeries can give a magical dimension to life-changing experiences. Faeries will give us answers, if only we know how to ask.

Asking for Faerie Healing

No one can ask for you; this is a step into self-empowerment and the first step along the illuminated pathway. There are many effective methods for asking for healing. The main thing to remember is that although asking is easy, listening for the answers may require a little more practice. Do not always expect the answers to be given at the time of asking, either. Remember that the faeries may thread your answers in their own magical way through your daily life.

Awakening to the possibility of magic makes listening all the easier. Answers and ways to heal may come to you in any form. Expect the unexpected! You may read something significant in a book or magazine, or see an aspect of a film that suddenly jumps out at you. You may experience the spiritual dimension of nature for yourself. Standing on the beach and just observing the waves lap over the shore can speak answers loud and clear to those who have attuned themselves to listening carefully.

Magical messages can be found in conversations, a walk in the park or even a crowded high street. Think of your life as a dream where you have to decipher the symbols within it to find the meaning. How magical it is to think that you are waking from a mundane dream into a faerie world! Once you have awoken to the faeries, it is like a knowledge that cannot be lost; you can never go back to the way you were before.

Here is a beautiful faerie healing story from Margaret who works with the ancient system of healing called Reiki.

Reiki Faeries

I used to rent space in a local salon to perform my Reiki treatments. Once during a Reiki healing session I was working on a woman patient when a strange thing happened during the treatment. I was working on my client, starting at the top of her head, when the next thing I remember is using the Reiki energy over her feet area. I had a whole load of missing time! When I had finished, instead of the hour session the woman had booked, I realized we had been in that room for over two hours!

I don't remember most of the healing but memories started to surface later. Over the next few days I began to recall, in my 'mind's eye', a journey. I felt that I was travelling through the universe and I could see stars. I wasn't able to see myself but I did see a group of fairies holding on to a silver cord and they were all giggling as we flew along. It sounded beautiful, like tiny bells jingling …. maybe those faeries had something to do with the healing and the missing time!

PRAYER

The faeries, like any other divine beings, will hear and respond to your prayers for healing and help. If you don't have a particular faerie in mind to address your prayer to, just saying, 'Dear faeries …' is fine. A time of quiet and solitude, if only for a few moments, is the best condition for prayerful time. You may also find that just by confiding in the faeries and knowing that they always listen will be of help too. Sometimes with prayer, answers can be instantaneous; at other times you may have to wait for a faerie-threaded answer. Most often it will be a combination of both.

Prayers are said to be 'talking to God' in the way that meditation is 'listening to God'. Faeries are God's helpers of the Earth and nature in the way that angels are God's helpers of humankind and the planets. Your faerie messages of prayer will all pass through God's hands first of all and be translated through His faerie helpers.

A FAERIE HEALING SPELL

In Chapter 17 there is a healing spell outlined in detail with guidance for you to try. Working a faerie healing spell is like active prayer. You may like to think of faerie spell-work as a prayer with added dynamite! When you are performing a spell you are being very precise with your request and actively calling upon specific faerie realms and beings to assist you and, most importantly, the aid of faerie magic. A prayer can be likened to a passive wish and a spell to a focused wish. The other difference between prayers and spells is that a spell usually takes a lot more preparation and effort.

The rituals that we use help us to spotlight our requests, as if we were looking through a magnifying glass. The rituals we use help us to focus our minds and concentrate on the task in hand.

You can work a faerie healing spell for yourself, for others or even for animals or locations. The person who needs healing does not need to be present. As long as you know their name and the condition that they need healing for, you can ask the faeries to send their healing energy directly to that person. If you would like to send healing to someone, it is a matter of courtesy to ask permission first, of course, although in emergencies it is OK to ask the 'higher self' or 'consciousness' of the person in question. In the case of animal or location healing this is not possible and you will just have to ask the faeries to send healing if it is appropriate. The faeries are extremely sensitive to animals and, of course, places, and they will know.

SPELL TIME

If there is an emergency, any time is suitable to send a healing spell. However, if there is time to plan working your spell, the optimum natural tide will magnify your spell's effectiveness. A simple guide for healing spell-work is on a full or waxing moon (the moon increasing to full). On a waning moon (the moon decreasing to a dark moon) you can work banishing magic, such as asking the faeries to help you banish an illness or particular condition which needs to decrease in size, such as a tumour or cyst, for example.

You might also like to use candles in your spell work. See Chapter 17 for more information.

MEDITATION

Faerie healing can also come from meditation, especially if you specifically ask for this. See Chapter 16 for a special healing faerie meditation that you can try for yourself.

The act of meditating can be a very healing experience in itself. Certain elements in a specific curative meditation can be included for this purpose. However, the faeries do communicate with us during meditation, and if you wish to ask a particular question this can be done during a meditation journey. Commonly the response may be given to you in symbols, rather like those in a dream. These symbols may be universal or may have meaning only for you. The most effective way to gain help from a healing meditation is to write your experience down in detail afterwards and ponder on it for a few days. You may find that by thinking over the experience the answers will come to you when you are least expecting it, or even when you are dreaming. If in doubt, the golden rule is always to ASK the faeries themselves to help you decipher your meditation messages. (See the Resources section for faerie CDs that will help you with your meditation.)

Faeries that Protect Us

It is appropriate to ask any benevolent faerie or the faeries in general for protection. There are also specific fey beings, such as many of the faerie kings and queens, as protection is one of their major roles. Help with this can be found in Chapter 6 if you would like protection from a particular faerie and would like to call upon him or her by name.

Faerie protection is afforded for a number of different purposes. You may like faerie protection for practical purposes, such as helping to safeguard your property, car or possessions or even for a person while travelling. Faerie protection can also be requested for such instances as nightmares and protecting yourself and others from someone who may wish you ill.

PRACTICAL PROTECTION

Here's a simple and effective way to help with additional safeguard to property, car or possessions etc. We say 'additional' here as, with any magical work, we must remember that we live in a physical world. This means that all precautionary common-sense measures to protect property etc. should be in place first. Think of this as a 'complementary faerie therapy'.

It is not wise to rely on magic alone for such matters, for it is only sensible to lock your door and install burglar alarms, especially if you live in a city area. However, for that extra peace of mind if you are away and have to leave your house for a while, or have to park your car in a less than congenial area, a little protection spell can make all the difference.

The Faerie Ring of Protection

This is easy to do and can also be performed practically anywhere. It is simple to remember and instantly effective. This method can be worked using faerie dust, handmade or purchased, or by using some finely chopped herbs with protective qualities. Examples of such herbs with faerie and protective traits are nettles, rosemary, cowslip, primrose, wood betony and garlic. You can use these herbs singly or in any combination or all at once; dried or fresh will do fine. The Faerie Ring of Protection also works well without faerie dust or herbs: that is why it can be performed anywhere and at any time. Some people prefer to use a physical focus such as faerie dust or herbs to help them visualize, but they are not crucial.

First, state your protection request to the faeries in general or a particular faerie by name. This should be in your own words, but could be something like this: 'Dear faeries, I ask you to surround…. (insert your protection recipient here) in a Faerie Ring of Protection. Blessed Be.'

It can be as simply worded as this, or longer if you desire. You may also like to ask for a specific date or a particular purpose – for example, if someone is going to have an operation on a certain date. The more focused you are with your request, the more successful you are likely to be. Then visualize a vibrant ring of sparkling white, silver or golden light around the intended recipient. Visualize it for a few moments, ensuring that the ring of light feels strong and is glowing. This is essentially your Faerie Ring of Protection in place. Once you have done this you may then like to sprinkle faerie dust or herbs in an actual ring around the thing that requires protection. If this is to be a permanent ring, repeating this exercise regularly (once a month, for instance) will help to maintain the strength of the spell.

If you would like to ask for protection for yourself or another person, then this is most easily done with the visualization method only. This is because people will move out of the physical faerie ring and then cease to be protected. A ring of light is at least portable!

A good time to use a physical ring is when you want to ask for protection while you are asleep, perhaps to guard against nightmares and so on. This can be performed in exactly the same way as the Ring of Protection. Do state the purpose for requiring protection. As with all magic, the more specific you are, the more effective your magic will be.

Alicen: I have used this type of faerie magic to help my six-year-old son. As is typical of many children of his age, he occasionally can't sleep for fear of ghosts and ghoulies and then has nightmares. One night recently when he was upset for this reason and he couldn't go to sleep I asked him if a Faerie Ring of Protection would help, as we seemed to have tried everything else I could think of to reassure him! I performed this for him and sprinkled sparkling faerie dust around his bed. This comforted him greatly and he fell asleep in minutes. Of course, for a child imagining ghosts, this act is more psychological than anything else, but if the thought of being surrounded by the protection of the good faeries comforts a young child to get a restful sleep, then why not?

This goes for grown-ups, too! The thought of being surrounded by the magic of the good faeries is incredibly comforting and, as a result, you should feel protected too. After all, love is the greatest force and that is what the faeries surround us with.

Jacky: I used a similar trick with my own daughters. They imagined a white light of protection around themselves, visualizing the light as a soft and fluffy cloud (or fog). It worked a treat!

CHAPTER 16

Guided Faerie Meditations

'... A purple shadow, sprinkled
With golden star-dust, twinkled ...'
MADISON JULIUS CAWEIN

What Is a Guided Meditation?

Meditation is simply extended imagining, where we allow our minds to break free from the inner voice which usually dominates our conscious thought. It is wakeful dreaming, where our imaginations can explore within given parameters. Meditation is halfway between waking and sleeping, while guided meditation can be likened to a daydream that has been set before you.

We have chosen to present guided meditation in this book because it is the easiest meditation method to master. It is rather like listening to a play on the radio with your eyes closed and being completely relaxed. A guided meditation is just one step up from this. All we are doing is adding a spiritual dimension to the play and asking you, as the listener, to follow the direction in your mind.

There is also a very significant reason why we have included a meditation chapter in this book. This is because our imagination is a special link to the Land of Faerie, as it is considered a place that exists within and without our beings. For this reason we can reach Faerie Land through our 'imaginations' by a direct route when we use meditation. A guided meditation asks us to imagine a setting or journey; this is our key to the faeries' realm.

There are three guided meditations set out here for you to try. You can read them through a couple of times and then follow the meditation from memory. Alternatively, you can read them out loud while recording your voice onto a tape. You can then play the tape and follow the meditation step by step without having to memorize it. The third and easiest method is to recruit a friend to read the guided meditation out to you slowly, while you follow it in your mind. Take it in turns to do this for each other.

The guided meditations we have created in this chapter have been especially written for those who have never meditated before and to provide a harmonious experience of the faeries and their realm.

How to Meditate with the Faeries

When beginning to meditate with the faeries there are several elements which will make your meditation experience more successful. Here is an example of a simple meditation routine which should bring about a positive faerie meditation experience.

Meditation can be done anywhere that is warm, comfortable, quiet, and where you will not be disturbed. Some people find that their temperature drops a little during meditation, so a light blanket and perhaps a pair of socks will make the experience more pleasant.

It can be a good idea to put the answerphone on and make sure that the TV and radio are turned off. If there are others in the house, do ask them to keep quiet whilst you do this and to respect your privacy and not disturb you.

To mark the transition from being in an everyday state to a more magical one, some people like to prepare the room or place in which they are to meditate. It is also possible to meditate outside when the weather permits. Lighting a special candle and/or incense and quietly playing relaxing music can set the scene. Making sure that you are comfortable and relaxed is one of the most important preparations.

Jacky: I like to use tea-lights or candles in jars, as I find these safer than open candles. There is nothing more disturbing than worrying whether the candle you have lit is safe whilst you meditate with your eyes closed!

Once you have prepared your place, the next step is to sit in a comfortable upright chair, or lie down (although you are more likely to fall asleep if you lie down). Close your eyes and relax your body and mind. Find the quiet place within yourself and dwell there until you feel ready to begin. Being ready includes silencing those insistent thoughts such as 'I really must change the light bulb in the hallway'! Just let these thoughts drift away. If you are new to meditating, you might find it useful to write a list of these persistent thoughts at the beginning of your meditation so that you can completely relax your mind. In time you will become more disciplined and be able to banish these thoughts before they even surface.

Once you have taken a few deep breaths, dropped your shoulders and relaxed yourself, it is a nice idea to ask for the assistance of your guardian angel on your meditation journey. Your guardian angel will always have your best interests at heart and it is a good thing to know that if they are there, you will always be on the right track. Faeries and angels are also linked very closely and work together with us, so it is quite appropriate to request your guardian angel when working with the faeries.

You can do this silently or out loud by just saying something like 'Dear guardian angel, I ask for your presence and guidance during my faerie meditation. Please protect me and keep me safe on my journey ...' As you are saying this you can also visualize your guardian angel standing behind you and surrounding you in a protective white or golden light.

Once you have done these few preparations, then you will be ready to begin. Here is a summary of the meditation routine for quick reference.

FAERIE MEDITATION ROUTINE

- Warn others you are going to meditate.
- Prepare yourself for meditation.
- Prepare your space.
- Make it magical!
- Sit or lie down and close your eyes.
- R-E-L-A-X …
- Invite your guardian angel.
- Meditation time.
- Thank your guardian angel.
- Open your eyes and perform a grounding exercise.
- Eat or drink something.
- Don't forget to leave the faeries a little gift!

Once you have become used to meditating with the faeries you can practise it whenever and wherever you wish. The more you meditate, the more wonderful your results will be. Meditation is also known to be a good way to relieve stress and feel more connected to yourself and the divine, resulting in feelings of wellbeing and increased harmony. Meditation is also a great way to develop your own psychic ability.

You do not have to limit meditation to designated times, but you can use it spontaneously and creatively at times of stress, crisis, illness and uncertainty, when it can give you a better perspective on situations or even simply comfort you when you are in need of it most.

GROUNDING EXERCISES – BACK TO EARTH!

After any type of meditation you will need to perform a simple grounding exercise. This is because while meditating, your imagination is extended much more than it would be during a normal day. In meditation your mind is allowed to free-fall, rather like dreaming. When we awake after a night's sleep we have breakfast, which among other functions actually helps to bring our awareness back from the dream-state. The same principles apply to meditation. It is always a good idea to eat and drink something after a meditation, to help us focus once more on earthly matters.

As well as eating and drinking a snack after meditating, it is also a good idea to run through a grounding exercise. The ones we have chosen in this chapter are both very straightforward and easy to remember. They should be used immediately after your meditation, before you begin anything else and get on with the rest of the day.

To ground yourself try:
- eating a slice of toast
- eating a piece of chocolate or a chocolate biscuit
- drinking a cup of tea with sugar (which is why we give tea to people in shock)
- taking your shoes off (and walking outside if you can), to 'earth yourself'
- holding a black crystal (obsidian, smoky quartz etc.).

Grounding Exercise One – Hands On

Sit cross-legged on the floor and place the palms of your hands either side of your body, pressing them flat on the floor. Simply imagine all the magical energy that you have used during the meditation draining down from your body, leaving through the palms of your hands and seeping into the Earth. You can visualize the energy as light of any colour that you wish, if this makes the exercise easier. When you have finished, clap your hands together a few times to disperse the energy. Then you're done!

Grounding Exercise Two – Dusting Yourself Down!

Working on the same principle as the above exercise – that all energy can leave your body and be absorbed into the Earth – here is a variation. Again visualize the energy you wish to disperse as a light in and around your body. In a standing position and beginning with your head, sweep your body in a downwards motion with the palms of your hands, as if you are actually brushing the energy off yourself. Imagine it is faerie dust falling away! Work with brisk strokes all the way down your body until you reach your feet, where you can sweep the energy into the porous earth.

Grounding Exercise Three – Become a Tree!

Some people find it easier to 'be' something else, so try this. Imagine yourself as strong and as tall as a tree. Imagine your branches reaching up to the sky, one branch and leaf at a time. Feel your trunk, wide and firmly settled on the Earth. See the colour brown on your trunk, old and well established. Feel how it is in control.

Feel your roots now winding down into the Earth. See as many roots in the Earth as there are branches in the sky. Feel those roots holding you in an upright position, and fixing you down to the Earth. Let the tree roots now take your energy down into the ground.

A MEDITATION FOR CALMING, SOOTHING AND HEALING

Alicen: The following mediation was given to me by the faeries when I was going through a time when I particularly needed some healing. Since that occasion I have often found that I am given this image and then I am reminded to use it once again.

At an unusually difficult time in my life quite recently, I lay in bed anguishing over something that had been troubling me. I really did lie awake for hours and finally it occurred to me that if I carried on in this way, I wouldn't get to sleep at all that night. So I asked the faeries for some help. As soon as I sent out this request, as if from nowhere I saw descend upon me a beautiful blanket made entirely of sparkling raindrops and starlight. This I knew to be a magical moment, as all my feelings changed at once, from being fretful to being at peace. I knew that the blanket had transformed my state of mind and, after watching the exquisite faerie covering in wonderment for a while, I fell into a deep and peaceful sleep.

On being enveloped by the faerie coverlet, I felt as if I had been given a fragment of Faerie Land to bask in. I had an instant knowing that all of our earthly worries and problems are merely that: earthly. There is no need to take them into the dream-state, when we may touch a piece of heaven every night and take a rest from our lives. The faerie coverlet is a reminder and an aid to restful, peace-inducing sleep.

I recommend it to those who are ill or in need of comfort at any time for any of life's worries! Although I was given this meditation as a faerie gift, I can also call upon it, if I feel the need, at any time I wish. You can do the same for yourself, and for others too. If you have a child who cannot sleep, or is ill, or if you feel that someone you are caring for would benefit from a healing sleep experience, then you can just ask them to close their eyes while you talk them through the visualization. This meditation is also so simple and easy to remember that you won't need to refer to the book once you have done it a couple of times.

The Faerie Coverlet of Dreams Meditation
> *'Every dewdrop and raindrop had a whole heaven within it.'*
> HENRY WADSWORTH LONGFELLOW (1807–82)

Unlike most meditations where you are asked to find a comfortable position, but not so comfortable that you fall asleep, in this meditation the sole objective is to drift into sleep at some point during the visualization! With this in mind, find yourself a comfortable place to either lie or recline, or just go to bed as normal. Ask your guardian angel to bless your meditation as before, and accompany you while you are sleeping.

Once you are comfortable, warm enough, relaxed and not likely to be disturbed, then close your eyes and take a few deep breaths. If there is anything specific you need healing for, or a problem that you need taking away for a while, request this now.

See at once a cloudless night's sky above you with stars glimmering brightly. For a few moments, just take in this spectacle and look at every detail in the starry sky.

After a while you notice a burst of brilliant white light directly above you. It twinkles and shimmers in the dark sky and begins to get bigger. You realize that it is coming closer to you, as if it is falling out of the sky, gently towards you. As the luminous light falls silently above, you begin to perceive its shape. It is a blanket made entirely of stars and sparkling raindrops, which has about it a radiant glow of glittering white light. It looks as if it has moonlight and starlight dancing around the edges of the coverlet. As the Faerie Coverlet of Dreams drifts towards you, it brings a sense of pure and powerful love, as it is an unconditional gift from the faeries. Know that you are worthy and ready to receive this gift, relax even deeper and begin to feel sleepy.

Study every detail of the luminescent coverlet as it drifts towards you. Every raindrop and star within it is a beautiful, restful dream encapsulated just for you, waiting to be dreamt. When you are ready, allow the Faerie Coverlet of Dreams to fall upon you and cover your whole body. Now is the time to drift into sleep whenever you feel ready. May you dream only beautiful dreams.

Once you have completed this exercise, if you are ever in need of faerie healing again, simply ask for the Faerie Coverlet of

Dreams to be sent to you. Visualizing this meditation should become easier each time that you do it. The Faerie Coverlet will never wear out!

MAKING YOUR OWN FAERIE COVERLET

If you are the creative type, maybe you could make a real faerie coverlet. This could be brought out in times of illness and family stress, or just laid out on the end of your bed. It can be as beautiful and magical as your creative mind can imagine. Use rainbow-coloured ribbons, gauzy 'faerie wing light' lace and silken flowers. Appliqué leaves cut from nature-strewn chintzes, stitched in faerie patches. My local sewing shop sells a range of iron-on faerie patches and I have no doubt that you will be able to find these in your own local craftshop or on the Internet. Make sure everything is sewn on well so that it is easy to wash.

If this project sounds just a little too daunting, have a go at making a faerie cushion. Stitch in sequins and crystal buttons with silver- and gold-coloured threads, and fill with dried scented herbs and potpourri including roses and lavender for a beautiful scented dreamtime and meditations.

The Magic Spider's Web Meditation

Everyone has seen the magical qualities of a spider's web, either strung with dewdrops at dawn or glazed with frost on a winter's day. Normally invisible, this is when they catch our attention and we can see their extraordinary beauty and intricacy. In this visible state they capture our imagination: poets have written about them, artists and photographers have seized this transient visible phase of a spider's web. It is no wonder, then, with all these magical, artistic and poetic characteristics, that spiders' webs are in faerie lore, a magical symbol of entry into the Land of Faerie. They share many aspects with the faeries' realm. A web is spun into a spiral shape, the traditional way to enter Faerie Land. The web is also constructed by spinning, a craft which has long been held sacred to the faeries. As mentioned earlier, a web is usually invisible unless water, in the shape of droplets or frost, is apparent. The Land of Faerie is also invisible and can often be entered through water or ice that is only visible at certain times. Thus a spider's web is our magical mirror onto Faerie Land, showing us when we can enter. The very fact that a spider's web looks magical is another clue to us that indeed they are.

By using your imagination we are going to show you how to activate this special doorway to Faerie Land, a very simple and effective way to begin a journey to the faeries. You don't need to find an actual web for this meditation, for your imagination is all that you need. Although we will tell you later on how to use this meditation if you find that you do stumble upon a dewy web.

Once you have closed your eyes and eased into a relaxed state, imagine that you are in an apple orchard. The time is dawn and you are comfortably seated on a warm rug at the base of an old apple tree. All around you the world is awakening. You hear birdsong carried on the light breeze and everything around you is bathed in the warm golden glow of the rising sun. Each blade of grass is hung with its own glistening dewdrop and the leaves of the apple tree glimmer in the honey-hued light.

Opposite where you are sitting is a very old apple tree, so ancient that moss and lichen cover its boughs with a velvet-green coat. In between its branches are suspended many spiders' webs, glittering with beaded dewdrops in the golden half-light.

Set your gaze upon one particular web which catches your eye the most. Now all you need to do is study it in every detail. See how the strands of the web are weighted down by the droplets of water. In every droplet see the light reflected. Make sure that you study the very tiny droplets as well as the large glassy ones.

Now follow with your eyes, from the outside of the web, through the whole spiral until you reach the very centre. Don't rush this part, but slowly and methodically reach the core. Once you have reached the centre, note if you feel any different. Common observations are that everything around the web appears insignificant or you just notice it less. You may have a sensation that you are being pulled or drawn into the centre of the web. Once at the central point you may feel a sense of deep peace, of stillness. At the core of the web lies a fragment of Faerie Land, a place where the outside world is excluded and the entrance to another realm lies waiting. You may set your gaze at the heart of the web for as long as you like and feel the calmness of residing there.

Once you feel that you would like to return, begin to retrace your steps with your eyes, back along the strands of the spiral until you reach the outside of the spiral web. Once this part of the exercise is completed you notice that the sun is higher in the sky and the magical time of dawn has lapsed. The dewdrops that once hung on the webs of the apple tree have now evaporated in the morning sun. The spiders' webs are once again invisible.

When you are ready you may open your eyes. Have a stretch and make sure that you feel properly back in everyday life. Perform one of the grounding exercises and it is also a good idea to eat or drink something to really bring yourself back to Earth. Leave a small gift out for the faeries in a special place, as your way of thanking them for your meditation experience.

Incidentally, if you happen upon a real spider's web when you are outside, you can of course do this meditation in a slightly different way with similar results. If you would like to try this, then just make sure that you will not be disturbed for a few moments so that you can concentrate.

Set your gaze upon the actual spider's web and follow the spiral inwards with your eyes, until you reach the centre. Rest your gaze on the centre for a few moments and retrace your tracks with your eyes, following the spiral outwards to the beginning of the web.

If you are doing this exercise with a real web you may have more profound results than if you follow an imaginary one in a meditation. You may find it interesting to compare the two methods and see when you are in a natural setting how nature interacts with your experience of the exercise.

MAKE A FAERIE 'DREAM CATCHER'

The Native Americans made 'dream catchers' of web-like construction to hang over the bed at night. The dream catchers would catch nightmares and protect the dreamer.

You can make your own faerie version to hang over your bed. Start with a wire or wooden hoop. Bind the whole hoop first (wrap your thread, wool or leather cord over and over the edge of the hoop to cover it all – you may wish to stitch or glue this in place). Then catch up a section of the binding all the way around, using a looping structure. Thread another loop through each hoop on every row as you work your way to the centre – much like a spider's web, with each loop connecting to the next (this doesn't have to be exact, but you may find it easier to use a needle to do this. If you find this too complicated, wind your thread over the hoop and gather the threads all together in the centre).

Place a hanging thread on the top of the hoop (a twist of wire works well to hang up your creation) and hang different lengths of cord onto the bottom. Use it like a mobile and place different objects from nature on the ends. Things to try:

- pebbles or stones with holes in
- shells
- seed heads

- crystals
- quartz crystal droplets (made for jewellery and light catchers)
- faerie dolls (Jacky bought some for her Christmas tree, but you could easily dress up small dolls with faerie dresses and wings).

Hang your creation over your bed or meditation area.

The Secret Onlooker Meditation

This meditation is like your ticket to a real faerie procession, or rade as they are known. We hope you will find that simply being in the presence of faeries is a breathtaking experience.

Once you have closed your eyes and you are feeling relaxed, imagine that you are in dense woodland. The time is dusk and the trees are creating long shadows upon the woodland floor. You are standing next to a large and extremely old oak tree. Its roots are so immense that some of them protrude out of the earth and you are able to sit on one of them. The trunk of the tree is entwined by ivy and vines which have woven their way throughout the branches and trunk of the oak. Adjacent to the oak tree is a leafy pathway that wends its way through the trees, flanked by bracken and brambles, ferns and even bluebells.

This is the time of the bluebells and they only grow in ancient woodlands, such as this one. A bluebell wood is also the special domain of the fey and esteemed in folklore as being blessed and graced by the faeries.

The nocturnal noises of the woodland begin with the first owl hooting, a deer rustling in the undergrowth, foraging for food, and a gentle breeze whispering through the leaves. This is the spellbinding atmosphere that only woodland at dusk can evoke. Take a few moments to take in all the twilight sounds and even smells of the woodland around you. Feel perfectly safe and calm in your natural surroundings.

Carried upon the breeze you begin to hear enchanting music. As the music fills your senses, the natural sounds of the woodland around you begin to fall away from your perception. The music has a peaceful and also unearthly quality. As you attune yourself to the lovely music, you see in the distance many lights appearing within the dense trees. The lights are many-coloured and appear to be bobbing towards you. Take this as the first sign of the coming of the elves …

As the lights draw nearer you see that they are luminous lantern lights illuminating the woodland foliage all around them. You now see that they are being carried by silent and majestic figures, the elven people themselves. Some of the elves, who are all human-sized, are on horseback and others walk alongside, wrapping their cloaks around them. As they draw nearer upon the pathway to where you are sitting you can see their sumptuous clothes and beautiful faces. They all wear long, flowing robes or dresses of the finest fabrics, cloaks of the softest velvet and luxurious silk. Their horses are gorgeous creatures; each one is highly-strung and walking as if on its tiptoes. Their splendid long, wild manes are plaited with tiny bells and their tails flow out behind them. Their elfin riders spread their velvet cloaks upon their horses' backs and have their feet placed in stirrups of gold. The whole procession is surrounded by an emanating auric light and they bring with them an overwhelming sense of love and peacefulness. To be in their presence is to be bathed in this light and the energy that they bring.

By now they are filing past you, quite absorbed in their own company and seemingly unaware of your proximity to them. As you watch them proceed past you, you notice their twinkling, slanting eyes and pointed ears protruding from their hair. Every single one of them, without exception, is radiantly beautiful with a composure known only to the fey. They are all talking and laughing amongst themselves.

Towards the end of the procession you spy two elfin figures, a male and a female, who are more finely dressed than the rest of the elfin court. Their cloaks are embroidered with sparkling threads and they wear crowns of glistening crystals upon their heads. These are the Elf King and Queen, and to be in their presence is an even more thrilling experience than being among the rest of the elven company.

Just as the Elf King and Queen ride past you, unexpectedly the Elf Queen quite deliberately turns her head towards you and, smiling, she sends you a knowing wink of her eye. This is her way of showing you that she knows you are watching and your presence is acknowledged and blessed.

The last few elfin folk file by, their long cloaks trailing behind along the woodland pathway. In a few moments they have gone and all that remains of their enchanted procession is the faint, beautiful music and the sight of their lantern lights bobbing in the distance. After a while only the natural sounds of the wood remain and, as the dusk has crept into darkness, the shadows are no more. Now is your time to leave the bluebell wood and, when you are ready, you may open your eyes.

Do make sure that you feel firmly grounded after this meditation by performing one of the grounding exercises in this chapter and drinking and eating a little something. Don't forget to leave the elven folk a little present as a gesture of gratitude for your meditation experience.

If you have enjoyed working with the faeries with the guided meditations in this chapter, then you can use your first experiences of faerie meditation to devise your own guided journey. Concentrating on one aspect and focusing on it in detail is the best approach. Also, keep the meditation simple. You may decide simply to imagine a pair of faeries' wings and use that as your meditation concept, studying them in detail or watching a scene of winged faeries dancing in a ring of mushrooms. The choice is yours and the only limit you have is your imagination.

So, take some large pieces of paper and write down your own faerie meditation. Add as much detail as you can. Initially it is this detail which makes your experience real – later you will naturally see all of these things around you anyway. Remember to finish the journey in the same place that you began it, as this is a key to coming back to reality. Be creative, as creativity is the most magical door to working with the faeries, and remind yourself to do a grounding exercise when you have finished … oh, and did we say have fun?

CHAPTER 17

∼≫

Wave Your Faerie Wand

'…But faeries have broke their wands, and wishing has lost its power!'
THOMAS HOOD (1799–1845)

Begin the Magic …

As everyone knows, even very small children, faeries are deeply associated with magic – so intrinsically that it is impossible to part them from this association. Faeries are magical, therefore they exist.

Hold on a minute – what exactly is real magic? The movies and fiction portray the idea that magic is something that happens instantly, fireworks, faerie dust and all. We are led to believe that with a wave of a wand just like Harry Potter's, Gandalf's or Mildred Hubble's … you get the picture. Real magic may not be instantaneous, but it is far more exciting because it is real!

The first thing that faeries wish us to understand is that magic does not just happen when you wave a wand; it is laced throughout your life, invisibly and enchantingly. Real magic is the raindrops held perfectly on a rose petal, the taste of snow, the breeze through your hair, watching the moonlight through the gap in your curtains as you drift off to sleep. Magic belongs to the real world and even us, for we are originally beings of nature – remember? Once we recognize that the whole of our lives is a magical happening, things begin to look quite different.

As Marcia Zina Mager, the author of *Believing in Faeries, A Manual for Grown Ups* quite accurately says, 'Search for magic everywhere in your life. The one and only rule of the Faery Realm: magic grows anywhere …'

Magic belongs to all of us, because it is a part of nature, just like us. Once we know this we can take one step further and make magic happen. Look through the eyes of a young child and you will see the magic like never before!

Lifting the Lid of the Teapot

Magic happens all by itself, every day, without us having to do anything. It is the sun rising, the grass growing, the colour of your eyes and the stars in the night sky. To make magic actively happen for us we need to 'Open the door' as Marina Medici says in her book *Good Magic*, wisely adding, 'There is magic under the teapot, in your shoestring … and in the wind outside, chanting to you.' The first step of making magic with the faeries is to recognize that there is enchantment within everything and to want to walk through the door marked M*A*G*I*C … every day of your life.

Before you walk through that sparkly, tantalizing door or lift the lid of the bewitchingly exciting teapot, just be aware that magic comes with a warning label. Yes, magic is fun, magic really does work, and magic can change your life. However …

THE WARNING LABEL ON MAGIC (OR '… AND NOW THE BORING BIT')

The following guidelines are for you to refer to when working spells, as later on in this chapter we will be giving you spells to try out. Never perform a spell just for the sake of it or because it seems an exciting thing to do. Always wait until you have a real need for a particular spell, as magic will always bring about change and is a responsibility. This does not mean that it shouldn't be fun to cast spells! Always think twice before you wave your wand, about whom the spell involves etc. Once you have become confident with these elementary spells, you can begin to devise your own. This is where 'The Warning Label on Magic' will become useful.

- Only work magic for good. If you don't, you will soon know about it.

- Magic always has consequences. Always think through what you are asking to happen. If it is going to harm anyone in any way, shape or form – just don't do it.

- Magic is a last resort. If you have a situation and you have exhausted all ordinary ways of solving it and there is still a problem left to solve, that is the time you may turn to magic.

- Magic is a loving and divine force; therefore it should always be used responsibly and with respect and love.

- Spells are wishes + ritual = magic.

- Financial gain, party tricks to make you look good, deception and manipulation of others are all big no-nos for using magic. If you cross that line into working magic for your own selfish motivation, then just be prepared to take the consequences. As in life, 'What goes around, comes around' is certainly true in magic. So, no trying to manipulate the free will of others (even if you think it is for their 'own good').

- Always be specific in your request when performing a spell. The universe will always give you exactly what you ask for – literally. Think twice about the wording of your spell, make sure you get it right, and ...be careful what you wish for!

The Secret Forces of Nature

Don't be too put off by the 'warning label'. As long as you have good intentions and behave responsibly, making magic should be a wonderful experience that enriches your life and, indeed, makes it more magical.

Marie Bruce in her book *Faerie Magick* suggests, 'When you bring magick into your life, your life in turn becomes magickal …' It has the power of transformation, growth, beauty, wisdom, fertility, release, completion, tranquility, healing, strength, cleansing … the list goes on. But magic can only manifest what nature can. It cannot change the shape of your face, give you a smaller bottom or turn a single coin into a wad of notes.

As Marina Medici reminds us, 'A good magician is like a good gardener. He knows that 'changing a rose into another flower is not possible'. Magic works entirely with nature and by its very being cannot work against it. Making magic happen for us towards a positive and intended outcome is very simple: ask the natural forces – in this case the faeries – to help us bring about a specific intent.

Magic is often shrouded in secrecy and complicated tools and rituals. There was a good reason for this – in ancient times, the ones performing the magic were the ones holding all the power. Naturally they didn't want the 'common people' to break out of their traditional roles. The more complicated the magic, the less chance of the workings being stolen. Many rituals were performed in secret or written in secret code.

The faeries would like everyone who is pure in their intentions to have the gift of magic. After all, everyone is capable of using magic and it doesn't have to be complicated. One of the members of the Golden Dawn Society, S L MacGregor Mathers, once summed up working magic as 'The Science of the Control of the Secret Forces of Nature'. One aspect of those secret forces is the faeries. Magic belongs to everyone, so let's get started!

In this chapter we are going to give you a beginning point at which to work your very own magic.

A Healing Faerie Wand

If the only tool that you ever own in faerie magic is a wand, you will still do very well. A wand is one of those magical tools that you will get a great deal of use from, and is a fundamental accompaniment to faerie magic. Its main purpose is to direct energy from you. A wand can be likened to a magical TV aerial. The TV aerial receives the signals and transmits them into the television set to create images and sounds. A wand is receiving energy from you which has come, with faerie help, from the ether. Then you direct the wand to transmit your intent into the world. A wand is really a device for transmitting and focusing magical energy.

Traditionally a wand's length is from the tip of your middle finger to your elbow. In the Harry Potter stories, J K Rowling got her research right when Mr Ollivander says, 'It's really the wand that chooses the wizard, of course.' People often find that their wand comes to them and not the other way around.

Jacky: A fan sent me a beautiful healing wand she had fashioned herself. Crystals were glued down the length in the order of the colours of the chakras ... a beautiful gift. Another wand – a long piece of clear quartz, finished with a perfect point and a rounded end, also arrived unexpectedly. At a crystal conference in Derbyshire, England, one of the stall-holders was packing up to go home when I admired the crystal wand on her stall. The stall-holder asked me how much money I had on me. It was beautiful but priced well outside my range – I only had enough cash to pay for half of its value and sadly she didn't take credit cards. 'I have to take these crystals all the way home to Scotland on the train tonight, and I'd rather not – I'll take the cash you have,' she said generously. I was stunned – she had literally given me the wand at half price ... a gift indeed. It seems that, just as in the Harry Potter stories, the wand had chosen me!

Wands are traditionally a fallen stick, fashioned and sometimes customized to suit the owner. Once you have set an idea firmly that you need a wand, don't be surprised if one comes to you. By this we mean that you may be given one as a present, you may find just the perfect stick on a walk in the woods, or a storm may blow the wand stick into your garden. For when you begin to live magically, magical things will begin to happen to you. It is the universe affirming to you that you're doing the right thing at the right time. Magical people do not believe that a coincidence is merely a coincidence. Everything is a magical happening and occurs for a reason, all part of life's big plan.

In this chapter we are going to explain how you can make your very own wand, one that is particularly suited for healing spells. There are many trees associated with the faeries and only a few of them are recommended for making faerie wands. Of these, the willow tree is one of the most potently magical woods akin to the faerie powers, and one of the willow's properties is healing.

It is perfectly possible to buy a willow wand from mystical shops and magical suppliers. However, the idea behind making your own magical tools is that the energy that you put into making them will make them more effective. Making your wand yourself will also bond you to it, causing it to have personal associations for you. It will also require your imagination which, as we already know, is the best route to contacting the faeries.

MAKE IT MAGICAL ...

Begin to think that you would like to have a wand. Perhaps leave a note out for the faeries, politely asking that a willow stick should come to you. Incidentally, if you live in a region where willow does not naturally grow, other suitable woods associated with the faeries are holly, oak, ash, hawthorn and hazel.

Don't rush this part of the process. Real magic doesn't happen instantaneously, but with the natural rhythm of life. If you happen to find a fallen stick and you know the tree that it came from, do thank the tree and the faeries that are the guardians of that tree, as in magical practice this is considered to be polite.

Once you have your willow stick, you may have to cut it to the right length. You can then set about fashioning it into a wand. Whether you strip the bark or not is entirely up to you, as willow bark is also considered to have magical properties. It is a good idea to make one end the handle part and the other end the wand tip. There are many ways to achieve this; it all depends on how decorated or simple you would like your wand to appear. The choice is yours. When working with faerie magic it is always best to stick to the most natural materials when fashioning and decorating your wand.

You Will Need

- A willow or other suitable stick
- a sharp knife
- sandpaper
- glue (optional)
- ribbon or leather thong
- copper wire
- materials for decoration (crystals, shells, feathers etc.).

If you do decide to decorate your wand, then the materials you could use are a ribbon wound around the wand from handle to tip in a spiral pattern. You could also use a leather thong. A spiral is a sacred symbol in faerie lore. If a spiral in any material or even copper wire is wound around the length of the wand, it acts as an energy path. This will enhance the magical potential of your wand.

You can also stick tiny shells, feathers and crystals to the wand. If you are feeling artistic you could paint it with faeries or even magical symbols, such as the spiral. for instance, or even images of trees and herbs etc.

Some people like to add a pointed crystal on the end of their wand – to concentrate the energy. Clear quartz is the most commonly used, but follow your own instincts as to the right crystal – or crystals – for you.

CONSECRATING YOUR WAND

Once you have decorated your wand, before you can use it for any magical purpose it should be consecrated. This is something that should be done to all magical tools before they are used. Consecration makes the tool sacred and sets it apart from ordinary, everyday implements. Your wand should then be treated as a very special tool and ideally be handled only by its owner and stored carefully. Some people like to wrap their wand in a silken scarf or in velvet.

Below is a wand consecration which you can use. After the consecration has been performed on your wand, it will be ready to use. This consecration need only be performed once in your wand's lifetime.

Faerie Wand Dedication and Meditation

Make sure that you will have a quiet time to yourself. Approach this in much the same way as you would a meditation (see Chapter 16). We have called this a Wand Dedication because not only will you be consecrating your wand, but dedicating it for the specific purpose of healing magic. This dedication has been specially written for those who have never performed any magic before. If you have completed the meditations in the previous chapter, then that is all the experience you will need.

Preparation – Prepare Your Faerie Altar

It is a nice idea to prepare a small table or to use a cloth on the floor (velvet or muslin is ideal) as your focal point in the dedication. You can decorate this space with all things faerie to make it a special occasion. You could sprinkle some glitter and flower petals on the cloth and then place on it a picture of a faerie, perhaps, some faerie wings, a bottle of faerie dust – anything that means faerie to you. Don't forget your faerie wand will have pride of place on your faerie altar.

Bring in the Four Elements

As well as your wand and faerie themes, you will need representatives of the four elements. This could be incense smoke for Air, a candle flame for the element of Fire, a bowl of spring water for Water and a pot of flowers or herbs for Earth.

Prepare Yourself

This is a magical occasion, so do put some effort into separating this happening from your everyday life. Wear something a little special that makes you feel magical. If it is something which, when you put it on, really captures your imagination, so much the better. In this experience you are entering a fragment of Faerie Land. As with all acts of magic, the more effort you put into it, the more wonderful and effective your magical experience will be. Remember that your imagination is the most potent tool to working magic and connecting with the faeries.

Bring a Gift of Thanks

It is also a nice idea to bring the faeries a gift as a gesture of thanks, for their help and the energy that they will bring to your wand dedication. On your faerie altar place a small bowl with honey, cake, milk, cream or bread especially for them.

Now You Are Ready to Begin ...

Stand before your faerie altar and tell the faeries why you are here. You may like to say the words below or use your own.

'Dear faeries of
Earth, Air, Water and Fire,
Please help me to dedicate my wand,
According to my desire.'

Once you have done this, sit down and take a few moments
to relax. Take some deep breaths and let your day slip away,
for this is now your special time to spend with the faeries.

Now you are going to create the simplest of magic
circles. For this you will need the help of your guardian angel.
Close your eyes and imagine your guardian angel standing
close behind you. If you can imagine them in as much detail
as possible, this will help you all the more. Once they are
firmly in your mind, you are going to ask them to protect you
during your magical work and also to help you to create a
magic circle. Ask this either in your own words or the words
below:

'Welcome, guardian angel of mine,
Help me to see a circle divine.
By my side, be you near,
Your loving presence always here.'

Now visualize a circle of beautiful white light around
yourself. This circle should also include within it your faerie
altar. See this as a really vibrant and glowing white light, with
faerie dust sparkling within it. See the light that surrounds you
glowing so strongly that it shines on your face and lights up
the room a little. Keep visualizing this light until you are
happy that it is luminous enough. Once you are content that
you have created a vivid magic circle, you may open your
eyes. Incidentally, if you find any part of this dedication
difficult to achieve, just close your eyes and ask your guardian
angel to help you a little more.

Now take your wand from the faerie altar and hold it in the hand that will usually be using it. First, wave your wand through the incense smoke and imagine your wand being imbued with the power of the Air elementals.

Second, pass your wand through the candle flame and imagine it being sparked with the energy of the Fire elementals.

Third, dip your wand lightly into the bowl of water and imagine the Water elementals sending their energy to your wand.

Last, touch your wand onto the earth in the pot of flowers or herbs and imagine the grounding energy of the Earth elementals being transmitted to your wand.

Now hold your wand before you and request all the elemental faeries to bring their own qualities to your wand. You may like to use the words below:

'Sylphs of Air, whisper your magic,
Salamanders of Fire, breathe your enchantment,
Undines of Water, sing your charms,
Gnomes of the Earth, bring your power.
Enliven this willow that makes my wand,
To heal and bring magic to those I am fond.'

Healing Wand Meditation

Still holding your wand, now close your eyes and see your willow wand in your mind's eye. Imagine your wand glowing with a pure blue light, which is the colour associated with healing. See this blue light sparkle and glitter with magical energy.

As you see this in your imagination a beautiful winged faerie appears next to your wand. She glides around it and watches the lovely blue sparkling light that you have created, as if she is bedazzled and fascinated. Then see her blow a kiss to your wand; upon her kiss is a shower of faerie dust she sends shimmering towards the wand. To your wand she has sent the sylph gift of empowerment. See her then disappear, as magically as she came.

Now you see appearing next to your wand a salamander elemental. She is an enchanting wispy creature, made entirely of rainbow hues of smoke. Her long hair billows all about her and her feet and hands taper away into trailing smoke. She begins to dance around your wand, watching in delight the blue sparkling lights that you have created around it. You then see her smoky hair curl its floaty, smoky locks around your wand. They create around your wand a spiral of blue smoke that looks very beautiful. As you continue to watch her, all her smoky being gradually fades away, along with her blue smoky spiral, until she finally disappears. To your wand she has sent the salamander gift of empowerment.

You see a light of shimmering green and blue appear next to your wand. Watch this light closely, as slowly but surely the form of a little female figure appears within the light. She is exceptionally beautiful and she has long, wet dark hair which has grown right down to her toes. She has feathery water weeds caught in her hair and a long green dress that has a shimmering iridescence, as if you could see many colours in it glistening and twinkling simultaneously. She tosses her wet hair and what look like a thousand glinting drops of water shower themselves over your wand. She smiles at you and then suddenly disappears. To your wand she has sent the undine gift of empowerment.

A red toadstool materializes next to your wand and, from behind it, the shy face of a gnome peeks out at you. He suddenly winks cheekily at you and pops back behind his toadstool. All you can see of him is his long beard trailing around the stem of the toadstool and the tips of his pointy red shoes. Again the friendly gnome peeks out from behind his toadstool. You now see that he has a little drawstring bag tied to his belt. He smiles and reaches into his bag and pulls out a handful of tiny red toadstools. These toadstools are gleaming with a brilliant red and green light that surrounds them. The gnome gives you another wink of his eye and then throws the handful of enchanted toadstools over to your wand. The toadstools flash and sparkle around the wand and then fade away, as if they were fungi fireworks! When you look over to the gnome, you see that he also has vanished, along with his toadstool. To your wand he has sent you the gnome gift of empowerment.

All the elemental faeries have now blessed and empowered your wand in their own unique ways. When you are ready you may now dissolve the image you have in your mind of your wand bathed in blue light. Open your eyes when you have done this.

Now place your actual wand on the faerie altar. Imagine all the four elemental faeries who helped you in your meditation leaving your circle. Ask them to do this by saying these words:

'Sylph, salamander, undine and gnome,
Blessings as you leave for your faerie home.'

Now also imagine that your guardian angel's presence disappears from behind you. At the same time, see the white circle of light that you created around you fading away. You may like to use your own words to thank your guardian angel, or the ones we have given below:

'Thank you, angel, for being here,
Your presence I hold very dear.'

This is now the end of your wand dedication and meditation. Your wand is now ready for any future magical work you may need for it, particularly healing. At the end of the chapter we have included a healing spell for you to try with your wand, if you so wish.

At the end of any magical work, it is always a good idea to eat or drink a little something and also complete a grounding exercise (please see Chapter 16 for these).

Candle Magic

Candle magic is one of the easiest forms of magic, and of course is connected with faerie magic as it uses flame as its focus, the domain of the fire elementals. Did you know that every time you blow out the candles on your birthday cake and make a wish, you are practising an echo of ancient candle magic?!

Working candle magic with the faeries is simple and effective. In this chapter we will guide you through the stages of performing this fun method of magic and, later on, we have written a Faerie Candle Meditation for you to try. With the guidelines we have set out for candle magic you can begin to devise your own spells, when the need arises.

FAERIE COLOURS

When performing magic using candles, the colour of the candle can enhance your magic greatly if chosen carefully. Every colour has different associations and magical meanings. Using the corresponding candle colour in a spell – for example, a pink candle for a love spell – will intensify your magical will and focus. This in turn should bring more effective spell results.

With this in mind, when you need to perform a spell using a candle, it is always best to find the colour most suited to your magical intent. However, that said, if you ever need to perform a spell in an emergency, a healing or protection spell for example, then a white candle will always suffice. If this is all you have in the cupboard, it will lend itself well to any spell work.

Candle Colours and Their Associations

Black	Completion, release, banishing
Brown	The gnomes and all Earth elementals, security, grounding, winter, the home, healing for animals
Gold	The sun, the Faerie King, masculinity, the god, good fortune, autumn, attraction
Dark blue	Healing, the undines and all Water elementals, dreams and sleep, peace, wisdom, knowledge
Sky blue	Healing, the undines and all Water elementals, calm, tranquillity, patience, understanding, health matters
Orange	Motivation, legal matters, success, imagination, energy, positivity
Pink	Love, friendship, honour, virtue, contentment, romance, femininity
Purple	Spiritual wisdom, ambition, inner strength, divination
Red	Love, summer, lust, passion, sex, life force, activity, courage, allure, the salamanders and all Fire elementals
Silver	The Faerie Queen, the goddess, femininity, the moon, the night, faerie magic
White	Purity, innocence, cleansing, peace, truth, childhood, protection, happiness, all-purpose magic
Yellow	The sylphs and all Air elementals, communication, creativity, attraction, examinations, happiness, laughter, concentration, artistic ability, wisdom, visions, divination
Green	Faerie Land and faeries, finances, security, career, fertility, luck, strength, growth, beauty

Let us take the example of the Faerie Candle Meditation featured in this chapter. This meditation is for bringing the faeries closer to you in your daily life. In effect, this meditation is inviting them to be your friend. Therefore we would choose a green candle for this spell, as this is the colour most strongly associated with the faeries.

TIMING

Whenever you work any kind of magic, when you choose to perform the spell will have a bearing on how successful the outcome will be. This is because magic is essentially a natural energy, and to make it work best for you it is best that your spell coincides with the most conducive natural tides. The most potent of these tides is the lunar one. The tides of the moon have a very strong pull and influence on faerie magic, so when considering when to perform your spell, always note the current phase of the moon. Below we have explained the cycles of the moon and their magical effect.

> '...*CHASTE ORB! as thro' the vaunted sky*
> *feather'ry clouds transparent sail...*'
> 'ODE TO THE MOON', MARY DARBY ROBINSON (1758–1800)

Moon Cycles

- New moon – This is when the moon is just beginning to appear in the night sky. You can see it as a slim crescent of light. All spells for new beginnings are perfect for this moon phase.

- Waxing moon – This is when the moon is growing to eventually become full. Each night you will see the crescent becoming larger. Any spells for making things happen and bringing something positive into your life are appropriate at this time.

- Full moon – This is the phase of the moon when it is completely visible. This night and indeed the night preceding and after the full moon are considered to be the most potent for working magic. Spells for fulfilment and completion are perfect for this most magical of moon phases. The faeries are also thought to delight in the full moon.

- Waning moon – This is the phase after the full moon, when it begins to grow smaller, night after night, and also diminish in strength. Only spells that are for banishing (for example, if you wanted to get rid of an illness) are performed at this time.

- Dark moon – This is the phase that lasts for three nights before the appearance of the new moon. At this phase the moon is not visible at all in the sky. This phase of the moon is considered a time for magical rest, when usually magic is not performed. It is a good time for reflection and meditation.

Days of the Week

These are also considered to have magical associations and can be taken into account when planning your candle magic spells. Especially noteworthy for faerie magic is the faeries' Sabbath day, which is Friday (although some sources say it is Wednesday). This is the day when the faeries have a rest from magic – and from making mischief too!

- Monday – This takes its name from the moon, so its associations are lunar influenced. Spells that involve the home and family, emotions, feminine matters and psychic abilities would be best performed on this day. The Faerie Queen presides over this day.

- Tuesday – The planet Mars rules over Tuesday. Spells that need courage or involve business, sexuality, war or positive action should be worked on this day.

- Wednesday – Mercury rules over Wednesday. Spells influenced by communication and all forms of creativity should be performed on this day.

- Thursday – The planet Jupiter presides over Thursday. Any spells for money matters, politics, business, success and travel are good on this day.

- Friday – The faeries' day of rest! Friday is ruled by Venus, who influences spells for love, friendship, fertility and new projects.

- Saturday – Originally 'Saturn's Day'. Saturn rules over protection, financial debts, responsibility and discipline.

- Sunday – Originally 'Sun's Day', this is of course governed by the sun. Spells for healing, strength, ambition and masculine matters are best on this day. The Faerie King presides over Sunday.

If you have an emergency spell to perform they can be cast whenever the call arises. For optimum results in all other spell work, planning the timing will increase the effectiveness of working with the natural forces.

Taking the example of our Faerie Candle Meditation, this would be best performed on either a waxing- or full-moon phase. This is because we wish to attract the faeries into your life. The most suitable day of the week would be Friday, for its influences on friendships and new projects. So make a date in your diary!

ANOINTING YOUR CANDLE

When it is time to perform your spell (and you have chosen a green candle in this case), it is also a common part of candle magic to 'anoint' the candle. This is really for the purpose of bringing your energy to the candle and transferring your intent to the candle. It is also a good idea, one that can be very creative, to carve words or symbols that represent your spell's intent into the candle. This makes your candle look really ready for a spell!

Olive oil is suitable for anointing your candle. Some people also add a drop of essential oil to this base oil appropriate for their spell. This may be an essential oil (aromatherapy oil) of a particular herb or flower which has a magical association akin to your spell intent. For your Faerie Candle Meditation, both rose and rosemary oil (but see the caution below) are known to attract faeries, and either would be suitable for this spell. Adding an essential oil is not a 'must have' at all; it's just an extra touch if you feel so inclined.

Once you have your oil and candle, close your eyes for a few moments and imagine that the oil and candle are being cleansed of any negative vibrations. Imagining a pure white light surrounding them can be helpful. Once you have done this, open your eyes. If you would like to carve any words or symbols into the candle, now is the time. For this meditation, the word FAERIE would be appropriate.

Now is the time to anoint your candle. While you are doing this, it is important to concentrate on your magical intent. In this case, it is to bring the faeries into your life. Imagine faeries all around you as you anoint the candle.

Anointing sounds very grand, but just means that you are covering the candle with your cleansed oil. To do this, dip your forefinger into the oil and then, beginning at the top of the candle in downward strokes, rub the candle with the oil, dipping your finger in the oil again as necessary, remembering to think of your magical intent as you do this. You will notice that your anointed candle ends up very slippery, so keep a cloth handy to wipe your hands afterwards, and keep your hands well away from your eyes.

Once your candle is anointed, then place it in a secure candle holder. Now you are ready to begin!

Magical Oils

There is a lot of good sense in using oils with smells that you like. If you enjoy your candle magic, then the energy is going to be a whole lot stronger! Of course, there are traditional associations too. You will find a good book on aromatherapy useful for your spell work – do ensure that you are not allergic to any of the following before you begin, as pure oils should be treated with respect. In most cases, only one or two drops are necessary.

If you're really not sure where to start, then you might find the following list useful:

• Bergamot – this orange-scented oil is commonly used to break away from or detach yourself from people you wish to move on from in your life. Perfect for confidence spells.

• Chamomile – wisdom, healing, calming and compassion.

• Citronella – perfect to raise your spirits and banish negativity. Citronella is a good oil for using in outdoor magic and it's helpful to keep the flies away!

• Coriander – traditionally used to promote out-of-body travel, and used in love magic.

• Eucalyptus – a powerful oil the ancients used in exorcisms! You can use it to cleanse and clear the energy of a room.

• Frankincense – this sacred oil is sometimes known as 'food for the gods'. It's the perfect choice for purification and raising the energy of your space. Often used in angel magic.

• Geranium – balances masculine and feminine energies and can be used for protection

- Lavender – always appropriate, this beautiful oil helps bring about deep inner peace and relaxation and is wonderful for spells relating to love and emotional issues.

- Pine – fertility and childbirth spells.

- Rose – roses are often associated with faeries anyway. Great for dream spells and seeing into the future. Is also used when grieving.

- Rosemary – traditionally used to open up your psychic abilities and perfect for cleansing and purifying your space, and used to help cross over to the afterlife after passing from the physical world. **Not recommended for use during pregnancy, or if suffering from high blood pressure.**

- Sandalwood – manifestation and prosperity.

- Vervain (Verbina) – the name *Verbina* is what the Romans called 'Altar plants'. Druids and sorcerers made full use of this plant. As an oil it is perfect for love spells, protection and, erm, controlling your bodily 'urges!'

A Faerie Candle Meditation

You will need:

- Candle colour – green
- Oil – rosemary (see warning above, however) or rose
- Moon phase – waxing or full
- Best day – Friday.

Place your candle before you and, using the guidelines in Chapter 16, prepare yourself for meditation. When you are fully prepared, always start a spell with a statement of intent. You are telling the faeries that you would like them to be with you in this magical experience and exactly how you would like them to help you. Light your candle and say:

'Come, faeries, elves, to my home,
As I'm here all alone.
Now in magic I believe,
For I'm ready to receive.'

Close your eyes and see yourself in your mind's eye sitting in your room, as you are now. Imagine that your floor begins to spread with dark green moss and bluebells covering the floor. Your room is beginning to resemble a woodland and you can even feel a pleasant breeze against your face and through your hair. The faeries are coming ... just a little more imagining and they will be here.

Imagine that you are surrounded by a circle of trees. These trees have knobbly hollows and twisted roots; they can be any species of tree that you care to imagine. They form a friendly circle around you, as if you are in a protective ring. You begin to hear birds in the boughs of the trees and the breeze rustling through the leaves. You can smell the earthy dampness of the velvety moss and the fresh scent of the blue-bells.

In front of you, in a circle, pops up a ring of fly agaric mushrooms, with their distinctive red caps and white spots: a magical faerie ring. Around the red-capped mushrooms you see lots of different-coloured lights bobbing up and down and in between the mushrooms. These are faerie lights and the faeries know that you are waiting for them. There are luminous spheres of gold, blue, green and red encircling you. They bring with them a wonderful energy of peacefulness and love.

After a while of watching these lovely lights dance within the circle, you begin to see that one of the lights is beginning to take on a form. Imagine seeing yourself holding out the palm of your hand and this sphere of light bouncing onto your palm. The sphere of light slowly transforms into a faerie that is made entirely of shimmering light. This form lasts only for a few seconds, but in that time you are able to discern its delicate limbs, features, flowing hair and beautiful wings. As soon as you have glimpsed the faerie, it vanishes and all that is left in your hand is a swirl of twinkling lights. As you look around you, your surroundings are once again your room; the woodland scene and the faerie ring are all gone. The faerie came just to give you a glimpse of things to come.

When you are ready, open your eyes and extinguish your candle. Perform one of the grounding exercises in Chapter 16 and don't forget to leave a small gift out for the faeries.

Over the cycle of the next month, the faeries should begin to make themselves known to you in your life.

Asking the Faeries for Magical Help

Once you have asked the faeries to come into your life, you may always call upon them for any help that you may need, be that magical or advice with mundane matters. Do remember to communicate with them regularly by leaving small gifts out for them, by working with them to help the environment, meditating with them and including them in your prayers and wishes. These are just a few ways to communicate with the faeries; for a multitude of ideas, please see Chapter 18.

Always invite the faeries to assist you when you are meditating or working any magic. They always like to be invited!

Finally, in this most magical of chapters, we have devised a healing spell where you can also make use of your willow wand and all the skills that you have learned so far.

A Healing Spell

You will need:

- Candle colour – blue
- Essential oil – rosemary or vervain (optional)
- Moon phase – waxing or full
- Best day – Sunday
- Magical tools – willow wand.

You will also need a photograph of the person/animal/situation that you are going to be sending healing to. Failing this, writing their name on a piece of paper in blue ink will suffice.

Again, this spell has been written for those who have little or no previous experience of magic. You just need to have completed one of the meditations in Chapter 16 and The Faerie Wand Dedication and Meditation in this chapter and you're ready to go! This spell is for healing for anyone who needs it in your life; it could even be a pet or yourself. The person who is intended to receive the healing doesn't need to be present, because you are going to send them the healing energy through the ether.

This spell can also be used for more non-specific healing work, such as sending healing for the environment, endangered species of animals, children in orphanages in a third-world country, all children who are suffering from terminal cancer. Of course, the list unfortunately goes on. This type of healing spell is equally valid, although your results cannot be so easily determined.

Preparation

Make ready a small table or cloth on the floor as your faerie altar. You will need on your table your blue candle in a holder, the anointing oil, your willow wand and a photograph of the healing recipient. Also a gift for the faeries in a small bowl. Decorate your faerie table in all things faerie, wear something special and prepare to be magical!

Light your healing candle. Stand before your faerie table and tell the faeries why you are here and why you need their help. You may like to use the words below:

'Come, faeries, to my circle new,
Surround with hue of healing blue.
Do help me in my healing task,
To send this light is what I ask.'

Once you have done this, sit down and take a few moments to relax. Let your faerie time begin and your earthly cares simply fall away, as if you can take them off like a cloak.

Create the magic circle with the help of your guardian angel, exactly as described in The Faerie Wand Dedication, saying;

'Welcome, guardian angel of mine,
Help me see a circle divine.
By my side be you near,
Your healing presence always here.'

Now visualize your circle of shimmering white light. Open your eyes and take your wand from your faerie table. With your wand you are going to direct healing light sent to you from the faeries and universal energy. Point the tip of your wand at the photograph or representation of the healing recipient. Now ask the faeries that this person receive your healing for the best possible outcome.

'Dear faeries, I ask of you,
Send healing and loving light to … please do.'

Now imagine that there is a gorgeously beautiful shaft of blue light above your head coming down, as if it has descended from the heavens. Imagine that lovely light as if it has tiny stars twinkling within it. Now see that glistening light drop down into your head and move slowly down through your body. Let it travel down your arms, into your hands and then the tips of your fingers and into the willow wand. See the wand glowing with the celestial light. Now imagine the blue light flowing effortlessly out of the tip of the wand and surrounding the photograph. Concentrate on this image for a few moments. Then imagine that person to be happy, healthy and healed, not in pain or ill as they may be now. Similarly, if you are asking for healing for a place, some animals or a situation, imagine a positive transformation; do not think of it as it is at the moment. Already believe that your healing recipient is transformed. Concentrate on this image for a few moments.

Then imagine that the healing energy you have sent into your wand is now shooting up into the ether and the heavens. Imagine that light swiftly and magically reaching its destination. How that person or situation is healed is not your concern, for the faeries will deal with that; just imagine the final outcome being positive. As Marie Bruce in her book *Faerie Magick* comments, '... magick will always work for your highest good ...'.

Once you have imagined the blue light shooting upwards, then place your wand back on your faerie table. Imagine the blue light, which came from the heavens and flowed through you, completely dissolving and then vanishing.

Now also imagine that the white light that surrounds you is dissolving into nothingness too. Once you have done this, acknowledge the faeries' help and that of your guardian angel.

> 'Guardian angel and faeries too,
> Blessings for your light of blue.
> To your secret realms you go,
> Of hidden wishes just you know.'

Now extinguish your healing candle. This marks the end of your healing spell. To make it even more effective, place your blue candle in a safe place and on three consecutive nights after this spell, burn down the candle a little each night, saying:

> 'Dear faeries, I ask of you,
> Send healing and loving light to … please do.'

Once you have completed the main spell here, don't forget to perform a grounding exercise and eat and drink a little something.

A Magical Beginning …

The exercises, meditations and spells we have introduced in this chapter and the one previously are a great beginning to working magically with the faeries. Once you have performed the healing spell a few times, you may feel confident, with the help of the Timing and Faerie Colours guides, to devise your own simple candle spells. You have all the basic information you need to begin working magically with the faeries. Don't forget, though, the 'warning label'! Also, remember to thank the faeries after working with them. Use magic responsibly and unselfishly and you are sure to have a lot of fun.

… Own the power!

CHAPTER 18

Communicating with the Faeries

'Do you believe in faeries'?
PETER PAN

The Magic Begins with You ...

Communicating with the faeries is a magical process, which very often begins with you. The faeries need to build their trust in you and, to a certain extent, vice versa. Communicating with the fey very much depends on a desire from you to get to know them better and begin to build a relationship. However, the old adage that 'the more you put in, the more you will get out' certainly applies to being friends with the fey kingdom. Although you may be the one who has to initiate contact, they will give back to you much more.

Throughout this book one of the main themes has been imagination and its connection to the faeries and their realm. This chapter is a glut of imagination! Here are lots of exercises and projects for you to try. We have listed so many that there is sure to be something for everyone. So see what takes your fancy and have a go!

The more creativity and imagination you use to approach these themes, the more strong and vibrant your connection to the faeries will be. We have chosen methods that are suitable for people who have never tried contacting the faeries before. If you have children, grandchildren, work with children etc. you will find that involving children in any of these fun projects will heighten your imagination and bring you closer to the fey. The way that children describe and experience things go beyond adults' capacity to imagine. Children will love getting involved in some of these projects too!

Remember, too, that the fey may not reply to your efforts in a conventional way. Look out for the messages in the awakening dream codes threaded through your life ... a truly magical journey.

Faerie Altar

Many faerie fans like to create a magical faerie altar at home. It is a wonderful way of expressing your interest and a perfect place to leave your faerie offerings. Each person of course will have their own ideas, but typical altars might include candles, aromatherapy oils, faerie figurines and paintings, flowers, shells, stones and pebbles, crystals and feathers.

If you like glitter and shine, then your winter altar could include an assortment of sparkly items borrowed from your Christmas tree. Summer altars might include terracotta pots of flowers; autumn, harvest fruits; and spring, bulbs and flowers. Let your imagination run away with you.

You don't need a large area to create your display. Consider a small coffee table or even a mantelpiece. Make sure objects are safely out of reach of small children and pets! Cover with a cloth, or layers of cloths, and add a garland of flowers (fresh or silk) or leaves. Add your candle or candles (in secure holders). You could vary the colours for each season or create altars for specific reasons, maybe one to help you move house or change jobs – using appropriate objects to help you focus your mind on your objective. (See Chapter 17 for more information on faerie altars.)

Faerie Art

Some of our special stories in this book have been shared by faerie artists. After having seen or felt faeries in their lives, many have been inspired to create beautiful artwork to illustrate what they have seen. Do you fancy having a go?

First you need to immerse yourself in faerie culture. You need to soak yourself in faerie energy. Do you have a pretty wood, sea shore or river bank which might be a possible faerie haunt? Dress appropriately (earth-coloured clothing in greens and browns is especially suitable – or whatever inspires you), and take some faerie gifts with you. You will also need a notepad and pen. It would certainly help if the weather was good ...

Find a quiet spot and sit down. If you want, you could play some relaxing, faerie-type music (Alicen has created the beautiful *Faerielore* with musician Llewellyn, and there are other musicians who have been inspired by the energy of the faeries).

Find somewhere comfortable to sit ...

Faerie Art Meditation

Close your eyes and ask for protection from your guides or guardian angel. Breathe in deeply through your nose, blowing out noisily through your mouth. In and out, about ten times ...

Now I want you to imagine you are surrounded by a bubble of light. See the rainbow colours which surround this bubble, and imagine each of the colours washing over you in turn ... green, purple, red, blue, brown ...

Watch as the bubble clears and becomes a screen in front of you. Ask your chosen faerie to appear in front of your screen so that you can take in every detail of their appearance.

What colour is your faerie? What clothing is the faerie wearing? What colours are around the faerie? Are aspects of nature appearing in your vision (flowers, seeds, weather ...

moss, even?). Soak up your vision fully. Feel the energy which is represented in your picture. Breathe in the colours and any sounds too.

When you are ready, bring back the rainbow colours to cover your screen ... feel yourself blend back into your natural surroundings. Feel the solid ground beneath your body and bring your awareness back to the here and now.

Thank your guides for their protection during your journey and begin to make notes or sketches on your notepad whilst your memories are fresh. You can use these notes to either create your artwork right there out in nature or take them home with you to make your faerie art in your own time. Use any of the following:

- paints (watercolours, acrylics or oils are great)

- pencils, coloured crayons, charcoal or any of the more modern textured media

- glue and sequins, beads, glitter ... or faerie dust (see instructions for making your own later in this chapter)

- you might want to include natural materials which you may have found at the time of the meditation, such as shells, bark, leaves and seed heads (remember always to ask permission from the faerie guardians before taking anything home with you – listen to their answer in your head)

- fabric including lace, gauze and natural cotton and wools; these can make your artwork beautifully tactile.

Most of all, have fun!

Faeries in the Bath

Well ... not literally, but there are some lovely ways in which to relax in the bath and feel connected to the Land of Faerie. This can lead to creative inspiration, more restful sleep and a sense of well-being. The most effective way to achieve this is by using essential oils and also dried flowers and herbs.

While you are running the bath water, just add a few drops of essential oil or a combination of your favourites into the running water. A lovely combination of a couple of faerie plants is lavender and rosemary (children love this too). Four drops of lavender and two of rosemary will make a beautiful bath experience. As you run the water, also ask the faeries (in your own words) to bring you closer to them. Please see Chapter 2 for plants associated with the faeries. If you are pregnant or using oils with children, always check the label on the bottle first or consult a qualified herbalist or aromatherapist to make sure that they are safe to use in the bath. Always dilute oils and never use them undiluted on your skin.

Flower petals and herbs can also be tied in a square of muslin material and strung to the tap while the water is running to infuse your bath in a magically relaxing infusion. Again, always check the suitability of the herbs and flowers that you would like to use, making sure they are safe to use near the skin (use particular caution when pregnant or if you have high blood pressure, as not all herbs and oils are suitable). If you are in a hurry, a handful of dried or fresh rose petals thrown into the bath water will always make it feel more magical and is another faerie favourite ... very extravagant!

To create an ambient and relaxing atmosphere, place a few aromatherapy candles in the bathroom – as before, rose and lavender are perfect. Simply lie back and relax ... Having a faerie bath also helps you to relax prior to meditations or any magical work, and also puts you in a magical frame of mind for rituals and faerie celebrations. Indulge at will.

Faerie Candles

You can use different candles and candle colours for your magical faerie work too, or even make your own. See Chapter 17 for more details of candle colours and how to use them in faerie magical spells.

Faerie Cooking

The faeries are known to love honey, nectar, milk, cream, cake and bread, and also the sweet things in life. If you make any recipes with these, then leaving a small piece as a gift for the faeries will please them very well, and hopefully stop them from helping themselves! I'm sure your children will love to help you make 'fairy cakes' – the smaller the better (try using the papers sold in confectioners for small home-made sweets). Decorate and enjoy.

Alicen: This year was the first year of 'World Fairy Day' initiated by international faerie artist, Jessica Galbreth. To celebrate, our two children and I made flower circlets for our hair and we decided to make one of the recipes from the Fairy Day website (see Resources pages). We chose to make fairy fudge and my daughter Morgan dutifully went on a shopping trip to the next-door shop to buy the ingredients. When she came back she had mistakenly bought margarine instead of butter. As we had never made fudge before, we decided to go ahead and see if it would make any difference, as we had limited time that day. Of course, with hindsight this was a bad move! The cooking process was hilarious, with cries of, 'Are you sure this looks right, Mummy?' and, 'Perhaps it might just take a bit longer to set?' Three days later and our 'sludge fudge', as we had now named it, was still – well – sludge. The children commented that they thought the faeries were laughing at us. I had a sneaking feeling that this was a very perceptive comment!

For faerie recipes, please see the Resources Directory for recommended books and websites. If my fudge is anything to go by, you will not want me to offer any recipes or cooking tips of my own (actually that goes for both of us)!

Faerie Dust ~ A 'Recipe' for Home-made Faerie Dust

(Of course, we don't suggest you actually 'eat' the faerie dust – it's just for fun!)

In a small lidded or corked glass jar (spice jars are an ideal size) put equal amounts of the following:

- very fine glitter (edible glitter is perfect too, though, and available from specialist cake shops)

- fine, clean sand

- favourite faerie dried flower petals (rose and lavender are good).

Put the flower petals in a pestle and mortar and grind until they are a fine powder. Add these in a bowl to the rest of the ingredients and mix well. Pour carefully into your glass jar. Don't forget to label your jar and then decorate it with ribbons, tiny bells, glitter, beads or minute crystals threaded onto a ribbon, for example. Make it feel magical.

A nice idea once you have made your faerie dust is to ask the faeries to bless it and imbue it with their faerie magic. This is best done on a full moon. Simply place the bottle on your faerie altar before you go to bed and request that the faeries do their work on it while you sleep.

A Book of Elfin

Why would you want a book of Elfin? This is a special book where you can:

- write down your faerie experiences
- record your dream accounts
- jot down your spells
- write letters to the faeries
- remember your meditation encounters
- stick down photographs taken on your faerie walks
- add your faerie drawings
- record your favourite faerie recipes and poetry.

It is a magical diary for all things faerie in your life. This book should be revered and kept so beautifully that you could even leave it as an heirloom for your children.

Choose a book that reminds you of the faeries. It may have a silver, green or purple cover, for instance, or a beautiful velvet cover. You can buy an attractive book from stationers or from a specialist maker of faerie books – yes, they exist, and many of their books have pretty shiny or sparkly covers! (See Resources Directory.)

Make a Book of Elfin

If you feel especially creative and have the time, you could buy some handmade paper (or make it) and sew the leaves of the pages together with silver thread, for example.

Once you have your Book of Elfin, do make sure that you decorate it. Try:

- any natural materials such as pressed flowers, grasses and leaves are good for borders for your writing

- faerie stickers

- draw pictures and/or cut them out from magazines to stick amongst your spells and poetry

- use coloured pencils, paints and silver- and gold-liquid pens to create that faerie feel. Your Book of Elfin should be a glimpse into your own personal view of Faerie Land. Beautiful, magical and enchanting are all watchwords for creating your very own Book of Elfin.

- tie your book closed with a beautiful metallic ribbon (silver or gold) – it helps to keep it neat and safe.

It is important to show your book only to others who share a love of faeries, for they do not like to be made fun of. Faerie secrets should not be shared lightly and you need to respect the faeries' ways too, when creating your book.

Faerie Letters

Jacky: When I was a child my sisters and I used to write letters to the faeries. Imagine the fun of writing teeny little letters with miniature writing and making the smallest envelopes. We used to use a magnifying glass to get the writing small enough (a hard and very sharp pencil made the smallest writing, but be careful not to smudge it). Perhaps you'll have your own ideas.

I am an angel teacher and often suggest to my students that they write to their angels and leave their messages under their pillow for the angels to find. I suggest trying the very same thing with the faeries ... in teeny, tiny writing, of course!

(See also Chapter 7 for more information on writing faerie letters.)

Faerie Music and Dancing

> '... *Eftsoones they heard a most melodious sound ...*'
> EDMUND SPENSER, *THE FAERIE QUEENE*, BOOK II

Uplifts and a sense of wellbeing can both be found through music and dancing. The faeries are well-known to adore both of these arts.

No special skills are needed for this one. Simply choose some music that you can't resist dancing to and find the best space to dance in. Music and dancing also engage your imagination.

The most important thing is not to worry about what you look like! Simply dance to the beat and let your mind wander. Sometimes that is all you need to allow yourself to plunge into your imagination and feel connected with the faeries. Wear loose and floaty clothes for full effect – and maybe wear or shake small bells or drums. We like to lock the door and close the curtains too!

It is also possible to visualize while you dance, even with your eyes open (a little like daydreaming). Here is a very simple visualization for you to try while you are dancing to the music of your choice.

Dancing Magically

Make sure that you warm up your body before starting to dance, so that you do not strain any muscles. While you are doing your warm-up, out loud or in your head, invite the faeries to come and dance with you, saying something like:

> 'I invite the faeries to take my hand,
> And dance me into Faerie Land.'

Once you have been dancing for a few moments, imagine that there are small winged faeries dancing all around you and enjoying the music, just as much as you are. If this works well for you, then build on this a little and imagine also a ring of scarlet-capped mushrooms around you in a Faerie Ring, for this is a portal to the Land of Faerie.

This is all that you need to do. Once you have this visualization established, then simply dance and keep on imagining. Some people then find that this is a kick-start to deeper imaginings, while others are happy to keep it simple. You may well receive more images, feelings and experiences while dancing with the faeries.

This is an exercise which is so free and simple that if you have ten minutes spare in your day, you can switch on the music and indulge in faerie therapy any time you feel the inclination!

Do treat this as a sacred act and perform a quick grounding exercise afterwards (see Chapter 16 for grounding exercises). This will ensure that you are fully earthed before you carry on with your day.

A Faerie Ring

The Faerie Ring is one of the most potent fey portals to their realm. It is very easy to create your own Faerie Ring either in your garden or home. Of course, a naturally occurring Ring is either a circle of mushrooms or a circle of darker grass amongst a patch of ordinary grass. The purpose of making your own Faerie Ring is to enhance your own faerie experiences.

There are dangers warned of, throughout faerie lore's history, of stepping into a Faerie Ring; it's thought to be a sure way of being captured by the faeries! However, this rule does not seem to apply if the Faerie Ring is made by you. In fact, almost the opposite seems to apply: the faeries welcome a ring made in their honour. They seem to be flattered and pleased that humans should do this. So if you do make a Faerie Ring, then they will certainly help you to use it to its best advantage.

An Indoor Faerie Ring

An indoor Faerie Ring of your own making is usually of a temporary nature, due to space restrictions, although this is of course a personal choice. Also, if you are using a ring for meditation and ritual or celebration purposes, then a temporary one may be easier. It can be constructed to suit your mood, time of year etc., but ultimately it's up to you.

Materials for making a Faerie Ring should be largely natural and not contain any metals, as a guideline. However, what you make your Faerie Ring from and how wide you make the diameter depend on your circumstances and personal preferences.

Here are some ideas of things to make a Faerie Ring from:

- home-made or shop-bought faerie dust (see page 303 for recipe or the Resources Directory for stockists of faerie dust)

- feathers, stones and sea shells

- moss – but be careful to take only a little of this natural resource and remember to water it regularly.

If you are using your Faerie Ring for a seasonal celebration, then you could use natural materials available to the season. Some examples are: swathes of holly and ivy for Yule, hawthorn blossom for May Eve/Beltaine, roses and summer flowers and foliage for the Midsummer Solstice.

Other ideas are dried berries, pine cones or nuts in their shells, all scattered in a circle. If fresh material isn't available, use dried flowers or leaves etc. Once you have your basic circle, you can also sprinkle faerie dust on it to add that extra sparkly touch!

If you want something you can use over and over again – especially with children – use a child's plastic hoop as a starting point and wrap a spiral of ribbon around the edge (gluing it down if necessary), then glue or tie on (with garden twine) lengths of silk flowers and leaves. It won't last forever, but with care will last for many happy hours of faerie play.

An Outdoor Faerie Ring

This has the scope for being an even more permanent feature in your garden because of the materials utilized. All of the above can be used for an outdoor Faerie Ring of a temporary nature. However, it is best not to use faerie dust outside as it contains glitter, which is not environmentally friendly.

For a more permanent outdoor ring you could use a number of faerie garden ornaments. If you have woods in your vicinity, go out looking for natural materials such as fallen wood in unusual shapes, or driftwood if you live by the sea. Large shells can also be collected and used to make a ring. Ask nature to help you out with this project and you will not be disappointed when you go hunting for finds.

If you are a city-dweller or your lifestyle does not allow you the luxury of time for long woodland walks, then garden centres are fantastic places for finding inspiration. They often have many ornamental pieces, made specifically for the outdoors, which you could create a ring with. Most suitable are wooden features and you can even source wooden mushrooms and toadstools, which are, of course, perfect! There are even specialist wood-turners who will create a tailor-made mushroom circle to your requirements. (See our Faerie Resources Directory at the back of the book.) ... Even one or two of these around the garden will certainly enhance your surroundings.

Once you have completed your Faerie Ring you will find lots of uses for it. It's a wonderful place to leave your faerie gifts and wishes. On fine days and evenings it would make a lovely place for meditation and visualization. You may even find it a welcome place to sit and relax after a busy day or as an escape from a chaotic household! This is your place where the peace of the faeries will always be there for you to find.

If you have children or even have them over to visit sometimes, you will soon discover that a Faerie Ring is a child-magnet! It is the perfect place for children to play and retreat into the world of their imaginations. Cats will also be drawn to your Faerie Ring, too. So if you aren't fond of cats or children (the faeries' natural favourites), then it may be best not to build one at all!

Have fun with your Faerie Ring and make it magical; light it up on summer evenings with candle lanterns. It is a natural place to feed the birds from all year round, and hedgehogs in winter. If you are connecting with nature you will also be reaching into the faeries' realm.

(For more information on creating a magical outdoor space, see Chapter 2.)

Faerie Oracle Cards

These are an invaluable tool if you would like comfort, reassurance and guidance from the faeries in a clear form. There are some very attractive packs available now, specifically focusing on faeries and their realms. Using them is like having a direct message-link to the fey, as each card gives you a short sentence or word to focus on – and, of course, a beautiful image.

You can buy many different sorts. Packs of cards (approximately the size of playing cards) contain words and phrases which you can use to give yourself a 'faerie reading.'

Many New Age shops sell these, and even your local bookshop might contain a pack or two – or, of course, you can always make your own.

Make Your Own Faerie Oracle Cards

Recycle card from old birthday or Christmas cards, or buy specially-shaped cards from stationers (the type used for business cards). You want around 50 so that you get a regular turnaround of the cards.

First of all, create your words and phrases, using a notepad and pen to keep a record. Try and incorporate positive and uplifting words which may be helpful in any given situation … the sort of helpful messages that the faeries might bring you. Take your time over this and really think through your phrases. Here are a few to start you off:

- Your faerie friends advise you to spend more time in nature today.

- Your Faerie Godmother wants to take care of you as you must take care of yourself.

- Your faerie wish is our command.

- We sprinkle magical faerie dust on your pets; give them extra attention today.

- Create an energizing space around you: add pretty objects from nature to your table or desk.

You might prefer to use shorter phrases or even single words like this:

- Faerie Love
- Faerie Support
- Faerie Guidance
- Faerie Housekeepers
- Faerie Finances
- Faerie Answers
- Faerie Kisses
- Faerie Health.

When you have decided on your text, add it to your cards by either writing in a special handwriting (such as calligraphy) or printing the text onto the cards using your computer. If you have chosen to get those special sheets of business cards, then these easily fit into your printer (do a test sheet first on ordinary paper).

If you are using recycled card, use sheets of stickers and write or print your words onto them before sticking them onto the card. Decorate the cards with drawings or paintings if you are particularly artistic, or maybe print off some copyright-free images from the Internet and use these. Many stationers and gift shops sell faerie stickers, so you might consider these as another option. Make sure you have fun!

You can use your Faerie Oracle Cards in any way you wish. Smaller cards can be selected from a dish or pretty bowl, or you could make a drawstring bag out of sparkly material and choose your cards from this. If you've made larger cards you might prefer to shuffle them and select one or more each day for daily help from your faerie guide, or pick one or more cards as an answer to specific questions.

Use your intuition to expand the meaning of each card. What thoughts enter your head as you look at your phrase? Does it instantly remind you of a situation you are dealing with (or should be dealing with) in your life? Look, too, at the pictures, to give you further clues to your faerie guidance. Go with your instincts – and remember that your faerie cards all contain positive and helpful suggestions and are not judgemental in any way.

(If you prefer to buy your cards, we have compiled a resource list of recommended oracle cards in the Faerie Resources Directory at the back of the book).

Faeries and Photography

Fancy having a go at photographing faeries?

> *Jacky:* 'Stop the car!' I yelled. My husband looked alarmed but I'd spotted a likely looking wooded area and wanted him to park the car.
>
> 'Do we have to?'
>
> 'Yes!'
>
> Armed with my digital camera, I set off to tour the park in search of the wee folk. My husband stayed in the car and the children were more interested in the swings than the fey. No sooner had I walked away from the car than my husband tipped back the seat and closed his eyes. He'd fallen asleep in seconds … some people just don't want to know about the unseen world!

Rule number one when you set off to photograph faeries is to ensure that your equipment is in order. I hadn't. I zoomed in on a likely looking daisy and nothing happened. The batteries needed changing in my camera. Did we have any spares? If there *had* been any faeries, I'd probably already missed the moment. Cursing to myself, I trudged back to the car to search for spare batteries. Luckily I managed to steal some from the portable DVD player on the back seat ... I'd explain later!

I realized that my chances of photographing anything remotely magical was limited. Children squealed in delight as their parents pushed them on swings. The small pond had several ducks with ducklings and I moved in close for a shot, so as to avoid the crisp packets and ice-cream sticks which were drifting around the edges of the pool. Nothing magical about that! A mother duck objected and I had to beat a hasty retreat, but I'd managed to get a couple of images before I left.

Over in the distance I noticed the wooded area I spied from the road, and decided to try my luck there. A path wound its way through the wood and the approach had a beautiful arch of trees to mark its entrance. I had to photograph it ... it looked so magical and I felt encouraged. The minute I stepped onto the path, the whole atmosphere changed. Whether in part due to the silence from the children's play area (the sound didn't seem to reach the wooded area) or whether there really was something different about the energy, I was not sure. It felt wonderful and I shivered in excitement!

Immediately I was drawn to a fallen tree, the knot of roots suggesting hidden worlds beneath. Sunlight seemed to twinkle upon the ground here. Were there faeries in this place? It certainly 'felt' like it.

A sound over to my left caught my attention. It was slight but something was scurrying close by. My eyes were drawn immediately to a large tree with several holes along the base. I was stunned when the teeniest of mice popped his head out from the largest of the holes! How brave he seemed as he scurried about. He grabbed at something on the ground, and then ran back inside his home. Almost immediately he appeared at the back of the tree ... but I was mistaken, for this was his mate! Both mice at once came around the front of the tree and almost posed for a second, willing me to take their photograph. So entranced was I that I had forgotten to take the shot.

The camera, although digital, is an old one and if there is a zoom facility with which to take close-up pictures, I haven't found it yet. I snapped away. The pair looked even more fun through the camera lens – but, alas, they were almost invisible on the print due to their small size.

I continued along the trail and a rabbit walked from one side of the path to the other. Birds sat calmly on nearby branches, and bees and butterflies flitted about my head. If there was a Faerie Land portal in this place, then I probably found it that day.

The very air around me seemed to glisten and shimmer, as the sun made its way through the leaves high up in the treetops. When you look through a camera lens everything appears different. I became aware of things I would normally miss, like the tiny pink flowers growing on the ground. I continued snapping away, finding delight in every shot.

Did I catch any faeries with my camera that day? It's hard to tell. Sometimes a smudge or speck could be something ... or nothing ... but another world was pushing its way through the veil of my consciousness that sunny afternoon and I couldn't wait to try other locations in the future.

Tips for a Successful Faerie Photo Shoot

Do you want to have a go? Here are a few tips:

1 First find a quiet place to shoot. The less disturbed by humans, the better the spot. I was lucky on this trip because I strayed onto a better site almost by accident, but I have since found many better places. Natural areas with old trees, flower meadows and places with a natural water source are good places to start. As well as a small duck pond, this woodland backed onto a lake, which certainly helped to create a wonderful relaxed feeling to the place.

2 I know I mentioned it before, but make sure your equipment is in order. Spare batteries if your camera needs them! Flash in working order, extra film and so on. If you find the perfect shot you'll be cross if you can't take the photo. You rarely get a second chance.

3 Faeries don't like to be hunted, so you need to be sneaky. Dress to blend in (natural earth colours like greens and browns) or take a chance and wear something pretty or sparkly to stand out – you might attract them to you!

4 Take your time, walk really slowly or sit and meditate for a while, even resting on a fallen log. Your state of mind is important, and a calm, chilled state helps your consciousness to shift ever so slightly, enabling you to see things you might normally miss.

5 Try looking down the camera lens as you walk along, or relax your eyes a little (into a sort of 'soft focus').

6 Use your camera in unusual ways. Hold your camera straight up into the canopy of leaves above you, or kneel down and photograph right beneath any exposed roots.

7 Follow butterflies and dragon flies – are you sure they're not faeries in disguise?

This reader is very experienced in faerie photography and has had a little more success than me! Here is Elliander's experience.

If You Go Down to the Woods Today

I like to go out in the forest and gather up stones from everywhere, picking up only the ones that feel right and placing my energy into them before putting them into my bag. I'll then go to a secluded place in the forest I like to call the 'Forest Ruins', basically an old bridge built for the water department which ended up being abandoned. The bridge is falling apart and it has the feeling of nature consuming building, rather than the other way around.

I go there with the stones I have gathered and use them to make a faerie ring with a large central stone for me to sit on. I'll open the circle by taking my hands and weaving energy around the bottom circle before walking three times around the top circle, both clockwise. I envision a spiral energy connecting them. Then I invoke the energies of the area, and talk to the fae.

The circle is a place of magic - but not magic in the traditional sense of control. I create it as magic (as in 'connection' and co-creation). I'll then come back and take pictures of it. I use a 35mm camera so I can prove it is real, and I will take many pictures of the same place, one after another, so I can prove that it isn't just a film distortion. The only alterations I have ever made are to crop and zoom in on an interesting structure, but I still leave the original also in view on the same page.

The results of my experiments are stunning, with many unusual light formations. On more than one picture I've caught a pink energy structure with a blue aura, which I believe to be a fae of some sort. There are also 'comet-like' energies, and I've even managed to film the 'energy pathways' in the wood.

While taking photographs one time I had a playful attitude, and thought to myself, *I wonder when I'll catch a fae on film?* I captured the fae on the very next photograph, which just goes to show how belief and the thoughts of the photographer make a difference to what appears in the shot!

You might also enjoy reading about the Cottingley faerie photographs in Chapter 9.

Faerie Spirals

As mentioned before, Faerie Spirals are symbols (as in the spider's web) of a pathway to Faerie Land. Walking along the spiral from the outside to the centre is meant to take you to the portal of Faerie Land. You can create your own Faerie Spiral in much the same way as the Faerie Ring mentioned earlier. These can also be permanent or temporary, outdoors or indoors: the choice is yours!

The Faerie Wishing Spiral

Alicen: Here at Orkney Faerie Museum and Gallery we have created a Faerie Spiral inside the museum, on the floor. This is a permanent spiral which we simply 'touch up' once a year to retain its sparkle!

This is how we made it, and how you can too:

First, choose a centrepiece; something that will complete the journey of the person who walks the spiral pathway. We found a very unusual large stone on the beach near our home and felt that this was a perfect central point. However, it could also be something like a small tree stump or log, for example. For the purposes of museum visitors we decided that our spiral was for making wishes. Visitors write their wish on small pieces of paper and then walk the spiral, all the while concentrating on their wish. When they reach the centre stone, they place their wish-paper in a little bowl next to a candle we have burning. When we've had enough visitors to fill the bowl of wish-papers, we take them into the house and burn them in the hearth, knowing that the wishes will reach the faeries by way of the smoke up the chimney.

Once we had our central stone, we made a spiral shape with glue on the floor. To this glue spiral base we stuck red rose petals and magical shapes from coloured sparkly paper. They're in the shape of spirals, stars, angels and more. We then added the final touch: faerie dust.

This spiral has brought a lot of enjoyment to many children and adults in our museum. We also know that the faeries take their responsibility seriously when they are given all those heartfelt wishes.

You can make your own version of this in your home very easily. If you make a temporary version with glitter and flower petals, this can be easily swept up afterwards. If you are lucky enough to have a garden or summerhouse, you can make a more permanent spiral using the method described above. Or you could ask a builder to lay a spiral path of cobbles or stones set into cement (include a few crystals or pretty shells). Make sure that, as at the museum, you have an interesting central point (a faerie figurine, a bench seat or a carved wooden mushroom would be great!).

A Faerie Spiral can also be used in a faerie ritual or celebration to mark your journey to the Land of Faerie. Simply walk the spiral very slowly and deliberately from the outside to the centre. While you are doing this you can read out some faerie-themed poetry, or just concentrate on your personal image of Faerie Land. Once you reach the centre, this is a perfect time to begin a faerie celebration, meditation or visualization. Once you have completed your chosen exercise, then do make sure that you walk the spiral outwards again. This helps to concentrate your mind on coming back to everyday reality.

(If you want some more fun ideas, then check out Chapter 12.)

Faerie Farewells

We hope you have enjoyed *A Fairy Treasury*. Remember that faeries and the faerie realms are real. If you want faeries and their magic to be a part of your life, it's up to you … it's as easy as opening up your imagination.

Bibliography and Recommended Reading

Over the course of many years, and hours of reading, there are lots of books which influence a writer. Naturally, most are long-forgotten when it comes to writing a bibliography; we want to thank the authors of these books just the same.

Here are some of the books we do remember:

Ted Andrews, *The Enchantment of the Faerie Realm* (Llewellyn Publications, 1993)

Cicely Mary Barker, *A Flower Fairies Journal* (Penguin, 1990)

———, *Flower Faeries of the Autumn, a celebration* (Penguin, 2002)

J M Barrie, *Peter Pan and Wendy* (Centenary Edition; Templar Publishing, 2004)

Betty Bib's Fairy Field Guide (Duncan Baird Publishers, 2005)

The Boy Who Saw True (Rider, 1953)

Katherine Briggs, *A Book of Fairies* (Penguin Books, 1997)

Marie Bruce, *Faerie Magick* (W Foulsham & Co Ltd, 2005)

Cinderella (Tormont Publications Inc, 1995)

Collins Concise Dictionary (Harper Collins, 1982)

Vivianne Crowley, *Wicca: The Old Religion in the New Age* (The Aquarian Press, 1989)

Scott Cunningham, *Cunningham's Encyclopedia of Magical Herbs* (Llewellyn Publications, 2002)

Maureen Duffy, *The Erotic World of Faery* (Avon Books, 1972)

Cassandra Eason, *A Complete Guide to Fairies & Magical Beings* (Judy Piatkus Publishers Limited, 2001)

W Y Evans-Wentz, *The Fairy-Faith in Celtic Countries* (New Page Books, 1911; 2004)

Anna Franklin, *The Illustrated Encyclopaedia of Fairies* (Vega, 2002)

Brian Froud, *Good Faeries/Bad Faeries* (Pavillion Books Ltd, 2000)

Brian Froud and Alan Lee, *Faeries* (Pavillion Books Ltd, 1995)

Brian Froud and Jessica Macbeth, *The Faeries' Oracle* (Simon & Schuster, 2000)

Alicen Geddes, *The Elfin Eclipse* (unpublished short story, 2005)

————, *The Faerie Mound* (unpublished short story, 2005)

Alicen and Neil Geddes-Ward, *Faeriecraft* (Hay House, 2005)

Demetra George, *Mysteries of the Dark Moon* (Harper Collins, 1992)

Rosemary Ellen Guiley, *Fairy Magic* (Element, 2004)

Martha Hamilton and Mitch Weiss, *Children Tell Stories: A Teaching Guide* (Richard C Owen Publishers Inc, 1990)

Marie Heaney, *Names Upon the Harp* (Faber & Faber, 2000)

John Keats, 'La Belle Dame Sans Merci', in *The Golden Treasury* (selected and arranged by Francis Turner Palgrave; Collins, 1861)

Sally Love, *Spells and Rituals Using Candle Magick* (Caxton Editions, 2001)

Edain McCoy, *A Witch's Guide to Faery Folk* (Llewellyn Publications, 1996)

Iain MacDonald, *On Holy Ground, A Guide to the Ecclesiastical Sites of Westray & Papa Westray* (Seabridge, 2006)

Marcia Zina Mager, *Believing in Fairies, A Manual for Grown-ups* (C W Daniel Company Ltd, 1999)

John Matthews, *The Secret Lives of Elves and Fairies* (Godsfield Press, 2005)

Marina Medici, *Good Magic* (MacMillan, 1988)

Jacky Newcomb, *An Angel Treasury* (HarperCollins, 2004)

Bansi Pandit, *Explore Hinduism* (Heart of Albion, 2005)

S K Robson (ed.), *An Illustrated Anthology of Fairy Poems* (Star Fire Books, 2006)

J K Rowling, *Harry Potter and the Philosopher's Stone* (Bloomsbury, 1997)

Howard Schwartz, *Elijah's Violin and Other Jewish Fairy Tales* (Oxford, 1994)

Gilly Sergiev, *How to Catch Faeries* (Fair Winds Press, 2002)

Edmund Spenser, 'The Faerie Queene', in *The Complete Works in Verse and Prose of Edmund Spenser* (Grosart, 1882)

Kisma K. Stepanich-Reidling, *Faery With Teeth* (1st Books, 2003)

Edmond Bordeaux Szekely (ed., trans.), *The Essene Gospel of Peace Book Two, The Unknown Books of the Essenes* (International Biogenic Society, 1981 [Sourced from www.thenazareneway.com])

J R R Tolkien, *The Lord of the Rings* (HarperCollins, 1991)

Doreen Valiente, *An ABC of Witchcraft Past and Present* (Robert Hale Ltd, 1973)

Doreen Virtue, *Healing with the Fairies* (Hay House, 2001)

———, *Earth Angels* (Hay House, 2002)

Websites

The Internet is a vast source of information, and many hundreds of websites were browsed whilst researching the book. Here are a few:

BBC Religion and Ethics – Religions, www.bbc.uk/religion

Elemental Kingdoms, www.orderofthewhitelion.com

Environmental Defence – Nature Watching Tips – Action Center, www.environmentaldefense.org/article.cfm

Gnostic Society Library, The, www.gnosis.org, Marsanes, The Nag Hammadi Library

Gods and goddesses of Celtic lands, www.scns.com

Iain Lowe, www.duach.co.uk/gallery.htm, artist

Indian Fairy Tales: The Ivory City and its Fairy Princess, www.sacred-texts.com

Islamic Account of Sulayman: Information from Answers.com, www.answers.com/topic/islamic-account-of-sulayman

Jewish Fairy Tales and Legends: The Fairy Frog, www.sacred-texts.com

Jinni – Columbia Encyclopedia, www.columbia.thefreedic-tionary.com/jinni

Origin and Evolution of Fairy Tales, www.bobhuang.com

Powell's Books – Jewish Fairy Tales, www.powells.com

www.undoit.org

Vattenfall – Tips for households, www.vattenfall.de

Wikipedia, the Free Encyclopedia, www.Wikipedia.org

CDs

To help you with your faerie meditations, you may also find the following useful:

Alicen Geddes, *Faerie Workshop* (Paradise Music, 2006)

———, *Journey to the Faerie Ring, A Guided Meditation* (Paradise Music, 2006)

Llewellyn, *FaerieLore, Journey to the Faerie Ring* (Paradise Music, 2006 [cover notes by Alicen Geddes])

———, *Journey to the Faeries* (New World Music, 2003)

Faerie Resources Directory

Faerie Magazines

Faerie

A quarterly magazine with stunning photography and artwork. A printed haven for all true faerie lovers. A US publication, but also distributed in the UK.
www.faeriemag.com

FAE *(Faeries and Enchantment)*

A UK faerie heaven publication with worldwide distribution. Gorgeous fantasy content and a wealth of information on faerie events. Also available as an app. www.faemagazine.com

The Magical Times

A UK publication with worldwide distribution. Features environment, natural health, spirituality and folklore, all with a faerie focus. www.themagicaltimes.com

Mermaids and Mythology

A quarterly UK publication with worldwide distribution. A mermaid lifestyle magazine with beautifully produced artwork and photography. The emphasis is on the ocean environment, but interviews and mer-fashion are also included.
www.mermaidmagazine.com

Faerie Websites

www.alicen-geddes.co.uk
The co-author's website, devoted to the world of faeries, elves and enchantment. Blogs, faerie FAQs, news, information on her books and spoken word CDs, and collaboration with her artist daughter, Morgan Geddes-Ward.

www.facebook.com/jackynewcombartistauthor
The co-author paints lovely faerie and angel images which are available on her Facebook page.

www.enchantedamerica.wordpress.com
A huge wealth of information focusing on faerielore in North America. The site has researched shops, places to visit, vintage faerie artwork and location-centred content. A well thought out compendium for those travelling in the USA with a faerie trail in mind.

www.faeriesight.wordpress.com
A large resource of book reviews, blogs, articles, events, art and clothes, to name but a few, are offered on this well-researched and hugely informative site.

www.fairiesworld.com
Described as 'A world guide to fairy art seen through the vision of those who believe and understand.' A fabulous guide to the abundance of work devoted to the fey. There are also pages on poems, fashion, fantasy creatures, famous faeries and more.

Faerie Artists and Sculptors

Mabel Lucie Attwell
www.mabellucieattwell.com

Cicely Mary Barker
www.flowerfairyprints.com

Jasmine Becket-Griffith
www.strangeling.com

Brian Froud
www.worldoffroud.com

Molly Harrison
www.mollyharrisonart.com

Howard David Johnson
www.howarddavidjohnson.com

Iain McCaig
www.iainmccaig.blogspot.co.uk

Arthur Rackham
www.artpassions.net

Linda Ravenscroft
www.lindaravenscroft.com

Josephine Wall
www.josephinewall.co.uk

Faerie Charities

Fairy Box

Donates gift boxes to children's wards, trains storytellers and supports holistic therapies and messages to help sick children in hospital. www.facebook.com/fairyboxcharity

The Fairyland Trust

A unique charity that helps to educate children in the conservation of the environment. www.fairylandtrust.org

The Woodland Trust

The UK's leading conservation charity, dedicated to protecting the UK's natural woodlands.
www.woodlandtrust.org.uk

Common Ground

This charity has been recognized internationally for its unique role in the arts and environmental fields. It links nature with the arts and culture by focusing on the positive actions people can make in their towns and cities, championing popular democratic involvement and inspiring celebration as a starting point for action to improve the quality of our everyday places.
www.commonground.org.uk

The National Trust

Conservation, heritage and education covering coastal areas and the countryside, as well as ancient monuments and buildings. www.nationaltrust.org.uk

Brighton Peace and Environment Centre

Provides practical information on how to make your home an environmentally friendly place. Its 'Environment and Sustainability Group' seeks to inform the public about human impacts (both good and bad) on the local and global environment. Based in Brighton, UK. www.bpec.org

Friends of the Earth
Well-known campaign group started in 1969 in San Francisco. It defends the environment and champions a healthy and just world. www.foe.org

Environmental Defense Fund
With over 500,000 members, this charity help find innovative, practical ways to solve the most urgent environmental problems. www.edf.org

Faerie Oracle Cards

The Faeries Oracle
Brian Froud and Jessica Macbeth, Simon & Schuster, 2001. Featuring the magical and enchanting art of Brian Froud as your guide, this deck takes you into the wise and wonderful world of the faeries. It's a beautifully designed divination set and contains everything you need to explore the mysterious faerie realm, including 66 cards and a 208-page illustrated book, which shows you how to read the cards with particular emphasis on connecting to and communicating with faeries.

Fairy Ring: An Oracle of the Fairy Folk
Anna Franklin and Paul Mason, Llewellyn Publications, 2002. Featuring faeries from Britain and Ireland divided into four seasons, or suits, so you can use the appropriate cards for the right time of year. Using the artistry of Paul Mason, author Anna Franklin guides you on how best to interpret the cards. Its full-sized guidebook includes fairy lore, upright and reversed card interpretations, and nine unique card layouts.

Magical Unicorns Oracle Cards
Doreen Virtue, Hay House Inc., 2005.
A 44-card oracle deck and guidebook using the loving
vibrations of the unicorns for magical and positive messages.
Highly recommended!

Faerie Festivals

Tintagel Arthurian Faery Ball and Fairy Fayre
The 3 Wishes Faery Festival
Both festivals are held in Cornwall, UK. www.faeryevents.com

Fairy & Human Relations Congress
Annual event in Washington, USA, aiming to improve
relations between humans and faeries. Includes workshops,
speakers and other guests. www.fairycongress.com

Faerieworlds
Renowned US-based festival celebrating the world of faeries
through music, art, imagination and celebration, featuring the
music of Woodland and the art of Brian and Wendy Froud.
www.faerieworlds.com

Maryland Faerie Festival
Celebrating the world of fae, with an atmosphere and
entertainment inspired by faerie folklore and literature, and,
of course, by the faeries themselves.
www.marylandfaeriefestival.org

Faerie-inspired CDs

Journey to the Faeries
Music by Llewellyn with accompanying notes by Alicen
Geddes-Ward, and illustrated by Neil Geddes-Ward.
www.newworldmusic.com and www.neilgeddesward.com

The Faerie Cottage
Music by Llewellyn and guided spoken meditation by Alicen
Geddes-Ward. www.neilgeddesward.com

Faerielore
Music by Llewellyn with sleeve notes by Alicen Geddes-Ward.
Includes wonderful visualizations. www.paradisemusic.co.uk

Journey to the Faerie Ring
A spoken guided meditation by Alicen Geddes-Ward,
including advice on how to meditate with the faeries
www.paradisemusic.co.uk

Faerie Workshop
Based on Alicen Geddes-Ward's successful Faeriecraft
workshops, this CD is intended for use with groups of people
or individuals who are passionate about faeries. Includes
music by Llewellyn. www.paradisemusic.co.uk

Other faerie-inspired music resources

Paradise Music
Mind, body and spirit music publisher, featuring many relaxing music and meditation CDs from musicians such as Llewellyn, Kevin Kendle, Chris Conway, Juliana and more. www.paradisemusic.co.uk

Woodland
An original Celtic-inspired music group featuring the song writing and poetic harmonies of Emilio and Kelly Miller-Lopez who play at the Faerieworlds festival, mentioned earlier in this directory, and elsewhere. www.woodlandmusic.net

www.llewellynandjuliana.com
Website of the well-respected New Age musician and composer Llewellyn, and his partner, Juliana. They sell millions of albums worldwide and have worked with many other musicians in their field, including producing Alicen Geddes-Ward's faerie meditation CDs and Jacky Newcomb's angel CDs.

Herbal organizations

National Institute of Medical Herbalists
One of the world's oldest professional bodies representing qualified herbalists. Established in 1864, it is the UK's leading authority on herbs and herb healing. Contact them for any advice when using herbs in any situation. www.nimh.org.uk

The American Herbalists Guild
The US equivalent of the UK National Institute above. www.americanherbalistsguild.com

Miscellaneous Resources

Be a Green Parent

The Green Parent website, home of the UK's leading green
lifestyle magazine, has lots of information and ideas for
anyone wishing to be a more natural parent, whether you
want to read articles on natural parenting or try out guilt-free
shopping. www.thegreenparent.co.uk

Edible Glitter for Faerie Cakes and Faerie Dust

CakeCraftShop stocks a truly exciting glitter range!
www.cakecraftshop.co.uk

ABOUT THE AUTHORS

 **Jacky Newcomb** is one of the UK's leading paranormal experiences experts and is known the world over as 'The Angel Lady'. She has appeared on many national television shows including ITV's *This Morning*, Channel Five's *Live with Gabby Logan* and *The Alan Titchmarsh Show*. She has appeared as an expert on radio shows all over the world and has published hundreds of articles in various publications. Jacky is a regular contributor to *Take a Break's Fate and Fortune* magazine and *Spirit and Destiny* magazine. She is *The Sunday Times* bestselling author of *An Angel Saved My Life* and *An Angel By My Side*, and the author of around 30 books on paranormal themes. Jacky is also a prolific painter; her work sells internationally. She paints angels, fairies, unicorns, spirit animals and art with healing themes.

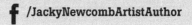 **f /JackyNewcombArtistAuthor**

www.jackynewcomb.com

ABOUT THE AUTHORS

Alicen Geddes is a writer and faerie priestess. She contributes regular articles to New Age and Wiccan magazines. She has appeared on TV and in magazines and has been described as the 'UK's leading exponent on faeries'.

Alicen is the author of four books and six spoken word relaxation CDs. Her latest work is children's fiction, *The Snoring Princess* (The Good Faerie Publishers, 2018), illustrated by her daughter Morgan Geddes-Ward. Alicen's numerous plays on magical themes for children and adults have been performed internationally and on TV.

Alicen has two grown up children and lives in Orkney with her partner Vernon. Together they have two horses, a cat, a dog and twenty or so eccentric ducks. She sometimes dips her toes into the world of grown ups, but can't admit to being one full time.

www.alicen-geddes.co.uk

HAY HOUSE

Look within

Join the conversation about latest products, events, exclusive offers and more.

  Hay House UK

  @HayHouseUK

  @hayhouseuk

  healyourlife.com

We'd love to hear from you!

Printed in the United States
by Baker & Taylor Publisher Services